GRAN*GIS* UK Publishing

Adapted and published by GRANGIS (Grand Register Library).
Online: www.grangis.com
E-mail: contact@grangis.com

In this version:
ISBN: 979-8-88559-038-9

Note: This is the original version (as it was originally enacted). Title, sub-title and the generated date is as marked on the pages.

AF719468

These notes refer to the Equality Act 2010 (c.15)

EXPLANATORY NOTES

EQUALITY ACT 2010

REVISION NOTES

INTRODUCTION

Background and summary

Background

Summary

Overview of the structure of the Act

Territorial extent and application

General

Scotland

Wales

Northern Ireland

Transposition of EU Directives

Commencement

COMMENTARY ON SECTIONS

PART 1: SOCIO-ECONOMIC INEQUALITIES

Section 1: Public sector duty regarding socio-economic inequalities

Effect

Background

Examples

Section 2: Power to amend section 1

Effect

Background

Examples

Section 3: Enforcement

Effect

Background

Example

PART 2: EQUALITY: KEY CONCEPTS

Chapter 1: Protected characteristics

Section 4: The protected characteristics

Effect

Background

Section 5: Age

Effect

Background

Examples

Section 6: Disability

Effect

Background

Examples

Section 7: Gender reassignment

Effect

Background

Examples

Section 8: Marriage and civil partnership

Effect

Background

Examples

Section 9: Race

Effect

Background

Examples

Section 10: Religion or belief

Effect

Background

Examples

Section 11: Sex

Effect

Section 12: Sexual orientation

Effect

Background

Examples

Chapter 2: Prohibited conduct

Section 13: Direct discrimination

Effect

Background

Examples

Section 14: Combined discrimination: dual characteristics

Effect

Background

Examples

Section 15: Discrimination arising from disability

Effect

Background

Examples

Section 16: Gender reassignment discrimination: cases of absence from work

Effect

Background

Example

Section 17: Pregnancy and maternity discrimination: non-work cases

Effect

Background

Examples

Section 18: Pregnancy and maternity discrimination: work cases

Effect

Background

Examples

Section 19: Indirect discrimination

Effect

Background

Examples

Section 20: Duty to make adjustments

Effect

Background

Examples

Section 21: Failure to comply with duty

Effect

Background

Examples

Section 22: Regulations

Effect

Background

Example

Section 23: Comparison by reference to circumstances

Effect

Background

Examples

Section 24: Irrelevance of alleged discriminator's characteristics

Effect

Background

Example

Section 25: References to particular strands of discrimination

Effect

Section 26: Harassment

Effect

Background

Examples

Section 27: Victimisation

Effect

Background

Examples

PART 3: SERVICES AND PUBLIC FUNCTIONS

Section 28: Application of this Part

Effect

Background

Section 29: Provision of services, etc.

Effect

Background

Examples

Section 30: Ships and hovercraft

Effect

Background

Section 31: Interpretation and exceptions

Effect

Background

Examples

PART 4: PREMISES

Section 32: Application of this Part

Effect

Background

Section 33: Disposals, etc.

Effect

Background

Examples

Section 34: Permission for disposal

Effect

Background

Example

Section 35: Management

Effect

Background

Examples

Section 36: Leasehold and commonhold premises and common parts

Effect

Background

Example

Section 37: Adjustments to common parts in Scotland

Effect

Background

Section 38: Interpretation and exceptions

Effect

Background

PART 5: WORK

Chapter 1: Employment, etc.

Section 39: Employees and applicants

Effect

Background

Examples

Section 40: Employees and applicants: harassment

Effect

Background

Example

Section 41: Contract workers

Effect

Background

Examples

Section 42: Identity of employer

Effect

Background

Example

Section 43: Interpretation

Effect

Background

Section 44: Partnerships

Effect

Background

Example

Section 45: Limited liability partnerships

Effect

Background

Examples

Section 46: Interpretation

Effect

Example

Section 47: Barristers

Effect

Background

Examples

Section 48: Advocates

Effect

Background

Examples

Section 49: Personal offices: appointments, etc.

Effect

Background

Examples

Section 50: Public offices: appointments, etc.

Effect

Background

Example

Section 51: Public offices: recommendations for appointments, etc.

Effect

Background

Example

Section 52: Interpretation and exceptions

Effect

Section 53: Qualifications bodies

Effect

Background

Examples

Section 54: Interpretation

Effect

Background

Example

Section 55: Employment service-providers

Effect

Background

Examples

Section 56: Interpretation

Effect

Example

Section 57: Trade organisations

Effect

Background

Examples

Section 58: Official business of members

Effect

Background

Example

Section 59: Interpretation

Effect

Example

Section 60: Enquiries about disability and health

Effect

Background

Examples

Chapter 2: Occupational pension schemes

Section 61: Non-discrimination rule

Effect

Background

Example

Section 62: Non-discrimination alterations

Effect

Background

Example

Section 63: Communications

Effect

Background

Chapter 3: Equality of terms

Section 64: Relevant types of work

Effect

Background

Examples

Section 65: Equal work

Effect

Background

Examples

Section 66: Sex equality clause

Effect

Background

Example

Section 67: Sex equality rule

Effect

Background

Example

Section 68: Sex equality rule: consequential alteration of schemes

Effect

Background

Example

Section 69: Defence of material factor

Effect

Background

Examples

Section 70: Exclusion of sex discrimination provisions

Effect

Background

Example

Section 71: Sex discrimination in relation to contractual pay

Effect

Background

Example

Section 72: Relevant types of work

Effect

Background

Section 73: Maternity equality clause

Effect

Background

Section 74: Maternity equality clause: pay

Effect

Background

Examples

Section 75: Maternity equality rule

Background

Examples

Section 76: Exclusion of pregnancy and maternity discrimination provisions

Effect

Background

Example

Section 77: Discussions about pay

Effect

Background

Examples

Section 78: Gender pay gap information

Effect

Background

Section 79: Comparators

Effect

Background

Example

Section 80: Interpretation and exceptions

Effect

Chapter 4: Supplementary

Section 81: Ships and hovercraft

Effect

Background

Section 82: Offshore work

Effect

Background

Example

Section 83: Interpretation and exceptions

Effect

PART 6: EDUCATION

Chapter 1: Schools

Section 84: Application of this Chapter

Effect

Background

Examples

Section 85: Pupils: admission and treatment, etc.

Effect

Background

Examples

Section 86: Victimisation of pupils, etc. for conduct of parents, etc.

Effect

Background

Examples

Section 87: Application of certain powers under Education Act 1996

Effect

Background

Example

Section 88: Disabled pupils: accessibility

Effect

Section 89: Interpretation and exceptions

Effect

Background

Examples

Chapter 2: Further and higher education

Section 90: Application of this Chapter

Effect

Background

Section 91: Students: admission and treatment, etc.

Effect

Background

Examples

Section 92: Further and higher education courses

Effect

Background

Example

Section 93: Recreational or training facilities

Effect

Background

Example

Section 94: Interpretation and exceptions

Effect

Background

Examples

Chapter 3: General qualifications bodies

Section 95: Application of this Chapter

Effect

Background

Section 96: Qualifications bodies

Effect

Background

Examples

Section 97: Interpretation

Effect

Background

Examples

Chapter 4: Miscellaneous

Section 98: Reasonable adjustments

Effect

Section 99: Educational charities and endowments

Effect

PART 7: ASSOCIATIONS

Section 100: Application of this Part

Effect

Background

Section 101: Members and associates

Effect

Background

Examples

Section 102: Guests

Effect

Background

Example

Section 103: Sections 101 and 102: further provision

Effect

Section 104: Selection of candidates

Effect

Background

Examples

Section 105: Time-limited provision

Effect

Background

Section 106: Information about diversity in range of candidates, etc.

Effect

Background

Example

Section 107: Interpretation and exceptions

Effect

Background

Examples

PART 8: PROHIBITED CONDUCT: ANCILLARY

Section 108: Relationships that have ended

Effect

Background

Examples

Section 109: Liability of employers and principals

Effect

Background

Examples

Section 110: Liability of employees and agents

Effect

Background

Examples

Section 111: Instructing, causing or inducing contraventions

Effect

Background

Example

Section 112: Aiding contraventions

Effect

Background

Example

PART 9: ENFORCEMENT

Chapter 1: Introductory

Section 113: Proceedings

Effect

Background

Chapter 2: Civil courts

Section 114: Jurisdiction

Effect

Background

Examples

Section 115: Immigration cases

Effect

Background

Section 116: Education cases

Effect

Background

Section 117: National security

Effect

Background

Section 118: Time limits

Effect

Background

Section 119: Remedies

Effect

Background

Chapter 3: Employment tribunals

Section 120: Jurisdiction

Effect

Background

Examples

Section 121: Armed forces cases

Effect

Background

Example

Section 122: References by court to tribunal, etc.

Effect

Background

Example

Section 123: Time limits

Effect

Background

Section 124: Remedies: general

Effect

Background

Example

Section 125: Remedies: national security

Effect

Background

Section 126: Remedies: occupational pension schemes

Effect

Background

Chapter 4: Equality of terms

Section 127: Jurisdiction

Effect

Background

Example

Section 128: References by court to tribunal, etc.

Effect

Background

Example

Section 129: Time limits

Effect

Background

Example

Section 130: Section 129: supplementary

Effect

Background

Examples

Section 131: Assessment of whether work is of equal value

Effect

Background

Example

Section 132: Remedies in non-pensions cases

Effect

Background

Example

Section 133: Remedies in pensions cases

Effect

Background

Section 134: Remedies in claims for arrears brought by pensioner members

Effect

Background

Section 135: Supplementary

Effect

Background

Chapter 5: Miscellaneous

Section 136: Burden of proof

Effect

Background

Example

Section 137: Previous findings

Effect

Background

Section 138: Obtaining information, etc.

Effect

Background

Section 139: Interest

Effect

Background

Example

Section 140: Conduct giving rise to separate proceedings

Effect

Background

Example

Section 141: Interpretation, etc.

Effect

PART 10: CONTRACTS, ETC.

Section 142: Unenforceable terms

Effect

Background

Example

Section 143: Removal or modification of unenforceable terms

Effect

Background

Example

Section 144: Contracting out

Effect

Background

Examples

Section 145: Void and unenforceable terms

Effect

Background

Examples

Section 146: Declaration in respect of void term, etc.

Effect

Background

Example

Section 147: Meaning of "qualifying compromise contract"

Effect

Background

Examples

Section 148: Interpretation

Effect

PART 11: ADVANCEMENT OF EQUALITY

Chapter 1: Public sector equality duty

Section 149: Public sector equality duty

Effect

Background

Examples

Section 150: Public authorities and public functions

Effect

Background

Section 151: Power to specify public authorities

Effect

Examples

Section 152: Power to specify public authorities: consultation and consent

Effect

Background

Section 153: Power to impose specific duties

Effect

Background

Section 154: Power to impose specific duties: cross-border authorities

Effect

Background

Section 155: Power to impose specific duties: supplementary

Effect

Background

Examples

Section 156: Enforcement

Effect

Background

Example

Section 157: Interpretation

Effect

Chapter 2: Positive action

Section 158: Positive action: general

Effect

Background

Examples

Section 159: Positive action: recruitment and promotion

Effect

Background

Examples

PART 12: DISABLED PERSONS: TRANSPORT

Chapter 1: Taxis, etc.

Section 160: Taxi accessibility regulations

Effect

Background

Examples

Section 161: Control of numbers of licensed taxis: exception

Effect

Background

Examples

Section 162: Designated transport facilities

Effect

Background

Example

Section 163: Taxi licence conditional on compliance with taxi accessibility regulations

Effect

Background

Examples

Section 164: Exemption from taxi accessibility regulations

Effect

Background

Example

Section 165: Passengers in wheelchairs

Effect

Background

Examples

Section 166: Passengers in wheelchairs: exemption certificates

Effect

Background

Example

Section 167: Lists of wheelchair-accessible vehicles

Effect

Background

Examples

Section 168: Assistance dogs in taxis

Effect

Background

Example

Section 169: Assistance dogs in taxis: exemption certificates

Effect

Background

Example

Section 170: Assistance dogs in private hire vehicles

Effect

Background

Examples

Section 171: Assistance dogs in private hire vehicles: exemption certificates

Effect

Background

Example

Section 172: Appeals

Effect

Background

Examples

Section 173: Interpretation

Effect

Chapter 2: Public service vehicles

Section 174: PSV accessibility regulations

Effect

Background

Example

Section 175: Offence of contravening PSV accessibility regulations

Effect

Background

Example

Section 176: Accessibility certificates

Effect

Background

Example

Section 177: Approval certificates

Effect

Background

Example

Section 178: Special authorisations

Effect

Background

Example

Section 179: Reviews and appeals

Effect

Background

Example

Section 180: Fees

Effect

Background

Example

Section 181: Interpretation

Effect

Chapter 3: Rail vehicles

Section 182: Rail vehicle accessibility regulations

Effect

Background

Example

Section 183: Exemptions from rail vehicle accessibility regulations

Effect

Background

Example

Section 184: Procedure for making exemption orders

Effect

Background

Section 185: Annual report on exemption orders

Effect

Background

Section 186: Rail vehicle accessibility: compliance

Effect

Background

Section 187: Interpretation

Effect

Background

Chapter 4: Supplementary

Section 188: Forgery, etc.

Effect

Background

PART 13: DISABILITY: MISCELLANEOUS

Section 189: Reasonable adjustments

Effect

Section 190: Improvements to let dwelling houses

Effect

Background

Examples

PART 14: GENERAL EXCEPTIONS

Section 191: Statutory provisions

Effect

Section 192: National security

Effect

Background

Example

Section 193: Charities

Effect

Background

Examples

Section 194: Charities: supplementary

Effect

Section 195: Sport

Effect

Background

Examples

Section 196: General

Effect

Section 197: Age

Effect

Background

Examples

PART 15: FAMILY PROPERTY

Section 198: Abolition of husband's duty to maintain wife

Effect

Background

Example

Section 199: Abolition of presumption of advancement

Effect

Background

Example

Section 200: Amendment of Married Women's Property Act 1964

Effect

Background

Example

Section 201: Civil partners: housekeeping allowance

Effect

Background

Example

PART 16: GENERAL AND MISCELLANEOUS

Section 202: Civil partnerships on religious premises

Effect

Background

Examples

Section 203: Harmonisation

Effect

Background

Example

Section 204: Harmonisation: procedure

Effect

Section 205: Crown application

Effect

Background

Example

Section 206: Information society services

Effect

Background

Section 207: Exercise of power

Effect

Background

Section 208: Ministers of the Crown, etc.

Effect

Background

Section 209: The Welsh Ministers

Effect

Background

Section 210: The Scottish Ministers

Effect

Background

Section 211: Amendments, repeals and revocations

Effect

Section 212: General interpretation

Effect

Background

Section 213: References to maternity leave, etc.

Effect

Background

Section 214: Index of defined expressions

Effect

Section 215: Money

Effect

Section 216: Commencement

Effect

Section 217: Extent

Effect

Section 218: Short title

Effect

Schedule 1: Disability: supplementary provision

Effect

Background

Example

Schedule 2: Services and public functions: reasonable adjustments

Effect

Background

Examples

Schedule 3: Services and public functions: exceptions

PART 1: CONSTITUTIONAL MATTERS: PARAGRAPHS 1-5

Effect

Background

Examples

PART 2: EDUCATION EDUCATION: PARAGRAPH 6

Effect

Background

Examples

Education: paragraph 7

Effect

Education: paragraph 8

Effect

Background

Education: paragraph 9

Effect

Background

Examples

Education: paragraph 10

Effect

Background

Education: paragraph 11

Effect

Background

Examples

PART 3: HEALTH AND CARE BLOOD SERVICES: PARAGRAPH 13

Effect
Background
Examples
Health and safety: paragraph 14
Effect
Background
Examples
Care within the family: paragraph 15
Effect
Background
Examples
PART 4: IMMIGRATION DISABILITY: PARAGRAPH 16
Effect
Background
Nationality and ethnic or national origins: paragraph 17
Effect
Background
Examples
Religion or belief: paragraph 18
Effect
Background
Examples
PART 5: INSURANCE, ETC. SERVICES ARRANGED BY EMPLOYER: PARAGRAPH 20

Effect

Background

Example

Disability: paragraph 21

Effect

Background

Examples

Sex, gender reassignment, pregnancy and maternity: paragraph 22

Background

Example

Existing insurance policies: paragraph 23

Effect

Background

Examples

PART 6: MARRIAGE GENDER REASSIGNMENT: ENGLAND AND WALES: PARAGRAPH 24

Effect

Background

Example

Gender reassignment: Scotland: paragraph 25

Effect

Background

Example

PART 7: SEPARATE AND SINGLE SERVICES SEPARATE SERVICES FOR THE SEXES: PARAGRAPH 26

Effect

Background

Example

Single-sex services: paragraph 27

Effect

Background

Examples

Gender reassignment: paragraph 28

Effect

Background

Example

Services relating to religion: paragraph 29

Effect

Background

Example

Services generally provided only for persons who share a protected characteristic: paragraph 30

Effect

Background

Examples

PART 8: TELEVISION, RADIO AND ON-LINE BROADCASTING AND DISTRIBUTION

Paragraph 31

Effect

Background

Examples

PART 9: TRANSPORT APPLICATION TO DISABILITY: PARAGRAPH 32

Effect

Background

Transport by air: paragraph 33

Effect

Background

Examples

Transport by land: paragraph 34

Effect

Background

Example

PART 10: SUPPLEMENTARY POWER TO AMEND: PARAGRAPH 35

Effect

Background

Schedule 4: Premises: reasonable adjustments

Effect

Background

Examples

Schedule 5: Premises: exceptions

Effect

Background

Examples

Schedule 6: Office-holders: excluded offices

Effect

Background

Example

Schedule 7: Equality of terms: exceptions

PART 1: TERMS OF WORK COMPLIANCE WITH LAWS REGULATING EMPLOYMENT OF WOMEN, ETC.

Background

PART 2: OCCUPATIONAL PENSION SCHEMES

Effect

Background

Schedule 8: Work: reasonable adjustments

Effect

Background

Examples

Schedule 9: Work: exceptions

PART 1: OCCUPATIONAL REQUIREMENTS

General: paragraph 1

Effect

Background

Examples

Religious requirements relating to sex, marriage etc., sexual orientation: paragraph 2

Effect

Background

Examples

Effect

Background

Example

Armed forces: paragraph 4

Effect

Background

Example

Employment services: paragraph 5

Effect

Background

Example

Interpretation: paragraph 6

Effect

PART 2: EXCEPTIONS RELATING TO AGE RETIREMENT: PARAGRAPH 8

Effect

Background

Examples

Applicants at or approaching retirement age: paragraph 9

Effect

Background

Examples

Benefits based on length of service: paragraph 10

Effect

Background

Examples

The national minimum wage: young workers: paragraph 11

Effect

Background

Examples

The national minimum wage: apprentices: paragraph 12

Effect

Background

Examples

Redundancy: paragraph 13

Effect

Background

Examples

Life assurance: paragraph 14

Effect

Background

Examples

Child care: paragraph 15

Effect

Background

Examples

Contributions to personal pension schemes: paragraph 16

Non-contractual payments to women on maternity leave: paragraph 17

Effect

Background

Examples

Benefits dependent on marital status: paragraph 18

Effect

Background

Examples

Provision of services, etc. to the public: paragraph 19

Effect

Background

Examples

Insurance contracts etc.: paragraph 20

Effect

Background

Example

Schedule 10: Accessibility for disabled pupils

Effect

Background

Example

Schedule 11: Schools: exceptions

PART 1: SEX DISCRIMINATION

Background
Admission to single-sex schools: paragraph 1
Effect
Examples
Single-sex boarding at schools: paragraph 2
Effect
Example
Single-sex schools turning co-educational: paragraphs 3 and 4
Effect
Examples
PART 2: RELIGIOUS OR BELIEF-RELATED DISCRIMINATION
Background
Schools with religious character, etc.: paragraph 5
Effect
Examples
Curriculum, worship etc.: paragraph 6
Effect
Background
Examples
Power to amend: paragraph 7
Effect
Background
PART 3: DISABILITY DISCRIMINATION PERMITTED FORM OF SELECTION: PARAGRAPH 8
Effect
Background
Example
Schedule 12: Further and higher education exceptions
PART 1: SINGLE-SEX INSTITUTIONS

Effect

Background

Admission to single-sex institutions: paragraph 1

Effect

Examples

Single-sex institutions turning co-educational: paragraphs 2 and 3.

Effect

Background

Examples

PART 2: OTHER EXCEPTIONS OCCUPATIONAL REQUIREMENTS: PARAGRAPH 4

Effect

Background

Example

Institutions with a religious ethos: paragraph 5

Effect

Background

Benefits dependent on marital status, etc.: paragraph 6

Effect

Background

Child care: paragraph 7

Effect

Background

Example

Schedule 13: Education: reasonable adjustments

Effect

Background

Examples

Schedule 14: Educational charities and endowments

Educational charities: paragraph 1

Effect

Background

Example

Educational endowments: paragraph 2Effect

Schedule 15: Associations: reasonable adjustments

Effect

Background

Examples

Schedule 16: Associations: exceptions

Single characteristic associations: paragraph 1

Effect

Background

Example

Health and safety: paragraph 2

Effect

Background

Example

Schedule 17: Disabled pupils: enforcement

PART 1: INTRODUCTORY

PART 2: TRIBUNALS IN ENGLAND AND WALES JURISDICTION: PARAGRAPH 3

Time for bringing proceedings: paragraph 4

Powers: paragraph 5

Procedure: paragraph 6

PART 3: TRIBUNALS IN SCOTLAND

PART 4: ADMISSIONS AND EXCLUSIONS

Background

Examples

Schedule 18: Public sector equality duty: exceptions

Effect

Background

Examples

Schedule 19: Public authorities

Effect

Schedule 20: Rail vehicle accessibility: compliance

Paragraphs 1 to 4

Rail vehicle accessibility compliance certificates: paragraph 1

Effect

Background

Regulations as to compliance certificates: paragraph 2

Effect

Background

Regulations as to compliance assessments: paragraph 3

Effect

Background

Fees in respect of compliance certificates: paragraph 4

Effect

Background

Paragraphs 5 to 12

Penalty for using rail vehicle that does not conform with accessibility regulations: paragraph 5

Effect

Background

Penalty for using rail vehicle otherwise than in conformity with accessibility regulations: paragraph 6

Effect

Background

Inspection of rail vehicles: paragraph 7

Effect

Background

Supplementary powers: paragraph 8

Effect

Background

Penalties: amount, due date and recovery: paragraph 9

Effect

Background

Penalties: code of practice: paragraph 10

Effect

Background

Penalties: procedure: paragraph 11

Effect

Background

Penalties: appeals: paragraph 12

Effect

Background

Forgery, etc.: paragraph 13

Effect

Background

Regulations: paragraph 14

Interpretation: paragraph 15

Effect

Background

Effect

Background

Examples

Schedule 22: Statutory provisions

Statutory authority: paragraph 1

Effect

Background

Examples

Protection of women: paragraph 2

Effect

Background

Examples

Educational appointments, etc: religious belief: paragraphs 3 and 4

Effect

Background

Examples

Crown employment, etc.: paragraph 5

Effect

Background

Examples

Schedule 23: General exceptions

Acts authorised by statute or the executive: paragraph 1

Effect

Background

Examples

Organisations relating to religion or belief: paragraph 2

Effect

Background

Examples

Communal accommodation: paragraph 3

Effect

Background

Examples

Training provided to non-EEA residents, etc: paragraph 4

Effect

Background

Example

Schedule 24: Harmonisation: exceptions

Effect

Schedule 25: Information society services

Effect

Background

Examples

Schedule 26: Amendments

Effect

Local Government Act 1988: paragraphs 1 to 4

Effect

Background

Examples

Equality Act 2006: paragraph 13

Effect

Background

Examples

Schedule 27: Repeals and revocations

Effect

Schedule 28: Index of defined expressions

Effect

HANSARD REFERENCES

These notes refer to the Equality Act 2010 (c.15) which received Royal Assent on 8 April 2010

EQUALITY ACT 2010

EXPLANATORY NOTES

REVISION NOTES

Revised Edition - August 2010

Page 175, paragraph 837 the examples have been revised to improve clarity.

Formatting and typographical errors have been corrected throughout.

INTRODUCTION

1. These explanatory notes relate to the Equality Act 2010 which received Royal Assent on 8 April 2010. They have been prepared by the Government Equalities Office, the Department for Work and Pensions (in respect of provisions relating to disability and pensions), the Department for Children, Schools and Families and the Department for Business, Innovation and Skills (in respect of provisions relating to education), the Department for Transport (in respect of provisions relating to disability and transport) and the Department for Business, Innovation and Skills (in respect of provisions relating to work exceptions). Their purpose is to assist the reader in understanding the Act. They do not form part of the Act and have not been endorsed by Parliament.

2. The notes need to be read in conjunction with the Act. They are not, and are not meant to be, a comprehensive description of the Act. So where a section or part of a section does not seem to require any explanation or comment, none is given.

Background and summary

Background

3. Domestic discrimination law has developed over more than 40 years since the first Race Relations Act in 1965. Subsequently, other personal characteristics besides race have been protected from discrimination and similar conduct, sometimes as a result of domestic initiatives and sometimes through implementing European Directives.

4. The domestic law is now mainly contained in the following legislation (where applicable, as amended):

   - the Equal Pay Act 1970;
   - the Sex Discrimination Act 1975;
   - the Race Relations Act 1976;
   - the Disability Discrimination Act 1995;
   - the Employment Equality (Religion or Belief) Regulations 2003;
   - the Employment Equality (Sexual Orientation) Regulations 2003;
   - the Employment Equality (Age) Regulations 2006;
   - the Equality Act 2006, Part 2;

- the Equality Act (Sexual Orientation) Regulations 2007.

5. The main European Directives affecting domestic discrimination legislation are:

   - Council Directive 2000/43/EC implementing the principle of equal treatment between persons irrespective of racial or ethnic origin;
   - Council Directive 2000/78/EC establishing a general framework for equal treatment in employment and occupation;
   - Council Directive 2004/113/EC implementing the principle of equal treatment between men and women in the access to and supply of goods and services;
   - European Parliament and Council Directive 2006/54/EC on the implementation of the principle of equal opportunities and equal treatment of men and women in matters of employment and occupation (recast). Also relevant in this context is Article 157 of the Treaty on the Functioning of the European Union.

6. In addition, in July 2008 the European Commission published a new draft Directive which would prohibit discrimination because of disability, religion or belief, sexual orientation and age, in access to goods and services, housing, education, social protection, social security and social advantage. This Directive is under negotiation.

7. In February 2005, the Government set up the Discrimination Law Review to address long-term concerns about inconsistencies in the current discrimination law framework. The Review was tasked with considering the fundamental principles of discrimination legislation and its underlying concepts, and the opportunities for creating a clearer and more streamlined framework of equality legislation which produces better outcomes for those who experience disadvantage.

8. In June 2007 the Department for Communities and Local Government published a consultation paper, A Framework for Fairness: Proposals for a Single Equality Bill for Great Britain. This was followed in June and July 2008 by two Command Papers published by the Government Equalities Office: Framework for a Fairer Future – the Equality Bill (Cm 7431); and The Equality Bill – Government Response to the Consultation (Cm 7454). In January 2009, the Government published the New Opportunities White Paper (Cm 7533) which, amongst other things, committed the Government to considering legislation to address disadvantage associated with socio-economic inequality.

9. The following further documents were published by the Government Equalities Office during the passage of the Bill that became the Equality Act: in April 2009, Equality Bill: Assessing the impact of a multiple discrimination provision (a summary of responses was published in October 2009); in June 2009, Equality Bill: Making it work - Policy proposals for specific duties; and in January 2010 Equality Bill: Making it work - Ending age discrimination in services and public functions.

Summary

10. The Act has two main purposes – to harmonise discrimination law, and to strengthen the law to support progress on equality.

11. The Act brings together and re-states all the enactments listed in paragraph 4 above and a number of other related provisions. It will harmonise existing provisions to give a single approach where appropriate. Most of the existing legislation will be repealed. The Equality Act 2006 will remain in force (as amended by the Act) so far as it relates to the constitution and operation of the Equality and Human Rights Commission; as will the Disability Discrimination Act 1995, so far as it relates to Northern Ireland.

12. The Act also strengthens the law in a number of areas. It:

- places a new duty on certain public bodies to consider socio-economic disadvantage when making strategic decisions about how to exercise their functions;
- extends the circumstances in which a person is protected against discrimination, harassment or victimisation because of a protected characteristic;
- extends the circumstances in which a person is protected against discrimination by allowing people to make a claim if they are directly discriminated against because of a combination of two relevant protected characteristics;
- creates a duty on listed public bodies when carrying out their functions and on other persons when carrying out public functions to have due regard when carrying out their functions to: the need to eliminate conduct which the Act prohibits; the need to advance equality of opportunity between persons who share a relevant protected characteristic and those who do not; and the need to foster good relations between people who share a relevant protected characteristic and people who do not. The practical effect is that listed public bodies will have to consider how their policies, programmes and service delivery will affect people with the protected characteristics;
- allows an employer or service provider or other organisation to take positive action so as to enable existing or potential employees or customers to overcome or minimise a disadvantage arising from a protected characteristic;
- extends the permission for political parties to use women-only shortlists for election candidates to 2030;
- enables an employment tribunal to make a recommendation to a respondent who has lost a discrimination claim to take certain steps to remedy matters not just for the benefit of the individual claimant (who may have already left the organisation concerned) but also the wider workforce;
- amends family property law to remove discriminatory provisions and provides additional statutory property rights for civil partners in England and Wales;
- amends the Civil Partnership Act 2004 to remove the prohibition on civil partnerships being registered in religious premises.

Overview of the structure of the Act

13. The Act consists of 16 Parts and 28 Schedules. The general arrangement of the Act is as follows:

PART	*SUMMARY*
Part 1	Imposes a duty on certain public bodies to have due regard to socio-economic considerations in making strategic decisions.
Part 2 including Schedule 1	Establishes the key concepts on which the Act is based including: • the characteristics which are protected (age, disability, gender reassignment, marriage and civil partnership, pregnancy and maternity, race, religion or belief, sex and sexual orientation); • the definitions of direct discrimination (including because of a combination of two relevant protected characteristics), discrimination arising from disability, indirect discrimination, harassment and victimisation.
	These key concepts are then applied in the subsequent Parts of the Act.
Part 3 including	Makes it unlawful to discriminate against, harass or victimise a person when providing a service (which includes the provision of goods or facilities) or when exercising a public function.

PART	***SUMMARY***
Schedules 2 and 3	
Part 4 including Schedules 4 and 5	Makes it unlawful to discriminate against, harass or victimise a person when disposing of (for example, by selling or letting) or managing premises.
Part 5 including Schedules 6, 7, 8 and 9	Makes it unlawful to discriminate against, harass or victimise a person at work or in employment services. Also contains provisions relating to equal pay between men and women; pregnancy and maternity pay; provisions making it unlawful for an employment contract to prevent an employee disclosing his or her pay; and a power to require private sector employers to publish gender pay gap (the size of the difference between men and women's pay expressed as a percentage) information about differences in pay between men and women. It also contains provisions restricting the circumstances in which potential employees can be asked questions about disability or health.
Part 6 including Schedules 10, 11, 12, 13 and 14	Makes it unlawful for education bodies to discriminate against, harass or victimise a school pupil or student or applicant for a place.
Part 7 including Schedules 15 and 16	Makes it unlawful for associations (for example, private clubs and political organisations) to discriminate against, harass or victimise members, associates or guests and contains a power to require political parties to publish information about the diversity of their candidates.
Part 8	Prohibits other forms of conduct, including discriminating against or harassing of an ex-employee or ex-pupil, for example: instructing a third party to discriminate against another; or helping someone discriminate against another. Also determines the liability of employers and principals in relation to the conduct of their employees or agents.
Part 9 including Schedule 17	Deals with enforcement of the Act's provisions, through the civil courts (in relation to services and public functions; premises; education; and associations) and the employment tribunals (in relation to work and related areas, and equal pay).
Part 10	Makes terms in contracts, collective agreements or rules of undertakings unenforceable or void if they result in unlawful discrimination, harassment or victimisation.
Part 11 including Schedules 18 and 19	Establishes a general duty on public authorities to have due regard, when carrying out their functions, to the need: to eliminate unlawful discrimination, harassment or victimisation; to advance equality of opportunity; and to foster good relations.
	Also contains provisions which enable an employer or service provider or other organisation to take positive action to overcome or minimise a disadvantage arising from people possessing particular protected characteristics.
Part 12 including Schedule 20	Requires taxis, other private hire vehicles, public service vehicles (such as buses) and rail vehicles to be accessible to disabled people and to allow them to travel in reasonable comfort.

PART	*SUMMARY*
Part 13 including Schedule 21	Deals with consent to make reasonable adjustments to premises and improvements to let dwelling houses.
Part 14 including Schedules 22 and 23	Establishes exceptions to the prohibitions in the earlier parts of the Act in relation to a range of conduct, including action required by an enactment; protection of women; educational appointments; national security; the provision of benefits by charities and sporting competitions.
Part 15	Repeals or replaces rules of family property law which discriminated between husbands and wives.
Part 16 including Schedules 24, 25, 26, 27 and 28	Contains a power for a Minister of the Crown to harmonise certain provisions in the Act with changes required to comply with EU obligations. It contains general provisions on application to the Crown, subordinate legislation, interpretation, commencement and extent. It also contains amendments to the Civil Partnership Act 2004 to allow civil partnership registrations to take place on religious premises that are approved for that purpose.

Territorial extent and application

General

14. The Act forms part of the law of England and Wales. It also, with the exception of section 190 and Part 15, forms part of the law of Scotland. There are also a few provisions which form part of the law of Northern Ireland.

15. As far as territorial application is concerned, in relation to Part 5 (work) and following the precedent of the Employment Rights Act 1996, the Act leaves it to tribunals to determine whether the law applies, depending for example on the connection between the employment relationship and Great Britain. However, the Act contains a power to specify territorial application of Part 5 in relation to ships and hovercraft (section 81) and offshore work (section 82). In relation to the non-work provisions, the Act is again generally silent on territorial application, leaving it to the courts to determine whether the law applies. However, in a limited number of specific cases, express provision is made for particular provisions of the Act to apply (or potentially apply) outside the United Kingdom. Thus, section 29(9) provides for the prohibitions in respect of the provision of services or the exercise of public functions to apply in relation to race and religion or belief to the granting of entry clearance, even where the act in question takes place outside the United Kingdom. Also, section 30 contains a similar power to that in Part 5 to specify the territorial application of the services provisions of Part 3 in relation to ships and hovercraft.

Scotland

16. The Act contains provisions that triggered the Sewel Convention in relation to Scotland. The Scottish Ministers can already impose specific equality duties on Scottish public bodies and on the devolved functions of cross-border bodies following appropriate consultation. Provisions in this Act replicate this situation. The Scottish Ministers will be able to impose specific duties on relevant Scottish bodies (sections 153 and 154) and by order to amend Part 3 of Schedule 19 which lists the relevant Scottish bodies to which the general public sector equality duty applies (section 151). A procedure will be specified in relation to imposition of specific duties on cross-border Scottish bodies added to Schedule 19 by a Minister of the Crown when a cross-border body is added to Part 4 of that Schedule. The procedure enables the Scottish Ministers to impose specific duties in relation to the devolved Scottish functions of the cross-border bodies. The Act

also contains a number of provisions which confer additional powers on the Scottish Ministers to make secondary legislation, for example: a power for the Scottish Ministers to add a relevant Scottish body to the bodies subject to the duty in section 1 to consider socio-economic inequalities and to make consequential amendments (section 2); the power to make regulations setting out a process for the making of adjustments to common parts of residential premises in Scotland (section 37); the power to make procedural rules for the hearing of disability discrimination claims by the Additional Support Needs Tribunals for Scotland (paragraph 10 of Schedule 17); the power, on the application of the governing body of an educational establishment (and if satisfied that it would be educationally beneficial) to modify an endowment whose benefits are restricted to persons of one sex (paragraph 2 of Schedule 14); the power to prescribe the regulator, qualifications body and relevant qualifications in Scotland (section 96); the power to make transitional exemption orders for single-sex education authorities or grant-aided schools in Scotland which alter their admissions arrangements so as to cease being a single-sex establishment (paragraph 4 of Schedule 11); a power to make regulations in relation to designated transport facilities (section 162).

17. The Sewel Convention provides that Westminster will not normally legislate with regard to devolved matters in Scotland without the consent of the Scottish Parliament. A Legislative Consent Motion in respect of the Act was passed by the Scottish Parliament on 28 January 2010.

Wales

18. Under the Welsh devolution settlement the subject matter of equal opportunities is not devolved to Wales. Section 2 of the Act provides a power for the Welsh Ministers to add any relevant Welsh body to the bodies subject to the duty in section 1 to consider socio-economic inequalities and to make consequential amendments. The Act also confers powers on the Welsh Ministers in relation to the public sector equality duty. Sections 153 and 154 give Welsh Ministers power to impose specific duties on relevant Welsh bodies and section 151 gives them power by order to amend Part 2 of Schedule 19 which specifies relevant Welsh bodies subject to the general public sector equality duty. A procedure is specified in relation to the imposition of specific duties on cross-border Welsh bodies added to Schedule 19 by a Minister of the Crown. The procedure enables the Welsh Ministers to impose specific duties in relation to the devolved Welsh functions of the cross-border bodies or provide for specific duties to be imposed by a Minister of the Crown only after consultation with the Welsh Ministers.

Northern Ireland

19. Equal opportunities and discrimination are "transferred matters" under the Northern Ireland Act 1998. As such, with a few exceptions the Act does not form part of the law of Northern Ireland. As a result, the Disability Discrimination Act 1995 (as amended), which extends throughout the United Kingdom, will remain in force for Northern Ireland as the repeal of that Act only forms part of the law of England and Wales and Scotland.

20. Section 82 enables an Order in Council to provide that Northern Ireland legislation applies in the case of persons in offshore work; and the provisions of section 105 amend the Sex Discrimination (Election Candidates) Act 2002 with the effect that the extension of the expiry date for women-only shortlists will apply in Northern Ireland as well as Great Britain.

Transposition of EU Directives

21. The Act does not itself implement EU Directives for the first time. It replaces earlier legislation which has implemented EU Directives, most of which is set out in paragraph 4 above.

Commencement

22. The following provisions will come into force on the day on which the Act is passed:

- the whole of Part 16 except sections 202 (which amends the Civil Partnership Act 2004 to allow civil partnership registrations to take place on religious premises), 206 (which brings Schedule 25 into effect) and 211 (which brings the Schedules of amendments and repeals into effect);
- section 186(2) which repeals Schedule 20 (on rail vehicle accessibility) if that Schedule is not brought into force before the end of 2010.

The remainder will be brought into force on a day or days appointed by commencement order made by a Minister of the Crown, or in the case of Part 15, an order made by the Lord Chancellor.

COMMENTARY ON SECTIONS

Part 1: Socio-Economic Inequalities

Section 1: Public sector duty regarding socio-economic inequalities

Effect

23. This section requires specified public bodies, when making strategic decisions such as deciding priorities and setting objectives, to consider how their decisions might help to reduce the inequalities associated with socio-economic disadvantage. Such inequalities could include inequalities in education, health, housing, crime rates, or other matters associated with socio-economic disadvantage. It is for public bodies subject to the duty to determine which socio-economic inequalities they are in a position to influence.

24. The duty applies to the listed public bodies, which have strategic functions – these include Government departments, local authorities and NHS bodies. In addition, the duty applies to other public bodies which work in partnership with a local authority to draw up the sustainable community strategy for an area, when they are drawing up that strategy. These partner public bodies are specified in the Local Government and Public Involvement in Health Act 2007.

25. Public bodies are required to take into account guidance issued by a Minister of the Crown when deciding how to fulfil the duty.

26. The duty does not require public bodies to consider how to reduce inequalities resulting from people being subject to immigration control.

Background

27. This is a new provision.

Examples

- The Department of Health decides to improve the provision of primary care services. They find evidence that people suffering socio-economic disadvantage are less likely to access such services during working hours, due to their conditions of employment. The Department therefore advises that such services should be available at other times of the day.
- Under the duty, a Regional Development Agency (RDA), when reviewing its funding programmes, could decide to amend the selection criteria for a programme designed to promote business development, to encourage more successful bids from deprived areas. The same RDA could also decide to continue a programme aimed at generating more jobs in the IT sector which, despite not contributing to a reduction in socio-economic inequalities, has wider economic benefits in attracting more well-paid jobs to the region. This decision would

comply with the duty, because the RDA would have given due consideration to reducing socio-economic inequalities.

- The duty could lead a local education authority, when conducting a strategic review of its school applications process, to analyse the impact of its campaign to inform parents about the applications process, looking particularly at different neighbourhoods. If the results suggest that parents in more deprived areas are less likely to access or make use of the information provided, the authority could decide to carry out additional work in those neighbourhoods in future campaigns, to ensure that children from deprived areas have a better chance of securing a place at their school of choice.

Section 2: Power to amend section 1

Effect

28. This section enables a Minister of the Crown or, in the case of Welsh or Scottish bodies, the Welsh or Scottish Ministers to make regulations amending the list of public bodies which are subject to the duty in section 1, and to limit or extend the functions of a listed body to which the duty applies. The duty can only be imposed on Welsh or Scottish bodies that carry out the same or a similar role to those carried out by a body listed in section 1.

29. It also enables the Welsh or Scottish Ministers to make other consequential amendments to section 1 which they consider are needed as a result of adding bodies to section 1. This includes adding a power for the Welsh or Scottish Ministers to issue guidance for Welsh or Scottish bodies respectively and to impose a requirement that those bodies take the relevant guidance into account. Where they issue guidance to bodies they have listed, the Welsh or Scottish Ministers can remove the requirement for those bodies to take into account guidance issued by a Minister of the Crown.

30. It also provides that a Minister of the Crown may not apply the duty to any devolved Welsh or Scottish functions.

Background

31. This is a new provision.

Examples

- A new public body is created in England to deal with regeneration. The Minister decides that it should give consideration to reducing socio-economic inequalities when making strategic decisions. The Minister makes regulations to add the body to the list in section 1.
- The Welsh Ministers decide they would like the duty to apply to local authorities in Wales, starting a year after the duty starts to apply in England. They consult the relevant Minister of the Crown, and make regulations to apply the duty to those bodies from their proposed commencement date.
- The Welsh Ministers then decide they would like to issue guidance to Welsh local authorities on how to fulfil the duty. They consult the relevant Minister of the Crown about this, and take into account the guidance the Minister of the Crown has issued in relation to English local authorities. They then issue their guidance, which Welsh local authorities must take account of in fulfilling the duty.

Section 3: Enforcement

Effect

32. This section ensures that individuals have no recourse to private law because of a failure by a public body to comply with the duty imposed by section 1. This means that individuals are not able to claim damages for breach of statutory duty for a breach of

this duty. However, this section does not prevent an individual from bringing judicial review proceedings against a public body which is covered by the duty, if he or she believes the public body has not considered socio-economic disadvantage when taking decisions of a strategic nature.

Background

33. This is a new provision.

Example

- An individual feels that the socio-economic disadvantages he faces should entitle him to a flat in a new social housing development, ahead of those whom he judges to be less disadvantaged. However, there is no provision in this Act for him to bring a case against the local council or other public body in such circumstances.

Part 2: Equality: Key Concepts

Chapter 1: Protected characteristics

Section 4: The protected characteristics

Effect

34. This section lists the characteristics that are protected by subsequent provisions in the Act.

Background

35. The protected characteristics listed are the same as those protected by previous discrimination legislation in Great Britain.

Section 5: Age

Effect

36. This section establishes that where the Act refers to the protected characteristic of age, it means a person belonging to a particular age group. An age group includes people of the same age and people of a particular range of ages. Where people fall in the same age group they share the protected characteristic of age.

Background

37. This section replaces a provision in the Employment Equality (Age) Regulations 2006.

Examples

- An age group would include "over fifties" or twenty-one year olds.
- A person aged twenty-one does not share the same characteristic of age with "people in their forties". However, a person aged twenty-one and people in their forties can share the characteristic of being in the "under fifty" age range.

Section 6: Disability

Effect

38. This section establishes who is to be considered as having the protected characteristic of disability and is a disabled person for the purposes of the Act. With Schedule 1 and regulations to be made under that Schedule, it will also establish what constitutes a

disability. Where people have the same disability, they share the protected characteristic of disability.

39. It provides for Ministers to issue statutory guidance to help those who need to decide whether a person has a disability for the purposes of the Act.

Background

40. This section, Schedule 1, and regulations to be made under Schedule 1 replace similar provisions in the Disability Discrimination Act 1995 and provisions in secondary legislation made under that Act.

Examples

- A man works in a warehouse, loading and unloading heavy stock. He develops a long-term heart condition and no longer has the ability to lift or move heavy items of stock at work. Lifting and moving such heavy items is not a normal day-to-day activity. However, he is also unable to lift, carry or move moderately heavy everyday objects such as chairs, at work or around the home. This is an adverse effect on a normal day-to-day activity. He is likely to be considered a disabled person for the purposes of the Act.
- A young woman has developed colitis, an inflammatory bowel disease. The condition is a chronic one which is subject to periods of remissions and flare-ups. During a flare-up she experiences severe abdominal pain and bouts of diarrhoea. This makes it very difficult for her to travel or go to work. This has a substantial adverse effect on her ability to carry out normal day-to-day activities. She is likely to be considered a disabled person for the purposes of the Act.

Section 7: Gender reassignment

Effect

41. This section defines the protected characteristic of gender reassignment for the purposes of the Act as where a person has proposed, started or completed a process to change his or her sex. A transsexual person has the protected characteristic of gender reassignment.

42. The section also explains that a reference to people who have or share the common characteristic of gender reassignment is a reference to all transsexual people. A woman making the transition to being a man and a man making the transition to being a woman both share the characteristic of gender reassignment, as does a person who has only just started out on the process of changing his or her sex and a person who has completed the process.

Background

43. This section replaces similar provisions in the Sex Discrimination Act 1975 but changes the definition by no longer requiring a person to be under medical supervision to come within it.

Examples

- A person who was born physically male decides to spend the rest of his life living as a woman. He declares his intention to his manager at work, who makes appropriate arrangements, and she then starts life at work and home as a woman. After discussion with her doctor and a Gender Identity Clinic, she starts hormone treatment and after several years she goes through gender reassignment surgery. She would have the protected characteristic of gender reassignment for the purposes of the Act.
- A person who was born physically female decides to spend the rest of her life as a man. He starts and continues to live as a man. He decides not to seek medical advice as he

successfully 'passes' as a man without the need for any medical intervention. He would have the protected characteristic of gender reassignment for the purposes of the Act.

Section 8: Marriage and civil partnership

Effect

44. This section defines the protected characteristic of marriage and civil partnership. People who are not married or civil partners do not have this characteristic.

45. The section also explains that people who have or share the common characteristics of being married or of being a civil partner can be described as being in a marriage or civil partnership. A married man and a woman in a civil partnership both share the protected characteristic of marriage and civil partnership.

Background

46. This section replaces similar provisions in the Sex Discrimination Act 1975.

Examples

- A person who is engaged to be married is not married and therefore does not have this protected characteristic.
- A divorcee or a person whose civil partnership has been dissolved is not married or in a civil partnership and therefore does not have this protected characteristic.

Section 9: Race

Effect

47. This section defines the protected characteristic of race. For the purposes of the Act, "race" includes colour, nationality and ethnic or national origins.

48. The section explains that people who have or share characteristics of colour, nationality or ethnic or national origins can be described as belonging to a particular racial group. A racial group can be made up of two or more different racial groups.

49. The section also enables a Minister of the Crown to amend the Act by order so as to add "caste" to the current definition of "race". When exercising this power, the Minister may amend the Act, for example by including exceptions for caste, or making particular provisions of the Act apply in relation to caste in some but not other circumstances. The term "caste" denotes a hereditary, endogamous (marrying within the group) community associated with a traditional occupation and ranked accordingly on a perceived scale of ritual purity. It is generally (but not exclusively) associated with South Asia, particularly India, and its diaspora. It can encompass the four classes (varnas) of Hindu tradition (the Brahmin, Kshatriya, Vaishya and Shudra communities); the thousands of regional Hindu, Sikh, Christian, Muslim or other religious groups known as jatis; and groups amongst South Asian Muslims called biradaris. Some jatis regarded as below the varna hierarchy (once termed "untouchable") are known as Dalit.

Background

50. This section replaces similar provisions in the Race Relations Act 1976. However, the power to add caste to the definition of race is a new provision.

Examples

- Colour includes being black or white.
- Nationality includes being a British, Australian or Swiss citizen.

- Ethnic or national origins include being from a Roma background or of Chinese heritage.
- A racial group could be "black Britons" which would encompass those people who are both black and who are British citizens.

Section 10: Religion or belief

Effect

51. This section defines the protected characteristic of religion or religious or philosophical belief, which is stated to include for this purpose a lack of religion or belief. It is a broad definition in line with the freedom of thought, conscience and religion guaranteed by Article 9 of the European Convention on Human Rights. The main limitation for the purposes of Article 9 is that the religion must have a clear structure and belief system. Denominations or sects within a religion can be considered to be a religion or belief, such as Protestants and Catholics within Christianity.

52. The criteria for determining what is a "philosophical belief" are that it must be genuinely held; be a belief and not an opinion or viewpoint based on the present state of information available; be a belief as to a weighty and substantial aspect of human life and behaviour; attain a certain level of cogency, seriousness, cohesion and importance; and be worthy of respect in a democratic society, compatible with human dignity and not conflict with the fundamental rights of others. So, for example, any cult involved in illegal activities would not satisfy these criteria. The section provides that people who are of the same religion or belief share the protected characteristic of religion or belief. Depending on the context, this could mean people who, for example, share the characteristic of being Protestant or people who share the characteristic of being Christian.

Background

53. This section replaces similar provisions in the Employment Equality (Religion or Belief) Regulations 2003 and the Equality Act 2006.

Examples

- The Baha'i faith, Buddhism, Christianity, Hinduism, Islam, Jainism, Judaism, Rastafarianism, Sikhism and Zoroastrianism are all religions for the purposes of this provision.
- Beliefs such as humanism and atheism would be beliefs for the purposes of this provision but adherence to a particular football team would not be.

Section 11: Sex

Effect

54. This section is a new provision which explains that references in the Act to people having the protected characteristic of sex are to mean being a man or a woman, and that men share this characteristic with other men, and women with other women.

Section 12: Sexual orientation

Effect

55. This section defines the protected characteristic of sexual orientation as being a person's sexual orientation towards:

    - people of the same sex as him or her (in other words the person is a gay man or a lesbian)

- people of the opposite sex from him or her (the person is heterosexual)
- people of both sexes (the person is bisexual).

56. It also explains that references to people sharing a sexual orientation mean that they are of the same sexual orientation.

Background

57. The definition is designed to replicate the effect of similar provisions in the Employment Equality (Sexual Orientation) Regulations 2003 and the Equality Act 2006.

Examples

- A man who experiences sexual attraction towards both men and women is "bisexual" in terms of sexual orientation even if he has only had relationships with women.
- A man and a woman who are both attracted only to people of the opposite sex from them share a sexual orientation.
- A man who is attracted only to other men is a gay man. A woman who is attracted only to other women is a lesbian. So a gay man and a lesbian share a sexual orientation.

Chapter 2: Prohibited conduct

Section 13: Direct discrimination

Effect

58. This section defines direct discrimination for the purposes of the Act.

59. Direct discrimination occurs where the reason for a person being treated less favourably than another is a protected characteristic listed in section 4. This definition is broad enough to cover cases where the less favourable treatment is because of the victim's association with someone who has that characteristic (for example, is disabled), or because the victim is wrongly thought to have it (for example, a particular religious belief).

60. However, a different approach applies where the reason for the treatment is marriage or civil partnership, in which case only less favourable treatment because of the victim's status amounts to discrimination. It must be the victim, rather than anybody else, who is married or a civil partner.

61. This section uses the words "because of" where the previous legislation contains various definitions using the words "on grounds of". This change in wording does not change the legal meaning of the definition, but rather is designed to make it more accessible to the ordinary user of the Act.

62. The section also provides that:

- for age, different treatment that is justified as a proportionate means of meeting a legitimate aim is not direct discrimination;
- in relation to disability it is not discrimination to treat a disabled person more favourably than a person who is not disabled;
- racial segregation is always discriminatory;
- in non-work cases, treating a woman less favourably because she is breast-feeding a baby who is more than six months old amounts to direct sex discrimination; and

- men cannot claim privileges for women connected with pregnancy or childbirth.

Background

63. The section replaces the definitions of direct discrimination in previous legislation and is designed to provide a more uniform approach by removing the former specific requirement for the victim of the discrimination to have one of the protected characteristics of age, disability, gender reassignment and sex. Accordingly, it brings the position in relation to these protected characteristics into line with that for race, sexual orientation and religion or belief in the previous legislation.

Examples

- If an employer recruits a man rather than a woman because she assumes that women do not have the strength to do the job, this would be direct sex discrimination.
- If a Muslim shopkeeper refuses to serve a Muslim woman because she is married to a Christian, this would be direct religious or belief-related discrimination on the basis of her association with her husband.
- If an employer rejects a job application form from a white man who he wrongly thinks is black, because the applicant has an African-sounding name, this would constitute direct race discrimination based on the employer's mistaken perception.
- If an employer advertising a vacancy makes it clear in the advert that Roma need not apply, this would amount to direct race discrimination against a Roma who might reasonably have considered applying for the job but was deterred from doing so because of the advertisement.
- If the manager of a nightclub is disciplined for refusing to carry out an instruction to exclude older customers from the club, this would be direct age discrimination against the manager unless the instruction could be justified.

Section 14: Combined discrimination: dual characteristics

Effect

64. This section provides for the discrimination prohibited by the Act to include direct discrimination because of a combination of two protected characteristics ("dual discrimination"). The protected characteristics which may be combined are age, disability, gender reassignment, race, religion or belief, sex and sexual orientation.

65. For a claim to be successful, the claimant must show that the less favourable treatment was because of the combination alleged, as compared with how a person who does not share either of the characteristics in the combination is or would be treated. A dual discrimination claim will not succeed where an exception or justification applies to the treatment in respect of either of the relevant protected characteristics - for example, where an occupational requirement in Schedule 9 (Work: exceptions) renders direct discrimination lawful.

66. The claimant does not have to show that a claim of direct discrimination in respect of each protected characteristic would have been successful if brought separately. A claimant is not prevented from bringing direct discrimination claims because of individual protected characteristics and a dual discrimination claim simultaneously (or more than one dual discrimination claim). Excluded from the scope of this section are circumstances involving disability discrimination in schools (claims in respect of which are heard by the Special Educational Needs and Disability Tribunals or equivalent specialist tribunals). This section enables a Minister of the Crown to make orders specifying further what a claimant does or does not need to show to prove dual

discrimination or further restricting the circumstances in which dual discrimination is prohibited by the Act.

67. As with any other type of prohibited conduct under the Act, proceedings or allegations (among other activities) relating to dual discrimination will constitute a "protected act" for purposes of victimisation (section 27). Moreover, public bodies must have due regard to the need to eliminate unlawful dual discrimination as part of the public sector equality duty (section 149).

Background

68. Previous legislation only allowed for claims alleging discrimination because of a single protected characteristic. This section allows those who have experienced less favourable treatment because of a combination of two relevant protected characteristics to bring a direct discrimination claim, such as where the single-strand approach may not succeed.

Examples

- A black woman has been passed over for promotion to work on reception because her employer thinks black women do not perform well in customer service roles. Because the employer can point to a white woman of equivalent qualifications and experience who has been appointed to the role in question, as well as a black man of equivalent qualifications and experience in a similar role, the woman may need to be able to compare her treatment because of race and sex combined to demonstrate that she has been subjected to less favourable treatment because of her employer's prejudice against black women.
- A bus driver does not allow a Muslim man onto her bus, claiming that he could be a "terrorist". While it might not be possible for the man to demonstrate less favourable treatment because of either protected characteristic if considered separately, a dual discrimination claim will succeed if the reason for his treatment was the specific combination of sex and religion or belief, which resulted in him being stereotyped as a potential terrorist.
- A black woman is charged £100 for insurance. As white men are only charged £50 for the same insurance, she alleges this is dual discrimination because of the combination of sex and race. By comparing the claimant's treatment with a white woman who also pays £100, or a black man who pays £50, the insurance company is able to demonstrate that the difference in premium is entirely due to sex, not race. The insurance exception in Schedule 3 means that insurance companies can lawfully set different premiums for women and men in certain circumstances so provided the exception applies in this case, the treatment does not constitute dual discrimination. The less favourable treatment is because of sex and an exception makes the sex discrimination lawful.

*Section 15: **Discrimination arising from disability***

Effect

69. This section provides that it is discrimination to treat a disabled person unfavourably not because of the person's disability itself but because of something arising from, or in consequence of, his or her disability, such as the need to take a period of disability-related absence. It is, however, possible to justify such treatment if it can be shown to be a proportionate means of achieving a legitimate aim. For this type of discrimination to occur, the employer or other person must know, or reasonably be expected to know, that the disabled person has a disability.

Background

70. This section is a new provision. The Disability Discrimination Act 1995 provided protection from disability-related discrimination but, following the judgment of the

House of Lords in the case of *London Borough of Lewisham v Malcolm [2008] UKHL 43*, those provisions no longer provided the degree of protection from disability-related discrimination that is intended for disabled people. This section is aimed at re-establishing an appropriate balance between enabling a disabled person to make out a case of experiencing a detriment which arises because of his or her disability, and providing an opportunity for an employer or other person to defend the treatment.

Examples

- An employee with a visual impairment is dismissed because he cannot do as much work as a non-disabled colleague. If the employer sought to justify the dismissal, he would need to show that it was a proportionate means of achieving a legitimate aim.
- The licensee of a pub refuses to serve a person who has cerebral palsy because she believes that he is drunk as he has slurred speech. However, the slurred speech is a consequence of his impairment. If the licensee is able to show that she did not know, and could not reasonably have been expected to know, that the customer was disabled, she has not subjected him to discrimination arising from his disability.
- However, in the example above, if a reasonable person would have known that the behaviour was due to a disability, the licensee would have subjected the customer to discrimination arising from his disability, unless she could show that ejecting him was a proportionate means of achieving a legitimate aim.

Section 16: ***Gender reassignment discrimination: cases of absence from work***

Effect

71. This section provides that it is discrimination against transsexual people to treat them less favourably for being absent from work because they propose to undergo, are undergoing or have undergone gender reassignment than they would be treated if they were absent because they were ill or injured. Transsexual people are also discriminated against in relation to absences relating to their gender reassignment if they are treated less favourably than they would be treated for absence for reasons other than sickness or injury and it is unreasonable to treat them less favourably.

Background

72. This section is designed to replicate the effect of a similar provision in the Sex Discrimination Act 1975.

Example

- A female to male transsexual person takes time off work to receive hormone treatment as part of his gender reassignment. His employer cannot discriminate against him because of his absence from work for this purpose.

Section 17: ***Pregnancy and maternity discrimination: non-work cases***

Effect

73. This section defines what it means to discriminate because of a woman's pregnancy or maternity, as distinct from her sex, in specified situations outside work. It protects a woman from discrimination because of her current or a previous pregnancy. It also protects her from maternity discrimination, which includes treating her unfavourably because she is breast-feeding, for 26 weeks after giving birth and provides that pregnancy or maternity discrimination as defined cannot be treated as sex discrimination.

Background

74. This section is designed to replicate the effect of similar provisions in the Sex Discrimination Act 1975 and extends the protection to cover discrimination in relation to public functions, education, and to associations, where no such protection previously existed.

Examples

- A café owner must not ask a woman to leave his café because she is breast-feeding her baby.
- A shopkeeper must not refuse to sell cigarettes to a woman because she is pregnant.
- A school must not prevent a pupil taking an exam because she is pregnant.

Section 18: Pregnancy and maternity discrimination: work cases

Effect

75. This section defines what it means to discriminate in the workplace because of a woman's pregnancy or pregnancy-related illness, or because she takes or tries to take maternity leave. The period during which protection from these types of discrimination is provided is the period of the pregnancy and any statutory maternity leave to which she is entitled. During this period, these types of discrimination cannot be treated as sex discrimination.

Background

76. This section is designed to replicate the effect of similar provisions in the Sex Discrimination Act 1975.

Examples

- An employer must not demote or dismiss an employee, or deny her training or promotion opportunities, because she is pregnant or on maternity leave.
- An employer must not take into account an employee's period of absence due to pregnancy-related illness when making a decision about her employment.

Section 19: Indirect discrimination

Effect

77. This section defines indirect discrimination for the purposes of the Act.

78. Indirect discrimination occurs when a policy which applies in the same way for everybody has an effect which particularly disadvantages people with a protected characteristic. Where a particular group is disadvantaged in this way, a person in that group is indirectly discriminated against if he or she is put at that disadvantage, unless the person applying the policy can justify it.

79. Indirect discrimination can also occur when a policy would put a person at a disadvantage if it were applied. This means, for example, that where a person is deterred from doing something, such as applying for a job or taking up an offer of service, because a policy which would be applied would result in his or her disadvantage, this may also be indirect discrimination.

80. Indirect discrimination applies to all the protected characteristics, apart from pregnancy and maternity.

Background

81. This section largely replaces similar provisions in previous legislation. It applies the EU definition of indirect discrimination, replacing pre-existing domestic definitions in the Sex Discrimination Act 1975 and the Race Relations Act 1976, to ensure uniformity of protection across all the protected characteristics in all areas where it applies. However, the extension of indirect discrimination to disability is new, coming after consultation following the judgment of the House of Lords in the case of *London Borough of Lewisham v Malcolm* [2008] UKHL 43, which concerned the interpretation of the provision on disability-related discrimination in the Disability Discrimination Act 1995.

Examples

- A woman is forced to leave her job because her employer operates a practice that staff must work in a shift pattern which she is unable to comply with because she needs to look after her children at particular times of day, and no allowances are made because of those needs. This would put women (who are shown to be more likely to be responsible for childcare) at a disadvantage, and the employer will have indirectly discriminated against the woman unless the practice can be justified.
- An observant Jewish engineer who is seeking an advanced diploma decides (even though he is sufficiently qualified to do so) not to apply to a specialist training company because it invariably undertakes the selection exercises for the relevant course on Saturdays. The company will have indirectly discriminated against the engineer unless the practice can be justified.

Section 20: Duty to make adjustments

Effect

82. This section defines what is meant by the duty to make reasonable adjustments for the purposes of the Act and lists the Parts of the Act which impose the duty and the related Schedules which stipulate how the duty will apply in relation to each Part. The duty comprises three requirements which apply where a disabled person is placed at a substantial disadvantage in comparison with non-disabled people. The first requirement covers changing the way things are done (such as changing a practice), the second covers making changes to the built environment (such as providing access to a building), and the third covers providing auxiliary aids and services (such as providing special computer software or providing a different service).

83. The section makes clear that where the first or third requirements involves the way in which information is provided, a reasonable step includes providing that information in an accessible format.

84. It sets out that under the second requirement, taking steps to avoid the disadvantage will include removing, altering or providing a reasonable means of avoiding the physical feature, where it would be reasonable to do so.

85. It also makes clear that, except where the Act states otherwise, it would never be reasonable for a person bound by the duty to pass on the costs of complying with it to an individual disabled person.

Background

86. This section replaces similar provisions in the Disability Discrimination Act 1995. However, the Act makes some changes to provide consistency across the reasonable adjustment provisions. It contains only one threshold for the reasonable adjustment duty – "substantial disadvantage" – in place of the two thresholds in the Disability Discrimination Act 1995. It also reflects current practice by applying the third requirement explicitly to employment. And it introduces consistency of language by

referring to "provision, criterion or practice" rather than "practice, policy or procedure" used in some provisions in the Disability Discrimination Act 1995. It also introduces greater transparency with the express references to providing information in accessible formats and to not passing on the costs of an adjustment which are explained above.

Examples

- A utility company knows that significant numbers of its customers have a sight impairment and will have difficulty reading invoices and other customer communications in standard print, so must consider how to make its communications more accessible. As a result, it might provide communications in large print to customers who require this.
- A bank is obliged to consider reasonable adjustments for a newly recruited financial adviser who is a wheelchair user and who would have difficulty negotiating her way around the customer area. In consultation with the new adviser, the bank rearranges the layout of furniture in the customer area and installs a new desk. These changes result in the new adviser being able to work alongside her colleagues.
- The organiser of a large public conference knows that hearing-impaired delegates are likely to attend. She must therefore consider how to make the conference accessible to them. Having asked delegates what adjustments they need, she decides to engage BSL/English interpreters, have a palantypist and an induction loop to make sure that the hearing-impaired delegates are not substantially disadvantaged.

*Section 21: **Failure to comply with duty***

Effect

87. This section has the effect that a failure to comply with any one of the reasonable adjustment requirements amounts to discrimination against a disabled person to whom the duty is owed. It also provides that, apart from under this Act, no other action can be taken for failure to comply with the duty.

Background

88. This section replaces similar provisions in the Disability Discrimination Act 1995.

Examples

- An employee develops carpal tunnel syndrome which makes it difficult for him to use a standard keyboard. The employer refuses to provide a modified keyboard or voice-activated software which would overcome the disadvantage. This could be an unlawful failure to make a reasonable adjustment which would constitute discrimination.
- A private club has a policy of refusing entry to male members not wearing a collar and tie for evening events. A member with psoriasis (a severe skin condition which can make the wearing of a collar and tie extremely painful) could bring a discrimination claim if the club refused to consider waiving this policy for him.
- A visually-impaired prospective tenant asks a letting agent to provide a copy of a tenancy agreement in large print. The agent refuses even though the document is held on computer and could easily be printed in a larger font. This is likely to be an unlawful failure to make a reasonable adjustment which would constitute discrimination.

*Section 22: **Regulations***

Effect

89. This section provides a power for a Minister of the Crown to make regulations about a range of issues relating to the reasonable adjustment duty, such as the circumstances

in which a particular step will be regarded as reasonable. This power also allows amendment of the Schedules referred to in section 20(13).

Background

90. This section replaces similar provisions in the Disability Discrimination Act 1995.

Example

- Regulations could be made about what is and what is not included within the meaning of a "provision, criterion or practice" if, for example, research indicated that despite statutory codes of practice there was quite a high level of uncertainty among employers and service providers about the extent of the duty and how it applied.

Section 23: Comparison by reference to circumstances

Effect

91. This section provides that like must be compared with like in cases of direct, dual or indirect discrimination. The treatment of the claimant must be compared with that of an actual or a hypothetical person – the comparator – who does not share the same protected characteristic as the claimant (or, in the case of dual discrimination, either of the protected characteristics in the combination) but who is (or is assumed to be) in not materially different circumstances from the claimant. In cases of direct or dual discrimination, those circumstances can include their respective abilities where the claimant is a disabled person.

92. The section also enables a civil partner who is treated less favourably than a married person in similar circumstances to bring a claim for sexual orientation discrimination.

Background

93. The section replicates similar provisions in previous legislation but also accommodates the new concept of dual discrimination.

Examples

- A blind woman claims she was not shortlisted for a job involving computers because the employer wrongly assumed that blind people cannot use them. An appropriate comparator is a person who is not blind – it could be a non-disabled person or someone with a different disability – but who has the same ability to do the job as the claimant.
- A Muslim employee is put at a disadvantage by his employer's practice of not allowing requests for time off work on Fridays. The comparison that must be made is in terms of the impact of that practice on non-Muslim employees in similar circumstances to whom it is (or might be) applied.

Section 24: Irrelevance of alleged discriminator's characteristics

Effect

94. This section provides that it is no defence to a claim of direct or dual discrimination that the alleged discriminator shares the protected characteristic (or one or both of the protected characteristics in a dual discrimination claim) with the victim. The discriminator will still be liable for any unlawful discrimination. The wording of the section is broad enough to cover cases of discrimination based on association or perception.

Background

95. Previous legislation only expressly provided that it was no defence to a claim of direct discrimination that the alleged discriminator shared the same religion or belief as the victim. This section makes clear that the same principle applies, as at present, for other protected characteristics and makes similar provision in relation to the new concept of dual discrimination.

Example

- An employer cannot argue that because he is a gay man he is not liable for unlawful discrimination for rejecting a job application from another gay man because of the applicant's sexual orientation.

Section 25: References to particular strands of discrimination

Effect

96. This section sets out what is meant by references to the types of discrimination referred to in the Act, so that references elsewhere in the Act to age, marriage and civil partnership, race, religious or belief-related, sex or sexual orientation discrimination, include references to both direct and indirect discrimination because of each of those characteristics respectively.

97. As well as direct and indirect discrimination, references to disability discrimination also include references to discrimination arising from disability and to a failure to comply with a duty to make reasonable adjustments; and references to gender reassignment discrimination also include discrimination within section 16 (gender reassignment discrimination: cases of absence from work). Finally, references to pregnancy and maternity discrimination have the meanings derived from sections 17 and 18.

Section 26: Harassment

Effect

98. This section defines what is meant by harassment for the purposes of the Act. There are three types of harassment. The first type, which applies to all the protected characteristics apart from pregnancy and maternity, and marriage and civil partnership, involves unwanted conduct which is related to a relevant characteristic and has the purpose or effect of creating an intimidating, hostile, degrading, humiliating or offensive environment for the complainant or of violating the complainant's dignity. The second type is sexual harassment which is unwanted conduct of a sexual nature where this has the same purpose or effect as the first type of harassment. The third type is treating someone less favourably because he or she has either submitted to or rejected sexual harassment, or harassment related to sex or gender reassignment.

Background

99. Previous legislation provided freestanding protection against harassment, but the first type of harassment described above was not defined in the same way for all the different protected characteristics to which it applied. In determining the effect of the unwanted conduct, courts and tribunals will continue to be required to balance competing rights on the facts of a particular case. For example, this could include balancing the rights of freedom of expression (as set out in Article 10 of the European Convention on Human Rights) and of academic freedom against the right not to be offended in deciding whether a person has been harassed.

Examples

- A white worker who sees a black colleague being subjected to racially abusive language could have a case of harassment if the language also causes an offensive environment for her.
- An employer who displays any material of a sexual nature, such as a topless calendar, may be harassing her employees where this makes the workplace an offensive place to work for any employee, female or male.
- A shopkeeper propositions one of his shop assistants. She rejects his advances and then is turned down for promotion which she believes she would have got if she had accepted her boss's advances. The shop assistant would have a claim of harassment.

Section 27: Victimisation

Effect

100. This section defines what conduct amounts to victimisation under the Act. It provides that victimisation takes place where one person treats another badly because he or she in good faith has done a "protected act", for example taken or supported any action taken for the purpose of the Act, including in relation to any alleged breach of its provisions. It also provides that victimisation takes place where one person treats another badly because he or she is suspected of having done this or of intending to do this.

101. A person is not protected from victimisation where he or she maliciously makes or supports an untrue complaint.

102. Only an individual can bring a claim for victimisation.

Background

103. This section replaces similar provisions in previous legislation. However, under the Act victimisation is technically no longer treated as a form of discrimination, so there is no longer a need to compare treatment of an alleged victim with that of a person who has not made or supported a complaint under the Act.

Examples

- A woman makes a complaint of sex discrimination against her employer. As a result, she is denied promotion. The denial of promotion would amount to victimisation.
- A gay man sues a publican for persistently treating him less well than heterosexual customers. Because of this, the publican bars him from the pub altogether. This would be victimisation.
- An employer threatens to dismiss a staff member because he thinks she intends to support a colleague's sexual harassment claim. This threat could amount to victimisation.
- A man with a grudge against his employer knowingly gives false evidence in a colleague's discrimination claim against the employer. He is subsequently dismissed for supporting the claim. His dismissal would not amount to victimisation because of his untrue and malicious evidence.

Part 3: Services and Public Functions

Section 28: Application of this Part

Effect

104. This section provides that this Part of the Act, which prohibits discrimination, harassment and victimisation by people who supply services (which includes goods and

facilities) or perform public functions, does not apply to discrimination or harassment of people in those circumstances because they are married or in a civil partnership or because of age if they are under 18.

105. It also states that, if an act of discrimination, harassment or victimisation is made unlawful by other Parts of the Act covering premises, work or education, then those provisions, rather than the provisions covering services and public functions, apply. Similarly, if the act in question results in a breach of an equality clause in a person's terms of work or a non-discrimination rule in an occupational pension scheme, this Part will not apply.

Background

106. This section generally reflects the position in previous legislation. However, since the prohibition on discrimination because of age in services and public functions will not be extended to the under 18s, this section explains that the provisions in this Part do not apply to under 18s in respect of the protected characteristic of age.

*Section 29: **Provision of services, etc.***

Effect

107. This section makes it unlawful to discriminate against or harass a person because of a protected characteristic, or victimise someone when providing services (which includes goods and facilities). The person is protected both when requesting a service and during the course of being provided with a service.

108. It also makes it unlawful to discriminate against, harass or victimise a person when exercising a public function which does not involve the provision of a service. Examples of such public functions include law enforcement and revenue raising and collection. Public functions which involve the provision of a service, for example, medical treatment on the NHS, are covered by the provisions dealing with services.

109. It also imposes the duty to make reasonable adjustments set out in section 20 in relation to providing services and exercising public functions. A person is considered to have discriminated against a disabled person if he or she fails to comply with the duty to make reasonable adjustments.

110. However, the prohibition on harassment when providing services or exercising public functions does not cover sexual orientation or religion or belief.

111. The prohibitions in this section apply, in relation to race or religion or belief, to any actions taken in connection with the grant of entry clearance to enter the United Kingdom, even if the act in question takes place outside the United Kingdom.

Background

112. Previous legislation provided some protection from discrimination, harassment and victimisation in the provision of services and the exercise of public functions. However, the protection was not uniform for the different protected characteristics. For example, there was no protection from discrimination in the exercise of public functions because of pregnancy and maternity or because a person is intending to undergo, is undergoing or has undergone gender reassignment. Also there was no protection for discrimination because of age, either in the provision of services or in the exercise of public functions.

113. This section replaces the provisions in previous legislation and extends protection so that it is generally uniform across all the protected characteristics covered by this Part. However, as under previous law, there is no express protection for harassment related to religion or belief or sexual orientation in either the provision of services or the exercise of public functions. Conduct that would otherwise have fallen within the definition of harassment may still amount to direct discrimination, as section 212(5) makes clear.

Examples

- A man and two female friends plan a night out at a local night club. At the entrance the man is charged £10 entry; the two women are charged £5 each. The owner explains the night club is trying to attract more women and has decided to charge them half the entrance fee. This would be direct sex discrimination.
- A company which organises outdoor activity breaks requires protective headwear to be worn for certain activities, such as white water rafting and rock climbing. This requirement could be indirectly discriminatory against Sikhs unless it can be justified, for example on health and safety grounds.
- A man who suffers from long-standing and serious health problems, including partial paralysis and a severe sight impairment, is imprisoned. On his imprisonment, the man is not allocated an adapted cell, despite being assessed as requiring one within 24 hours of arriving at prison. Instead, he is allocated a standard cell. This would be discrimination resulting from a failure to make reasonable adjustments to take account of a person's disability.
- A black man goes into a bar to watch a football match. He is served a pint of beer and takes a seat at an empty table. Whilst watching the football match the bartender and a number of customers make racist remarks about some of the footballers on the pitch. When the man complains he is then called a number of derogatory names. This would be harassment because of race.

Section 30: Ships and hovercraft

Effect

114. This section provides that the services provisions will only apply to ships and hovercraft in the way set out in regulations made by a Minister of the Crown. The section also provides that in relation to the exercise of public functions that do not involve providing a service to the public, section 29(6) applies to ships and hovercraft in all cases except disability discrimination for which regulations will be needed.

115. As ships and hovercraft may be constantly moving between waters under the jurisdiction of different States or be outside the jurisdiction of any State, such regulations are needed to give certainty for people who provide or receive services in relation to ships and hovercraft about whether the services and public functions provisions apply.

Background

116. Previous legislation specified the territorial application of the services provisions, dealing specifically with ships and hovercraft (for example, section 36 of the Sex Discrimination Act 1975 and section 27 of the Race Relations Act 1976). As the Act is silent on the territorial application of the services provisions, regulations made under this section will ensure that there is clarity about when and on which ships and hovercraft the services provisions apply.

Section 31: Interpretation and exceptions

Effect

117. This section explains what is meant by the terms "provision of a service" and "public function" in the Act. The definition of a "public function" is that which applies for the purposes of the Human Rights Act 1998. The public functions provisions apply only where what is being done does not fall within the definition of a "service".

118. This section also explains that refusing to provide or not providing a service includes providing a person with a service of different quality, or in a different way (for example

hostile or less courteous) or on less favourable terms than the service would normally be provided.

119. This section provides that where an employer arranges for another person to provide a service to a closed group of employees, then the members of that closed group are to be treated as a section of the public for the purposes of their relationship with the service-provider. This means that if the service-provider discriminates against members of that group, the prohibitions in this Part apply. However, the employer is not to be treated as a service-provider, despite facilitating access to the service. Instead, his or her conduct in respect of his or her employees is to be governed by the provisions in Part 5 (work).

120. Further details of how the reasonable adjustments duty applies in relation to providing services and exercising public functions are contained in Schedule 2.

121. The exceptions which apply to this Part of the Act are contained in Schedule 3.

Background

122. Much of what is contained in this section has its origins in previous legislation, but this is now brought together in an interpretation section rather than in the substantive provisions as was the case in the previous legislation. The subsection concerning employers arranging for provision of services to their employees by another person is new.

Examples

- Services include the provision of day care, the running of residential care homes and leisure centre facilities, whether provided by a private body or a local authority.
- Public functions not involving the provision of a service include licensing functions; Government and local authority public consultation exercises; the provision of public highways; planning permission decisions; and core functions of the prison service and the probation service.
- The definition of refusing to provide a service covers, for example, a bank which has a policy not to accept calls from customers through a third party. This could amount to indirect discrimination against a deaf person who uses a registered interpreter to call the bank.
- An employer arranges for an insurer to provide a group health insurance scheme to his employees. The insurer refuses to provide cover on the same terms to one of the employees because she is transsexual. This would be treated as direct discrimination in the provision of services by the insurer against the employee in the same way as if the insurance was available to the general public. However, if it was the employer, rather than the insurer, who decided that the transsexual employee should not be able to access the group health insurance scheme, such discrimination in the employee's access to benefits in the workplace would be covered by the provisions of Part 5 (work).

Part 4: Premises

Section 32: Application of this Part

Effect

123. This section provides that this Part of the Act, which prohibits discrimination, harassment and victimisation in relation to the disposal, management and occupation of premises, does not make it unlawful to discriminate against or harass people in those circumstances because they are married or in a civil partnership or because of age.

124. It also states that, if an act of discrimination, harassment or victimisation is made unlawful by other Parts of the Act covering work or education, then those provisions, rather than the provisions covering premises, apply. Further, where accommodation is

provided either as a short-term let or where it is provided as part of a service or public function, Part 3 (services and public functions) applies instead of this Part. If the act in question results in a breach of an equality clause in a person's terms of work or a non-discrimination rule in an occupational pension scheme then these provisions will not apply.

Background

125. This provision broadly reflects the position in the previous legislation, which gave protection from discrimination in the disposal and management of premises across all the protected characteristics with the exception of age and marriage and civil partnership.

Section 33: Disposals, etc.

Effect

126. This section makes it unlawful for a person who has the authority to dispose of premises (for example, by selling, letting or subletting a property) to discriminate against or victimise someone else in a number of ways including by offering the premises to them on less favourable terms; by not letting or selling the premises to them or by treating them less favourably.

127. It also makes it unlawful for a person with authority to dispose of premises to harass someone who occupies or applies for them. The Act does not however make it unlawful to harass someone because of sexual orientation or religion or belief when disposing of premises.

Background

128. This section replaces similar provisions in previous legislation. Conduct that would otherwise have fallen within the definition of harassment may still amount to direct discrimination, as section 212(5) makes clear.

Examples

- A landlord refuses to let a property to a prospective tenant because of her race. This is direct discrimination when disposing of premises.
- A vendor offers her property to a prospective buyer who is disabled at a higher sale price than she would to a non-disabled person, because of the person's disability. This is direct discrimination when disposing of premises.

Section 34: Permission for disposal

Effect

129. This section makes it unlawful for a person whose permission is needed to dispose of premises (for example, to sell, let or sublet a property) to discriminate against or victimise someone else by withholding that permission. It also makes it unlawful for such a person to harass someone who seeks that permission, or someone to whom the property would be sold or let if the permission were given. The Act does not however make it unlawful to harass someone because of sexual orientation or religion or belief by withholding permission to dispose of premises.

130. This section does not apply where permission to dispose of premises is refused by a court in the context of legal proceedings.

Background

131. This section replaces similar provisions in previous legislation.

Example

- A disabled tenant seeks permission from his landlord to sublet a room within his flat to help him pay his rent. The landlord tells him that he cannot because he is disabled. This is direct discrimination in permission for disposing of premises.

Section 35: Management

Effect

132. This section makes it unlawful for a person who manages premises to discriminate against or victimise someone who occupies the property in the way he or she allows the person to use a benefit or facility associated with the property, by evicting the person or by otherwise treating the person unfavourably. It also makes it unlawful for a person who manages a property to harass a person who occupies or applies to occupy it. The Act does not however make it unlawful to harass someone because of sexual orientation or religion or belief in the management of premises.

Background

133. This section replaces similar provisions in previous legislation.

Examples

- A manager of a property restricts a tenant's use of a communal garden by setting fixed times when she can use the garden because she is undergoing gender reassignment, while allowing other tenants unrestricted access to the garden. This would be direct discrimination in the management of premises.
- A manager of a property refuses to allow a lesbian tenant to use facilities which are available to other tenants, or deliberately neglects to inform her about facilities which are available for the use of other tenants, because she had previously made a claim of discrimination against the manager. This would be victimisation.
- A manager of a property responds to requests for maintenance issues more slowly or less favourably for one tenant than similar requests from other tenants, because the tenant has a learning disability. This would be direct discrimination in the management of premises.

Section 36: Leasehold and commonhold premises and common parts

Effect

134. This section imposes the reasonable adjustments duty on those who let premises, commonhold associations, and those who are responsible for the common parts of let or commonhold premises in England and Wales. This section also defines who is responsible for common parts, defines common parts and includes a power to prescribe premises to which the requirements do not apply.

Background

135. Part of this section replaces similar provisions in the Disability Discrimination Act 1995 relating to let premises and premises to let. The provisions relating to common parts are new.

Example

- An agency used by a landlord to let and manage leasehold premises is a controller of premises under this provision and therefore is under the duty to make reasonable adjustments for disabled people, such as making information about the property available in accessible formats.

Section 37: Adjustments to common parts in Scotland

Effect

136. This section confers a power on the Scottish Ministers to make regulations entitling disabled people to make disability-related alterations to the common parts of some residential property in Scotland.

137. This section also sets out what matters the regulations may provide for; provides that the Scottish Ministers must consult a Minister of the Crown before exercising the power; and defines "common parts" and "relevant adjustments".

Background

138. This provision is new. It is intended to facilitate disability-related alterations to the common parts of residential premises in Scotland where the premises are the disabled person's only or main home. Provision for disabled people in tenanted property in Scotland was made in the Housing (Scotland) Act 2006, but in relation to common parts those provisions cover only the consent required from the person's landlord and not that required from other common owners. As the process for obtaining consent from common owners will need to fit into, and operate within, the Scottish devolved areas of property and housing, land registration and civil justice, it is considered appropriate to confer a power on the Scottish Ministers to permit them to make the necessary provision by means of secondary legislation.

Section 38: Interpretation and exceptions

Effect

139. This section explains what is meant by terms used in this Part. In particular it sets out the kinds of property transactions meant by "disposing of premises" in the case of premises which are subject to a tenancy, and defines what is meant by "tenancy". It also makes it clear that the provisions apply to tenancies made before as well as after the Act.

140. The details of how the reasonable adjustments duty applies in relation to "let premises", "premises to let", "commonhold land" and "common parts" of let or commonhold premises are contained in Schedule 4.

141. The exceptions which apply to this part of the Act are contained in Schedule 5.

Background

142. This section replaces similar provisions in previous legislation.

Part 5: Work

Chapter 1: Employment, etc.

Section 39: Employees and applicants

Effect

143. This section makes it unlawful for an employer to discriminate against or victimise employees and people seeking work. It applies where the employer is making arrangements to fill a job, and in respect of anything done in the course of a person's employment. In respect of discrimination because of sex or pregnancy and maternity, a term of an offer of employment which relates to pay is treated as discriminatory where, if accepted, it would give rise to an equality clause or if an equality clause does not apply, where the offer of the term constitutes direct or dual discrimination. It also

imposes the reasonable adjustments duty set out in section 20 on employers in respect of disabled employees and applicants.

Background

144. This section replaces similar provisions in previous legislation.

Examples

- An employer decides not to shortlist for interview a disabled job applicant because of her epilepsy. This would be direct discrimination.
- An employer offers a woman a job on lower pay than the set rate because she is pregnant when she applies. She cannot bring an equality clause case as there is no comparator. However, she will be able to claim direct discrimination.
- An employer refuses to interview a man applying for promotion, because he previously supported a discrimination case against the employer brought by another employee. This would be victimisation.
- An employer enforces a "no beards" policy by asking staff to shave. This could be indirect discrimination, because it would have a particular impact on Muslims or Orthodox Jews.

Section 40: Employees and applicants: harassment

Effect

145. This section makes it unlawful for an employer to harass employees and people applying for employment. It also makes the employer liable for harassment of its employees by third parties, such as customers or clients, over whom the employer does not have direct control. Liability in relation to third party harassment will however only arise when harassment has occurred on at least two previous occasions, the employer is aware that it has taken place, and has not taken reasonable steps to prevent it happening again.

Background

146. This section is designed to replicate the effect of provisions in the Sex Discrimination Act 1975 as regards harassment by employers, and extend to the other protected characteristics (apart from marriage and civil partnership and pregnancy and maternity) the position in relation to employer liability for sex harassment under that Act.

Example

- A shop assistant with a strong Nigerian accent tells her manager that she is upset and humiliated by a customer who regularly uses the shop and each time makes derogatory remarks about Africans in her hearing. If her manager does nothing to try to stop it happening again, he would be liable for racial harassment.

Section 41: Contract workers

Effect

147. This section makes it unlawful for a person (referred to as a principal) who makes work available to contract workers to discriminate against, harass or victimise them. Contract workers are separately protected from discrimination by their employer (for example, the agency for which they work and which places them with the principal) under section 39. This section also imposes a duty on the principal to make reasonable adjustments for disabled contract workers (in addition to the duty on the contract worker's employer).

Background

148. This section is designed to replicate the effect of provisions in previous legislation, while codifying case law to make clear that there does not need to be a direct contractual relationship between the employer and the principal for this protection to apply.

Examples

- A hotel manager refuses to accept a black African contract worker sent to him by an agency because of fears that guests would be put off by his accent. This would be direct discrimination.
- A bank treats a female contract worker less well than her male counterparts, for example by insisting that as she is a woman she should make coffee for all meetings. This would be direct discrimination.

Section 42: Identity of employer

Effect

149. This section provides that police constables and police cadets are treated as employees for the purposes of this Part of the Act. It identifies the relevant employer as either the chief officer (or, in Scotland, the chief constable) or the responsible authority as defined in section 43, depending on who commits the act in question.

150. Constables serving with the Civil Nuclear Constabulary are treated as employees of the Civil Nuclear Police Authority.

151. A constable seconded to the Serious Organised Crime Agency (SOCA) or Scottish Police Services Authority (SPSA) is treated as employed by SOCA or SPSA.

152. A constable at the Scottish Crime and Drugs Enforcement Agency (SCDEA) is treated as employed by the Director General of SCDEA.

Background

153. This section is designed to replicate the provisions in previous legislation and extends coverage to constables at SPSA and SCDEA. It also removes the requirement to pay out of police funds compensation and related costs arising from the personal liability of chief officers (or in Scotland, chief constables) for acts which are unlawful under the Act. Payments of compensation and related costs arising from the personal liability of chief officers (or in Scotland, chief constables) will instead be dealt with by the Police Act 1996 and the Police (Scotland) Act 1967, as for all other police officers.

Example

- A chief officer refuses to allocate protective equipment to female constables. The chief officer would be treated as the employer in a direct discrimination claim.

Section 43: Interpretation

Effect

154. This section explains what is meant by terms such as "chief officer" and "relevant Act" used in section 42.

Background

155. This section replaces similar provisions in previous legislation, but includes some additional terms, such as those relevant to the SPSA and SCDEA.

Section 44: Partnerships

Effect

156. This section makes it unlawful for firms (and those intending to set up a firm) to discriminate against, harass or victimise their partners, or people seeking to be partners in the firm. Activities covered by these provisions could include the offering of partnerships or giving existing partners access to opportunities such as training and/or transfers to other branches of the firm. It imposes on firms and people setting up firms a duty to make reasonable adjustments for disabled partners and prospective partners.

157. In the case of limited partnerships, these prohibitions only apply in relation to those partners who are involved with the operation of the firm (general partners).

Background

158. Because partners are mainly governed by their partnership agreements, rather than by employment contracts, separate provisions are needed to provide protection from discrimination, harassment and victimisation for partners in ordinary and limited partnerships. This section is designed to replicate the effect of provisions in previous legislation but also to provide consistent protection in respect of race (whereas previously the protection of colour and nationality differed in some respects from that of race and ethnic or national origin).

Example

- A firm refuses to accept an application for partnership from a black candidate, who is qualified to join, because he is of African origin. This would be direct discrimination.

Section 45: Limited liability partnerships

Effect

159. This section makes it unlawful for a limited liability partnership (LLP), or a group of people setting up an LLP, to discriminate against, harass or victimise a member (or prospective member). Activities covered by these provisions include offers of membership or access to opportunities that the LLP makes available to its members. It imposes on LLPs a duty to make reasonable adjustments for disabled members and prospective members.

Background

160. LLPs are distinct from general and limited partnerships, so separate provisions are needed to provide protection from discrimination, harassment and victimisation for their members. This section is designed to replicate the effect of provisions in previous legislation but also to achieve the same consistency in respect of race as is provided in section 44.

Examples

- An LLP refuses a member access to use of a company car because he has supported a discrimination or harassment claim against the LLP. This would be victimisation.
- An LLP refuses a Muslim member access to its child care scheme because all the other children who attend the scheme have Christian parents. This would be direct discrimination.

Section 46: Interpretation

Effect

161. This section explains what is meant by terms used in sections 44 and 45. As well as defining the types of partnership to which these provisions apply, it establishes what is meant by expulsion from a partnership.

Example

- A gay partner in a firm who, because of constant homophobic banter feels compelled to leave his position as a partner, can claim to have been expelled from the partnership because of his sexual orientation. Should an employment tribunal agree with him, the firm could be found to be in breach of these provisions in a similar way to how the employment tribunal would find for an employee who wins a claim for constructive dismissal.

Section 47: Barristers

Effect

162. This section makes it unlawful for a barrister or a barrister's clerk to discriminate against, harass or victimise a pupil (a trainee barrister) or tenant (including a squatter or door-tenant) in the barristers' chambers, or people seeking to be a pupil or tenant, in relation to the professional relationship between them. It also imposes on barristers a duty to make reasonable adjustments for disabled pupils and tenants.

163. It also makes it unlawful for a person instructing a barrister (for example, a client or instructing solicitor) to discriminate against, harass or victimise a barrister in relation to the giving of instructions.

Background

164. This section replaces provisions in previous legislation providing similar protection for barristers, pupils, tenants and prospective pupils or tenants in barristers' chambers. However, it no longer protects clients and clerks from discrimination by barristers because they can respectively seek redress under the "services" provisions or under other work provisions (section 39 and section 41) of the Act.

Examples

- A barrister treats a female pupil less favourably than his male pupils by allowing her to be involved in a narrower range of cases, because of assumptions about the kind of cases women can handle competently. This would be direct discrimination.
- A clerk gives instructions to a Christian barrister in his chambers in preference to a Hindu barrister, because he fears that the barrister's religion would prevent him representing a Christian client properly. This would be direct discrimination.

Section 48: Advocates

Effect

165. This section makes it unlawful for practising advocates and their clerks to discriminate against, harass or victimise devils (trainee advocates) or members of the stable (a group of advocates working in shared premises) or people seeking to be a devil or member, in respect of the professional relationship between them. It imposes on advocates a duty to make reasonable adjustments for disabled devils and stable members.

166. It also makes it unlawful for a person instructing an advocate (for example, a direct access client or instructing solicitor) to discriminate against, harass or victimise an advocate in relation to the giving of instructions.

Background

167. This section replaces similar provisions in previous legislation. However, as with the section on barristers, this section no longer protects clients and clerks from discrimination by advocates because they can respectively seek redress under the "services" provisions or under other work provisions (section 39 and section 41) of the Act.

Examples

- An advocate treats one devil less favourably than another by refusing to allow him to be involved in a particular case because he fears the devil's sexual orientation may affect his involvement in the case. This would be direct discrimination.
- An advocate puts pressure on a stable member to leave because the member is disabled and the advocate does not want to make reasonable adjustments. This would be direct discrimination.

Section 49: Personal offices: appointments, etc.

Effect

168. This section makes it unlawful to discriminate against, harass or victimise people who are or wish to become personal office-holders. These provisions apply in so far as other work provisions do not – this means that where office-holders are also employees, they will be protected by the provisions dealing with employment in respect of their employment relationship. In respect of sex or pregnancy and maternity discrimination, a term of an offer of an appointment to office which relates to pay is treated as discriminatory where, if accepted, it would give rise to an equality clause or, if that is not the case, where the offer of the term constitutes direct or dual discrimination.

169. Personal office-holders are people who perform a function personally at a time and place specified by another person and who, in return, are entitled to payment (other than expenses or compensation for lost income). Section 52(4) provides that, where a personal office is a public office at the same time, it is to be treated as a public office only.

170. An office-holder can be appointed by one person and then an entirely different person can be responsible for other matters, for example for providing facilities for the office-holder to perform his or her functions. Because of this, the section prohibits both the person who makes the appointment and any relevant person from discriminating against, victimising or harassing the office-holder. The relevant person is the person who is responsible for the act complained of in each case.

171. This section places a duty to make reasonable adjustments on a person who makes the appointment and any relevant person in relation to the needs of disabled people who seek or hold personal offices.

Background

172. This section is designed to replicate the effect of provisions in previous legislation.

Examples

- A company board refuses to appoint a candidate as director because she is black. This would be direct discrimination.
- A company terminates the appointment of a director because it is discovered that she is pregnant. This would be direct discrimination.

Section 50: Public offices: appointments, etc.

Effect

173. This section makes it unlawful to discriminate against, harass or victimise people who are or wish to become public office-holders. Like the personal office- holder provisions above, these provisions apply in so far as other work provisions do not. This means that where public office-holders are also employees, they will be protected by the provisions dealing with employment in respect of their employment relationship. In respect of sex or pregnancy and maternity discrimination, a term of an offer of an appointment to office which relates to pay is treated as discriminatory where, if accepted, it would give rise to an equality clause or if that is not the case where the offer of the term constitutes direct or dual discrimination.

174. Public office-holders are people appointed by, on the recommendation of, or with the approval of, a member of the executive branch of Government, such as a Government Minister, or people who are appointed on the recommendation, or subject to the approval of, either of the Houses of Parliament, the National Assembly for Wales, or the Scottish Parliament.

175. A public office-holder can be appointed by one person and then an entirely different person can be responsible for other matters, for example for providing facilities for the office-holder to perform his or her functions. Because of this, the section prohibits both the person with the power to make the appointment and any relevant person from discriminating against, victimising or harassing the office- holder. The relevant person is the person who is responsible for the act complained of in each case (but does not include either of the Houses of Parliament, the National Assembly for Wales or the Scottish Parliament).

176. This section also places on the person who has the power to make an appointment and any relevant person a duty to make reasonable adjustments for disabled people seeking or holding public offices.

Background

177. This section is for the most part designed to replicate the effect of provisions in previous legislation. It also extends protection from discrimination, harassment and victimisation to those appointed on the recommendation or approval of law-making bodies such as the Scottish Parliament and the Welsh Assembly.

Example

- A Government Minister with the power to appoint the non-executive board members of a non-departmental public body fails to appoint a candidate because he is gay. This would be direct discrimination.

Section 51: Public offices: recommendations for appointments, etc.

Effect

178. This section makes it unlawful for a person with power to make recommendations about or approve appointments to public offices to discriminate against, harass or victimise people seeking or being considered as public office- holders in respect of the recommendation or approval process. It also imposes a duty on the person with the power to make a recommendation or approve an appointment to make reasonable adjustments for disabled people who seek or are being considered for appointment to public offices.

179. This section does not apply in respect of all public offices, only those to which the appointment is made on the recommendation or approval of a member of the executive

or where the appointment is made by a member of the executive on the recommendation or approval of a relevant body (for example, a non-departmental public body).

Background

180. This section is for the most part designed to replicate the effect of provisions in current legislation. It also extends protection from discrimination, harassment and victimisation to those appointed by a member of the executive on the recommendation or with the approval of a non-departmental public body (in respect of that appointment or recommendation).

Example

- It would be direct discrimination for the Government Minister responsible for approving the appointment of members of the BBC Trust to refuse to approve the appointment of a person because he has a hearing impairment.

Section 52: Interpretation and exceptions

Effect

181. This section explains the meaning of various terms, such as "relevant person", used in sections 49, 50 and 51. It provides that appointment does not include election, meaning elected offices will not constitute personal or public offices for the purpose of these sections.

182. It also stipulates that termination of an appointment includes the expiration of the appointment period or where unreasonable conduct of the relevant person causes the office-holder to terminate the appointment. But it does not count as termination if after expiry of the appointment the person's appointment is immediately renewed on the same terms.

Section 53: Qualifications bodies

Effect

183. This section makes it unlawful for a qualifications body (as defined in section 54) to discriminate against, harass or victimise a person when conferring relevant qualifications (which includes renewing or extending a relevant qualification). It provides that applying a competence standard to a disabled person is not disability discrimination, provided the application of the standard is justified. It also imposes a duty on qualifications bodies to make reasonable adjustments for disabled people.

Background

184. This section replaces similar provisions in previous legislation. It also extends the protection to cover discrimination in the arrangements made for determining upon whom a relevant qualification should be conferred.

Examples

- A body which confers diplomas certifying that people are qualified electricians refuses to confer the qualification on a man simply because he is gay. This would be direct discrimination.
- An organisation which maintains a register of professional tradespeople refuses to include a person's details on the register because her name does not sound English. This would be direct discrimination.

Section 54: Interpretation

Effect

185. This section explains the meaning of various terms used in section 53. In particular, it defines a qualifications body as a body which can confer any academic, medical, technical or other standard which is required to carry out a particular trade or profession, or which better enables a person to do so by, for example, determining whether the person has a particular level of competence or ability.

186. It also makes clear that bodies such as schools, institutions of further and higher education and education authorities which confer qualifications such as A Levels and GCSEs are not qualifications bodies for the purposes of section 53.

Background

187. This section is designed to replicate the effect of similar provisions in previous legislation.

Example

- Examples of qualifications bodies are the Public Carriage Office (which licenses cab drivers in London), the British Horseracing Authority and the General Medical Council. Also included is any body which confers a diploma on people pursuing a particular trade (for example, plumbers), even if the diploma is not strictly necessary to pursue a career in that trade but shows that the person has reached a certain standard.

Section 55: Employment service-providers

Effect

188. This section makes it unlawful to discriminate against, harass or victimise a person when providing an employment service. It also places a duty on providers of employment services to make reasonable adjustments for disabled people. The duty is an anticipatory duty except for providers of a vocational service, so that in relation to the provision of vocational services, employment service-providers do not need to deal in advance with reasonable adjustments for disabled people. Employment services and vocational services are defined in section 56.

Background

189. This section replaces the separate provisions for vocational training, employment agencies and assisting persons to obtain employment in previous legislation with a single provision covering all these aspects.

Examples

- A company which provides courses to train people to be plumbers refuses to enrol women because its directors assume that very few people want to employ female plumbers. This would be direct discrimination.
- An agency which finds employment opportunities for teachers in schools offers placements only to white teachers based on the assumption that this is what parents in a particular area would prefer. This would be direct discrimination.
- An agency advertises job vacancies on its website. It will need to have the website checked for accessibility and make reasonable changes to enable disabled people using a variety of access software to use it.

Section 56: Interpretation

Effect

190. This section explains what the provision of an employment service includes (such as the provision of training for employment or careers guidance), and what it does not include (such as education in schools), for the purposes of section 55.

Example

- Examples of the types of activities covered under this section include providing CV writing classes, English or Maths classes to help adults into work; training in IT/keyboard skills; or providing work placements.

Section 57: Trade organisations

Effect

191. This section makes it unlawful for a trade organisation to discriminate against, harass or victimise a person who is, or is applying to be, a member. It also requires trade organisations to make reasonable adjustments for disabled people.

192. A trade organisation is an organisation of workers (such as a trade union) or employers (such as the Chambers of Commerce); or an organisation whose members carry out a particular trade or profession (such as the British Medical Association, the Institute of Civil Engineers and the Law Society).

Background

193. This section is designed to replicate the effect of similar provisions in previous legislation. It also extends the protection to cover discrimination in the arrangements made for determining to whom membership should be offered.

Examples

- A trade union restricts its membership to men. This would be direct discrimination.
- An organisation of employers varies membership subscriptions or access to conferences because of a person's race. This would be direct discrimination.

Section 58: Official business of members

Effect

194. This section makes it unlawful for local authorities to discriminate against, harass or victimise their members in relation to providing access to facilities such as training which relate to the carrying out of their official business. This does not apply to election or appointment to posts within the local authority. It imposes a duty on local authorities to make reasonable adjustments for disabled members.

Background

195. This section extends protection previously in the Disability Discrimination Act 1995 to all protected characteristics.

Example

- A local authority does not equip meeting rooms with hearing loops for a member who has a hearing impairment, in order to enable her to take full part in the business for which she has been elected. This would be discrimination if provision of hearing loops were considered to be a reasonable adjustment.

Section 59: Interpretation

Effect

196. This section explains the meaning of various terms used in section 58. In particular, it lists the various bodies which are included in the term "local authority" and provides a power for a Minister of the Crown to add to this list of bodies. It also explains what is meant by reference to the carrying-out of official business by members of a local authority.

Example

- A local authority member who is considering an application for planning permission while sitting on a council's Planning Committee would be undertaking "official business".

Section 60: Enquiries about disability and health

Effect

197. Except in the situations specified in this section, an employer must not ask about a job applicant's health until that person has been either offered a job (on a conditional or unconditional basis) or been included in a pool of successful candidates to be offered a job when a suitable position arises. The specified situations where health-related enquiries can be made are for the purposes of:

    - finding out whether a job applicant would be able to participate in an assessment to test his or her suitability for the work;
    - making reasonable adjustments to enable the disabled person to participate in the recruitment process;
    - finding out whether a job applicant would be able to undertake a function that is intrinsic to the job, with reasonable adjustments in place as required;
    - monitoring diversity in applications for jobs;
    - supporting positive action in employment for disabled people; and
    - enabling an employer to identify suitable candidates for a job where there is an occupational requirement for the person to be disabled.

198. The section also allows questions to be asked where they are needed in the context of national security vetting.

199. Where an employer makes a health or disability-related enquiry which falls outside the specified situations, he or she would be acting unlawfully under the Equality Act 2006. Together with Schedule 26, this section gives the Equality and Human Rights Commission (EHRC) an enforcement role. (Section 120(8) ensures that only the EHRC can enforce a breach of this provision.). This means, for example, that the EHRC would be able to conduct an investigation if there was evidence that a large employer might be routinely asking prohibited questions when recruiting.

200. Where the employer asks a question not allowed by this section and rejects the applicant, if the applicant then makes a claim to the employment tribunal for direct disability discrimination, it will be for the employer to show that it had not discriminated against the candidate.

201. As well as applying to recruitment to employment, the section also applies to the other areas covered by Part 5 of the Act, such as contract work, business partnerships, office-holders, barristers and advocates.

Background

202. This is a new provision. The Disability Discrimination Act 1995 did not prevent an employer from making health- or disability- related enquiries of applicants for a job, although it did make it unlawful to use the result of such enquiries to discriminate against a candidate because of his or her disability. This provision will limit the making of enquiries and therefore help to tackle the disincentive effect that an employer making such enquiries can have on some disabled people making applications for work.

Examples

- Applicants are asked on an application form whether they have a disability that requires the employer to make a reasonable adjustment to the recruitment process. This is to allow, for example, people with a speech impairment more time for interview. This enquiry would be permitted.
- An applicant applies for a job in a warehouse, which requires the manual lifting and handling of heavy items. As manual handling is a function which is intrinsic to the job, the employer is permitted to ask the applicant questions about his health to establish whether he is able to do the job (with reasonable adjustments for a disabled applicant, if required). The employer would not be permitted to ask the applicant other health questions until he or she offered the candidate a job.

Chapter 2: Occupational pension schemes

Section 61: Non-discrimination rule

Effect

203. This section requires that every occupational pension scheme is to have a non-discrimination rule read into it. The rule prohibits “a responsible person” from discriminating against, harassing or victimising a member or a person who could become a member of the scheme.

204. A responsible person is a scheme trustee or manager, an employer, and the person responsible for appointing a person to a public office, where the office-holder can be a scheme member.

205. The rule does not apply to pension rights built up or benefits payable for periods of service before the commencement of this section. Periods of service prior to this date will be subject to the previous discrimination legislation.

206. Where there has been a breach of a non-discrimination rule, proceedings may be brought against the person responsible for the breach under Part 9 of the Act. The provisions in Part 9 do not prevent the investigation or determination of any matter in accordance with Part 10 of the Pension Schemes Act 1993 (investigations: the Pensions Ombudsman) by the Pensions Ombudsman as the Ombudsman’s investigations are not legal proceedings.

207. Pension credit members are not protected from discrimination because their rights are derived from an order of the court, rather than directly from employment.

208. It would not be a breach of a non-discrimination rule if an employer or the trustees or managers maintain certain practices or make decisions in relation to age that are specified by order by Ministers.

209. The non-discrimination rule does not apply where an equality rule operates or would operate, but for the exceptions in Part 2 of Schedule 7.

Background

210. Occupational pension schemes were already required by previous legislation to have non-discrimination rules in respect of age, disability, religion or belief and sexual orientation. This provision establishes non-discrimination rules in respect of race, gender reassignment, marriage and civil partnership, and sex.

211. Exceptions to the non-discrimination rule in relation to age were set out in Schedule 2 to the Employment Equality (Age) Regulations 2006 (SI 2006/1031).

Example

- A disabled person is refused membership of an occupational pension scheme because the trustees believe it is not in her best interest to join. This is because she has a short life expectancy and is unlikely to build up a reasonable pension. Although the trustees believe they are acting reasonably, they may be liable to challenge because they have breached the non-discrimination rule.

Section 62: Non-discrimination alterations

Effect

212. This section gives trustees and managers of an occupational pension scheme the power, by resolution, to alter their scheme's rules to conform to the non-discrimination rule in section 61.

213. They may use the power if:

   - they lack powers to alter the rules for that purpose, or
   - procedures for altering the rules, including obtaining consent, are unduly complex or would take too long.

Background

214. This section is based on similar provisions which allowed trustees and managers to secure conformity with the non-discrimination rules in the Disability Discrimination Act 1995, the Employment Equality (Religion or Belief) Regulations 2003, the Employment Equality (Sexual Orientation) Regulations 2003 and the Employment Equality (Age) Regulations 2006.

Example

- Changes to the scheme rules of a large scheme require consultation with all the members before they may be made. This is impracticable, particularly as some deferred members cannot be traced. Scheme trustees may make the necessary alteration to scheme rules relying on this power.

Section 63: Communications

Effect

215. This section applies to sections 61, 120, 126 and paragraph 19 of Schedule 8, in their application to communications, to a disabled person who is:

   - entitled to the present payment of dependants' or survivors' benefits under an occupational pension scheme, or
   - entitled to a pension derived from a divorce settlement (pension credit member).

Background

216. This section replaces provisions in the Disability Discrimination Act 1995.

Chapter 3: Equality of terms

Section 64: Relevant types of work

Effect

217. Chapter 3 of Part 5 of the Act contains provisions designed to achieve equality between men and women in pay and other terms of employment where the work of an employee and his or her comparator – a person of the opposite sex - is equal. It does so by providing for a sex equality clause to be read into the employee's contract of employment. This is designed to ensure parity of terms between the employee and his or her comparator. A similar provision – referred to as a sex equality rule – is implied into the terms of pension schemes.

218. This section explains that the sections mentioned which impose the equality clause and equality rule apply to employees, office-holders and, by virtue of subsection (3) of section 83, members of the armed forces, where one person's work is equal to the work of another.

Background

219. This is a new provision that is designed to clarify to whom the equality clause and equality rule provisions of the Act apply. It should be read together with section 79. The references to comparator (and its definition in section 79) clarify, but do not widen the choice of comparator available in previous legislation for the purpose of a claim for breach of an equality clause or rule. As was the case under previous law, a comparator has to be a real person and not a hypothetical one. Section 64(2) is a new provision which is intended to ensure that the effect of pre-existing case law *Macarthy's Ltd v Smith (C 129/79; [1981] 1 All ER 111; [1980] ECR 1275)* is maintained: that a comparator need not be someone who is employed at the same time as the person making a claim under these provisions, but could be a predecessor in the job.

Examples

- A female employee can compare her work with that of a male colleague employed by the same employer.
- A male police officer can compare his work with that of a female police officer in the same force.

Section 65: Equal work

Effect

220. This section sets out when the work of two people, whose work is being compared, is taken to be equal so that an equality clause or equality rule can operate. For work to be equal, a claimant must establish that he or she is doing like work, work rated as equivalent or work of equal value to a comparator's work. The section also sets out the factors which determine whether a person's work is within one of these categories. The fact that a discriminatory job evaluation study has been carried out which gives different values to the work of men and women is not an obstacle to the operation of an equality clause if an evaluation that set the same values for men and women would have found the jobs to be of equal value.

Background

221. This section is designed to replicate the substance of definitions contained in the Equal Pay Act 1970.

Examples

- Male and female supermarket employees who perform similar tasks which require similar skills will be doing like work even though the men may lift heavier objects from time to time. This is because the differences are not of practical importance in relation to their terms of employment.
- A job evaluation study rated the jobs of women and their better paid male comparators as not equivalent. If the study had not given undue weight to the skills involved in the men's jobs, it would have rated the jobs as equivalent. An equality clause would operate in this situation.

Section 66: Sex equality clause

Effect

222. This section requires that a sex equality clause be read into the terms under which people are employed. The effect of this is that any term in the contract which is less favourable than that of the comparator of the opposite sex is modified so as to ensure that both have the same effect. Where the comparator benefits from a term which is not available to the employee, the effect of the sex equality clause is to include such a term in the employee's contract of employment.

223. A sex equality clause will operate similarly on the terms of a person who is an appointee to an office or a member of the armed forces, as it does in relation to an employee.

224. Subsection (3) is intended to ensure that the provisions relating to equality of terms at work and the provisions governing pension schemes in sections 67 and 68 operate effectively together so that action can be taken against an employer as it could against a trustee, to ensure, for example that a defence that operates in relation to one, will operate in relation to the other.

225. Where a job evaluation study has rated the work of an employee and comparator as equivalent, the equality clause will give the employee the benefit of all of the comparator's terms, including those which have not been determined by the rating of the work.

Background

226. This section is designed to replicate the effect of definitions contained in the Equal Pay Act 1970.

Example

- A male employee's contract includes a term that he can use his employer's car for private purposes. His female comparator who does equal work does not benefit from this term. A sex equality clause will have the effect of including in her contract a term corresponding to that of her male comparator.

Section 67: Sex equality rule

Effect

227. This section requires that every occupational pension scheme is to have a sex equality rule read into it.

228. The rule requires that men and women are treated equally to comparable members of the opposite sex in relation both to the terms on which they are permitted to join the scheme, and to the terms on which they are treated once they have become scheme members.

229. The rule, insofar as it applies to the terms on which a person is treated once he or she has become a member of the scheme, does not apply to pensionable service before 17 May 1990. This was the date of the European Court's decision in *Barber v Guardian Royal Exchange Assurance Group (C 262/88; [1991] 1 QB 344; [1990] ECR I-1889)*, which established that occupational pensions were pay for the purposes of what was Article 119 of the Treaty of Rome (now Article 157 of the Treaty on the Functioning of the European Union). Where the application of the rule relates to the terms on which a person becomes a member of the scheme, it has effect from 8 April 1976. This was the date of the judgment in *Defrenne v Sabena (C 43/75; [1981]1 All ER 122; [1976] ECR 455)*, where the Court, in holding that the principle of equal pay was directly effective, indicated that what was Article 119 of the Treaty of Rome should not be applied to periods of service prior to the judgment.

230. Where there has been a breach of a term modified by a sex equality rule, proceedings may be brought against the person responsible for the breach under Part 9 of the Act.

Background

231. The section replaces equivalent equal treatment provisions in section 62 of the Pensions Act 1995.

Example

- A scheme rule requires employees to work full time before they may join the scheme. There may be a breach of the equality rule because the scheme rule may have an adverse impact on female employees, who are less able to comply with the requirement to work full-time.

Section 68: Sex equality rule: consequential alteration of schemes

Effect

232. This section gives trustees and managers of an occupational pension scheme the power, by resolution, to alter scheme rules to conform to the sex equality rule in section 67.

233. They may use the power if:

- they lack the power to alter rules; or
- procedures for altering rules, including obtaining consent from another person (for example the employer), are unduly complex or would take too long.

234. In line with section 67, where the operation of an equality rule relates to the terms on which a person becomes a member of the scheme, any alteration made relying on this section may only have effect from 8 April 1976. Where the alteration relates to a term on which a member of the scheme is treated, reliance on this section may have effect only from 17 May 1990.

Background

235. The section replaces equivalent equal treatment provisions in section 65 of the Pensions Act 1995.

Example

- The scheme rules of a large scheme require consultation with all the members before an amendment to the rules may be made. This is impracticable, particularly as some deferred members cannot be traced. Scheme trustees may make the necessary alterations to scheme rules relying on this power.

Section 69: Defence of material factor

Effect

236. As a general rule, if the work of a worker and a comparator of the opposite sex is equal but their terms are not, the sex equality clause takes effect. Section 69 provides that neither a sex equality clause nor a sex equality rule will apply if the employer can show that the difference in terms is due to a material factor which is relevant and significant and does not directly or indirectly discriminate against the worker because of her sex.

237. If there is evidence that the factor which explains the difference in terms is not directly discriminatory but would have an adverse impact on people of her sex (that is, without more, it would be indirectly discriminatory), the employer must show that it is a proportionate means of meeting a legitimate aim or the sex equality clause will apply. For these purposes, the long-term objective of reducing pay inequality will always count as a legitimate aim.

238. Subsection (4) deals with the application of the material factor defence to occupational pension schemes.

Background

239. The Equal Pay Act 1970 and Pensions Act 1995 made similar provision permitting employers and trustees to objectively justify differences to which an equality clause or rule would otherwise apply. This section draws those separate provisions into one section and clarifies the way in which they are to be applied. The reference in the previous legislation to a difference being "genuinely" due to a material factor has not been repeated in this section since the adverb added nothing to the meaning of the requirement, which is that the employer's obligation is to show that the reason for the difference is genuine and not a sham. The section incorporates the effect of EU law in respect of objective justification of indirectly discriminatory factors.

240. The reference to an employer's long-term objective of reducing pay inequality between men and women always being considered a legitimate aim is new.

Examples

- An employer introduces a bonus payment to encourage staff doing the same work to work a new night shift to maximise production. Only a small number of female staff can work at night and the bonus payments go almost entirely to male employees. Despite the disparate effect on the female employees, the employer's aim is legitimate and the payment of a bonus to night workers is a proportionate way of achieving it.
- A firm of accountants structures employees' pay on the basis of success in building relationships with clients (including at after-hours client functions). Because of domestic responsibilities, fewer women than men can maintain regular client contact and women's pay is much lower. The employer is unable to show the way it rewards client relationship building is proportionate, taking into account the disadvantage to women employees.
- In imposing a new pay structure which seeks to remove pay inequalities between men and women employees, and to accommodate the interests of all the various groups, an employer includes measures which seek to protect the pay of the higher paid group for a short period of time. The intention to remove pay inequalities is a legitimate aim, and the question will be whether the imposition of the particular temporary pay protection arrangements is a proportionate means of achieving it.

Section 70: Exclusion of sex discrimination provisions

Effect

241. This section ensures that the sex discrimination provisions of the Act do not apply where an equality clause or rule operates (or would operate in the absence of a defence of material factor or the exceptions set out in Part 2 of Schedule 7).

242. The sex discrimination provisions prohibit sex discrimination in relation to non-contractual pay and benefits such as promotion, transfer and training and in relation to offers of employment or appointment.

243. The equality of terms provisions operate only in relation to the terms of a contract of employment, the terms of appointment to a personal or public office and the terms of service of members of the armed forces.

Background

244. This provision brings together sex discrimination and equality of terms provisions previously found in the Equal Pay Act 1970 and the Sex Discrimination Act 1975 and explains how they work together.

Example

- A female sales manager is entitled under her contract to a bonus every year in proportion to the number of sales her team achieves. She discovers that a male sales manager for the same firm doing the same job has a contract which includes a larger bonus payment in relation to the same number of sales. Her claim will be dealt with under the equality clause provisions.

Section 71: Sex discrimination in relation to contractual pay

Effect

245. This section deals with sex discrimination in relation to contractual pay in circumstances where a sex equality clause would not operate. This could be because there is no comparator doing equal work with whom a claimant can compare his or her pay or other terms. The section ensures that indirect sex discrimination in respect of contractual pay can be challenged only by means of an equality clause. However, the section for the first time enables a person who is treated less favourably than others by being paid less because of the person's sex or a combination of two protected characteristics including sex to pursue a claim for direct or dual discrimination where an equality clause does not operate.

Background

246. The section replaces similar provision in the Sex Discrimination Act 1975 which ensured that the sole remedy in respect of claims made about sex discrimination in contractual pay matters was obtained through the Equal Pay Act 1970. This required that the comparator be a real person. This section however contains a new provision designed to allow claims to be brought where a person can show evidence of direct sex discrimination or dual discrimination (where sex is one of the protected characteristics in the combination) in relation to contractual pay but is unable to gain the benefit of a sex equality clause due to the absence of a comparator doing equal work.

Example

- An employer tells a female employee "I would pay you more if you were a man" or tells a black female employee "I would pay you more if you were a white man". In the absence of any male comparator the woman cannot bring a claim for breach of an equality clause but she can bring a claim of direct sex discrimination or dual discrimination (combining sex and race) against the employer.

Section 72: Relevant types of work

Effect

247. This section sets out the types of work that are covered by the provisions for pregnancy and maternity equality set out in the sections which follow.

Background

248. This section replaces various provisions in the Equal Pay Act 1970, which set out who is covered by the pregnancy and maternity equality requirements.

Section 73: Maternity equality clause

Effect

249. This section requires that a woman's contract must be read as including a maternity equality clause. Section 74 sets out how a maternity equality clause modifies a woman's pay. No comparator is required in these cases.

250. A maternity equality clause is capable of affecting the terms of an occupational pension scheme but only in the way a maternity equality rule (as described in section 75) would. This ensures that the provisions relating to pregnancy and maternity equality of terms at work and the provision governing pension schemes in section 75 operate effectively together.

Background

251. This section reflects provisions of the Equal Pay Act 1970.

Section 74: Maternity equality clause: pay

Effect

252. This section sets out how and when a maternity equality clause affects a woman's pay while she is on maternity leave.

253. Firstly, the maternity equality clause is designed to ensure that any pay increase a woman receives (or would have received if she had not been on maternity leave) is taken into account in the calculation of her maternity-related pay where her terms do not already provide for this.

254. Secondly, a maternity equality clause will operate to ensure that pay, including any bonus, is paid to the woman at the time she would have received it if she had not been on maternity leave.

255. Thirdly, a maternity equality clause will provide for a woman's pay on her return to work following maternity leave to take account of any pay increase which she would have received if she had not been on statutory maternity leave.

Background

256. This section is designed to replicate the effect of provisions previously in the Equal Pay Act 1970.

Examples

- Early in her maternity leave, a woman receiving maternity-related pay becomes entitled to an increase of pay. If her terms of employment do not already provide for the increase to be reflected in her maternity-related pay, the employer must recalculate her maternity pay to take account of the increment.
- A woman becomes entitled to a contractual bonus for work she undertook before she went on maternity leave. The employer cannot delay payment of the bonus and must pay it to her when it would have been paid had she not been on maternity leave.

Section 75: Maternity equality rule

Effect

257. This section introduces a maternity equality rule into all occupational pension schemes.

258. The effect of the rule is that any period when a woman is on maternity leave should be treated as time when she is not, in particular in relation to any rule of an occupational pension scheme which can be applied in respect of:

    - scheme membership,
    - accrual of scheme rights, and
    - determination of benefits.

259. The section makes similar provision in relation to any discretion under scheme rules which can be exercised in a way that treats a period of maternity leave differently from time when a woman is not on maternity leave.

260. The woman's contributions to the scheme during maternity leave need be determined only by reference to the amount she is paid during maternity leave.

261. The provisions of the section apply only to women on unpaid ordinary maternity leave where the expected week of confinement began on or after 6 April 2003.

262. The provisions of the section apply only to a woman on unpaid additional maternity leave where the expected week of confinement began on or after 5 October 2008 and they do not apply to the accrual of scheme rights.

263. Where there has been a breach of a term modified by a maternity equality rule, proceedings may be brought against the person responsible for the breach under Part 9 of the Act.

Background

264. This section replaces the previous provisions on "unfair maternity provisions" in paragraph 5 of Schedule 5 to the Social Security Act 1989 and replicates aspects of Regulations 9 and 18A of the Maternity and Parental Leave etc Regulations 1999.

Examples

- A woman who is on maternity leave will be entitled to continuing membership of the scheme throughout the period of maternity leave whether or not she is paid.
- A woman who is paid whilst on maternity leave will be entitled to accrue rights in a scheme as though she were paid her usual salary but she will only be required to make contributions based on her actual pay.

Section 76: Exclusion of pregnancy and maternity discrimination provisions

Effect

265. This section provides that the pregnancy and maternity discrimination provisions of the Act do not apply where a maternity clause or rule operates.

266. The maternity discrimination provisions prohibit discrimination in relation to non-contractual pay and benefits such as promotion, transfer and training and in relation to offers of employment or appointment.

267. The maternity equality clause provisions operate only in relation to terms of a contract of employment, the terms of appointment to a personal or public office and the terms of service of members of the armed forces and do so by including an equality clause to modify terms governing maternity-related pay.

Background

268. This provision explains the relationship between the two sets of provisions and is intended to ensure that they provide seamless protection against pregnancy and maternity-related inequality.

Example

- A woman who is in line for promotion tells her employer that she is pregnant. The employer tells the woman he will not promote her because she is likely to be absent on maternity leave during a very busy period. This will be direct pregnancy discrimination.

Section 77: Discussions about pay

Effect

269. This section is designed to make unenforceable terms of employment, appointment or service that prevent or restrict people from disclosing or seeking to disclose their pay to others, or terms that seek to prevent people from asking colleagues about their pay, where the purpose of any disclosure is to find out whether there is a connection between any difference in pay and a protected characteristic. Any action taken against an employee by the employer as a result of conduct protected by this section is treated as victimisation within the meaning of section 27, as applied in the sections listed in the table in subsection (5).

270. Generally, discussions about pay would take place between colleagues, but this section makes it clear that protection extends more widely so as to include,; for example;, disclosures made to a trade union official or anyone else, provided that it is made with a view to finding out whether any pay differences may be connected with a protected characteristic.

Background

271. This section is new. It is intended to ensure that there is greater transparency and dialogue within workplaces about pay.

Examples

- A female employee thinks she is underpaid compared with a male colleague. She asks him what he is paid, and he tells her. The employer takes disciplinary action against the man as a result. The man can bring a claim for victimisation against the employer for disciplining him.

- A female employee who discloses her pay to one of her employer's competitors with a view to getting a better offer could be in breach of a confidentiality clause in her contract. The employer could take action against her in relation to that breach.

Section 78: Gender pay gap information

Effect

272. This section enables a Minister of the Crown to make regulations requiring private and voluntary sector employers with at least 250 employees in Great Britain to publish information about the differences in pay between their male and female employees. The regulations may specify, among other things, the form and timing of the publication, which will be no more frequently than annually. The regulations may also specify penalties for non-compliance. Employers who do not comply with the publication requirements could face civil enforcement procedures or be liable for a criminal offence, punishable by a fine of up to £5,000.

Background

273. This is a new provision. The Government wants larger private and voluntary sector employers in Great Britain to publish information on what they pay their male and female employees, so that their gender pay gap (the size of the difference between men and women's pay expressed as a percentage) is in the public domain.

274. The Government's aim is for employers regularly to publish such information on a voluntary basis. To give voluntary arrangements time to work, the Government does not intend to make regulations under this power before April 2013. The power would then be used only if sufficient progress on reporting had not been made by that time.

Section 79: Comparators

Effect

275. This section sets out the circumstances in which employees and others are taken to be comparators for the purposes of Chapter 3. A person who claims the benefit of a sex equality clause or sex equality rule must be able to show that his or her work is equal to that of the chosen comparator. The application of Article 157 of the Treaty on the Functioning of the European Union, which has direct effect, will ensure that existing case law on the breadth of possible comparisons is carried forward, so that, for example, in relevant circumstances the concept of a comparator will include a predecessor doing the same job.

276. If two persons share the same employer and work at the same establishment, each may be a comparator for the other.

277. If two persons work at different establishments but share the same employer and common terms and conditions of employment apply, each may be a comparator for the other.

278. A person can also be a comparator for another in either of the above circumstances if one is employed by a company associated with the other's employer. Subsection (9) defines when employers are taken to be associated.

279. A person holding a personal or public office may be a comparator for another person holding a personal or public office if the same person is responsible for paying both of them.

280. A person holding the office of constable is treated for the purposes of Chapter 3 as holding a personal office for the purpose of determining who can be that person's comparator.

281. The section also defines when staff of the Houses of Parliament may be taken to be each other's comparators.

Background

282. These provisions generally reflect the effect of provisions in previous legislation.

Example

- A woman is employed by a company at a factory. A man works for the same company at another factory. Common terms of employment apply at both establishments. The woman may treat the man as a comparator, if they are doing equal work (as defined in section 65).

Section 80: Interpretation and exceptions

Effect

283. This section explains the meaning of terms used in Chapter 3 of Part 5 of the Act. It also gives effect to Schedule 7, which sets out exceptions to the equality of terms provisions.

Chapter 4: Supplementary

Section 81: Ships and hovercraft

Effect

284. This section provides that the employment provisions in Part 5 will apply to seafarers and the crew of hovercraft only in the way set out in regulations made by a Minister of the Crown.

Background

285. The Act is silent on the territorial application of the employment provisions. While this approach is acceptable for most workers, who at any given time are within either the territory of the United Kingdom or some other territory, seafarers work on ships that may be constantly moving between waters under the jurisdiction of different States. This section will allow the Minister to say how and when the employment provisions apply to seafarers on ships and crew on hovercraft in accordance with international law and custom and the global practices of the shipping industry. The Minister may make provision with regard to ships outside Great Britain.

286. This section replaces provisions in previous legislation concerning its application to seafarers.

Section 82: Offshore work

Effect

287. This section contains a power to make an Order in Council in relation to work on board offshore installations. The power may be used to apply Part 5 (with or without modification) to those working on such installations. The power may also be used in relation to any corresponding Northern Ireland legislation (with or without modification).

Background

288. This section will enable protection to be extended to workers on offshore installations, such as oil and gas rigs and renewable energy installations (generally wind farms), to reflect the extent of previous discrimination legislation.

Example

- Offshore workers are typically workers (either employees, contract workers, partners, members of an LLP, or personal or public office-holders) on oil and gas rigs located in the sea within the area of the United Kingdom Continental Shelf (UKCS), and on renewable energy installations (generally wind farms) within the part of the UKCS known as the Renewable Energy Zone.

Section 83: Interpretation and exceptions

Effect

289. This section explains the meaning of various terms used in Part 5 of the Act. In particular, it defines what is meant by "employment" and provides that people serving in the armed forces and people who work for the Crown and in the Houses of Commons and Lords are to be regarded as employed for the purposes of this Part of the Act.

Part 6: Education

Chapter 1: Schools

Section 84: Application of this Chapter

Effect

290. This section provides that this Chapter of the Act, which prohibits discrimination, harassment and victimisation in the field of education in schools, does not apply to discrimination or harassment of people in those circumstances because of age or marriage and civil partnership.

Background

291. This replicates the position in previous legislation and in, addition, extends protection because of gender reassignment and pregnancy and maternity to pupils in schools.

Examples

- It is not unlawful discrimination for a school to organise a trip for pupils in one year group, but not for pupils in other years.
- It is not unlawful discrimination for a school to allow older pupils to have privileges for which younger pupils are not eligible, such as more choice of uniform or the right to leave school during the lunch period.

Section 85: Pupils: admission and treatment, etc.

Effect

292. This section makes it unlawful for the responsible body of a school to discriminate against, harass or victimise a pupil or prospective pupil in relation to the terms on which it offers him or her admission, by not admitting him or her, or in the way it treats the pupil once admitted. The responsible body for a maintained school is the local authority or the governing body, and for an independent educational institution or a non-maintained special school is the proprietor.

293. It also imposes on the responsible body of a school the duty to make reasonable adjustments for disabled pupils and prospective disabled pupils.

294. However, the prohibition on harassment of pupils or prospective pupils does not cover gender reassignment, sexual orientation or religion or belief.

Background

295. This section is primarily designed to replicate the effect of provisions in current legislation applying to schools. In addition, it extends protection from discrimination to transsexual pupils and pupils who become pregnant.

Examples

- A school refuses to let a gay pupil become a prefect because of his sexual orientation. This would be direct discrimination.
- A selective school imposes a higher standard for admission to applicants from an ethnic minority background, or to girls. This would be direct discrimination.
- A pupil alleges, in good faith, that his school has discriminated against him because of his religion (for example claiming that he is given worse marks than other pupils because he is Jewish), so the school punishes him by making him do a detention. This would be victimisation.
- A teacher ridicules a particular pupil in class because of his disability, or makes comments which have the result of making the girls in the class feel embarrassed and humiliated. This would be harassment.

Section 86: Victimisation of pupils, etc. for conduct of parents, etc.

Effect

296. This section protects children in schools from being victimised as a result of a protected act (such as making or supporting a complaint of discrimination) done by their parent or sibling. The aim is to prevent parents being discouraged from raising an issue of discrimination with a school because of worry that their child may suffer retaliation as a result.

297. Where a parent or sibling maliciously makes or supports an untrue complaint, the child is still protected from victimisation, as long as the child has acted in good faith. But, in common with the general approach to victimisation, where a child has acted in bad faith, he or she is not protected, even where a parent or sibling makes or supports an untrue complaint in good faith.

Background

298. This section is designed to replicate the effect of provisions in the Disability Discrimination Act 1995 and extend the protection to cover all characteristics protected under this Chapter.

Examples

- The parent of a pupil complains to the school that her daughter is suffering sex discrimination by not being allowed to participate in a metalwork class. The daughter is protected from being treated less favourably by the school in any way because of this complaint.
- A pupil brings a case against his school claiming that he has suffered discrimination by a member of staff because of his sexual orientation. The pupil's younger brother, at the same school, is protected against any less favourable treatment by the school because of this case, even if it is later found that the older brother was not acting in good faith.

Section 87: Application of certain powers under Education Act 1996

Effect

299. This section enables the Secretary of State to give directions, using powers under the Education Act 1996, to require a maintained school or a non-maintained special school to comply with its duties under section 85. It enables the Secretary of State to require a school to stop a discriminatory practice or policy even if no complaint has been brought by an individual pupil or prospective pupil.

Background

300. Sections 496 and 497 of the Education Act 1996 empower the Secretary of State to give directions to local education authorities and to governing bodies of maintained schools to prevent them exercising their functions under the Education Acts unreasonably, or to require them to perform statutory duties where they are not doing so. This power has already been extended to require compliance with the law on sex discrimination, and this section extends those powers to all the protected characteristics covered by section 85.

Example

- The governing body of a school refuses as a matter of policy to let disabled pupils participate in school trips because of the extra risk management required. The Secretary of State could direct the governing body to change its policy so as to make reasonable adjustments to enable disabled pupils to participate.

Section 88: Disabled pupils: accessibility

Effect

301. This section introduces Schedule 10 which requires local authorities and schools to prepare and implement accessibility strategies and plans. These will increase disabled pupils' access to the curriculum and improve the physical environment and the provision of information. They are explained in more detail in the notes to that Schedule.

Section 89: Interpretation and exceptions

Effect

302. This section explains what is meant by terms used in this Chapter, such as "school" and "pupil". It also makes it clear that the prohibitions in the Chapter do not apply to anything done in relation to the content of the school curriculum. This ensures that the Act does not inhibit the ability of schools to include a full range of issues, ideas and materials in their syllabus and to expose pupils to thoughts and ideas of all kinds. The way in which the curriculum is taught is, however, covered by the reference to education in section 85(2)(a), so as to ensure issues are taught in a way which does not subject pupils to discrimination. This section also gives effect to Schedule 11 which provides some exceptions to the provisions in this Chapter.

Background

303. This section is designed to replicate the effect of an exception relating to discrimination because of religion or belief in the Equality Act 2006, and extends it to other protected characteristics.

Examples

- A school curriculum includes teaching of evolution in science lessons. This would not be religious discrimination against a pupil whose religious beliefs include creationism.

- A school curriculum includes The Taming of the Shrew on the syllabus. This would not be discrimination against a girl.

Chapter 2: Further and higher education

Section 90: Application of this Chapter

Effect

304. This section provides that this Chapter of the Act, which prohibits discrimination, harassment and victimisation in the field of education in institutions providing further and higher education, does not make it unlawful to discriminate against or harass people in those circumstances because of marriage or civil partnership status.

Background

305. This section is designed to replicate the effect of provisions in the Sex Discrimination Act 1975.

Section 91: Students: admission and treatment, etc.

Effect

306. This section makes it unlawful for universities, colleges and other institutions in the higher and further education sectors to discriminate against, harass or victimise a student or someone who wants to become a student in relation to the arrangements it makes in deciding who to admit, the terms on which a person is admitted and the way a person is treated when admitted. Subsection (3) of section 91 specifically makes it unlawful to discriminate when considering conferring qualifications to disabled people who are not enrolled at the institution.

307. It also imposes on the responsible body of such an institution the duty to make reasonable adjustments for disabled students and prospective students.

Background

308. This replicates the position in previous legislation.

Examples

- A college refuses admission to a man who applies to be a student, because he is gay. This would be direct discrimination.
- A university refuses to provide residential accommodation to Jewish or Muslim students. This would be direct discrimination.
- A college puts an age limit on access to a particular course. This would be direct discrimination, unless the college could show that the age limit was objectively justified.

Section 92: Further and higher education courses

Effect

309. This section makes it unlawful for local authorities securing further and higher education, and maintained schools providing further education, to discriminate against, harass or victimise a person in relation to deciding who to enrol, or in the way it provides any services when the person has been enrolled. It also imposes on them the duty to make reasonable adjustments when offering such facilities and services to disabled people.

Background

310. This section is designed to replicate the effect of provisions in the Disability Discrimination Act 1995, and to extend protection to all the protected characteristics covered by this Chapter.

Example

- A school puts on a 10-week evening educational course for local adults but prevents applicants from enrolling who are disabled or gay. This would be direct discrimination.

Section 93: ***Recreational or training facilities***

Effect

311. This section makes it unlawful for local authorities providing any recreational or training facilities to discriminate against, harass or victimise a person in terms of deciding who should be provided with any facilities and the terms on which the facilities are provided. It also imposes on them the duty to make reasonable adjustments when offering such facilities and services to disabled people.

312. The recreational and training facilities concerned are those provided in England under sections 507A or 507B of the Education Act 1996 and include things like centres, parks and sports facilities.

Background

313. These provisions are designed to replicate the effect of provisions in the Disability Discrimination Act 1995 and to extend protection to all the protected characteristics covered by this Chapter.

Example

- A local authority which puts on a summer camp for children from local schools refuses an application from a child simply because that child is disabled or a Muslim. This would be direct discrimination.

Section 94: ***Interpretation and exceptions***

Effect

314. This section explains what is meant by terms used in this Chapter, such as "student" and "university". It also makes it clear that the prohibitions in the Chapter do not apply to anything done in relation to the content of the curriculum. This ensures that the Act does not inhibit the ability of institutions in the higher and further education sectors to include a full range of issues, ideas and materials in their syllabus and to expose students to thoughts and ideas of all kinds. The way in which the curriculum is taught is, however, covered by the reference to education in section 91(2)(a), so as to ensure issues are taught in a way which does not subject students to discrimination or harassment.

315. It also gives effect to Schedule 12 which provides exceptions to the provisions in this Chapter.

Background

316. These provisions are new, but are based on an exception relating to discrimination because of religion or belief in education in schools in the Equality Act 2006, and explicitly extend it to education in higher and further education institutions across all the protected characteristics covered by this Chapter.

Examples

- A college course includes a module on feminism. This would not be discrimination against a male student.
- A university requires students to use a computer for projects or essays. This would not be indirect discrimination against a member of a sect which rejects the use of modern technology.

Chapter 3: General qualifications bodies

Section 95: Application of this Chapter

Effect

317. This section provides that this Chapter of the Act, which prohibits discrimination, harassment and victimisation by qualifications bodies, does not make it unlawful for such bodies to discriminate against or harass people in the circumstances covered because of marriage or civil partnership status.

Background

318. This section is designed to replicate the effect of similar provisions in previous legislation subject to modifications that include placing a responsibility on the appropriate regulator.

Section 96: Qualifications bodies

Effect

319. This section makes it unlawful for a qualifications body to discriminate against, harass or victimise a person in the arrangements it makes for deciding on whom to confer qualifications, and the terms on which those qualifications are conferred. Qualifications bodies are defined in section 97.

320. It also places a duty on qualifications bodies to make reasonable adjustments for disabled people. The section includes a power for a Minister of the Crown, the Secretary of State, Scottish Ministers and Welsh Ministers to designate an "appropriate regulator", which may then specify matters which are not subject to the reasonable adjustments duty. For example, it could be specified that the requirement to achieve a particular mark to gain a particular qualification is not subject to reasonable adjustments. The appropriate regulator may also specify which reasonable adjustments should not be made. For example, it may be appropriate to allow additional time to complete the exam or to provide a reader, but not to give an exemption from part of an exam. In doing so, the appropriate regulator must have regard to the need to minimise the extent to which disabled persons are disadvantaged, and the need to protect the integrity of, and maintain public confidence in the qualification. It is important that the disabled candidate knows that his or her qualification will be as highly regarded as other people's qualifications, and will not be regarded as inferior because reasonable adjustments have been made. Before specifying any such matter, the regulator must consult anyone it thinks appropriate and it must publish the specified matters.

Background

321. These provisions are designed to make similar provision to those in the Disability Discrimination Act 1995 and to extend protection to all the protected characteristics covered by this Chapter. There are some changes to the provisions concerning when reasonable adjustments do not need to be made for disabled candidates. Previously, awarding bodies were not required to make reasonable adjustments to a competence standard, but there was some confusion as to what was a competence standard in these

qualifications. Under these provisions it is the regulator that will make the decision, after consultation, about what cannot be reasonably adjusted and – as noted in paragraph 320 above - will be under specific duties in making that decision. This will create more transparency and consistency in the application of reasonable adjustments.

Examples

- A qualifications body refuses to allow a girl to undertake a GCSE in woodwork because of her sex. This would be direct discrimination.
- A visually impaired candidate is granted a modified paper (enlarged font) by a qualifications body in order that she can read her English GCSE exam.
- The regulator publishes, after appropriate consultation, a requirement that qualifications bodies cannot make reasonable adjustments by granting an exemption from components of the qualification which exceed a specified percentage of the total marks.
- The regulator publishes, after appropriate consultation, a requirement on qualifications bodies not to use a specific reasonable adjustment, such as a reader in the independent reading element of a GCSE English exam. This would not be unlawful discrimination against a disabled candidate who would otherwise have been entitled to this specific adjustment.

Section 97: Interpretation

Effect

322. This section explains what is meant by terms used in section 96. It defines a qualifications body as an authority or body which awards a qualification, and sets out what it is not. It also defines a qualification as a certificate or authorisation of a set description.

Background

323. This section is designed to replicate the effect of provisions in previous legislation.

Examples

- Edexcel is an example of a qualifications body.
- A GCSE is an example of a qualification.

Chapter 4: Miscellaneous

Section 98: Reasonable adjustments

Effect

324. This section introduces the provisions of Schedule 13, concerning the making of reasonable adjustments to ensure that disabled pupils are not placed at a substantial disadvantage in comparison with non-disabled pupils. These provisions are explained in more detail in the notes to that Schedule.

Section 99: Educational charities and endowments

Effect

325. This section introduces the provisions of Schedule 14, concerning educational charities which restrict benefits to a single sex and providing for such restrictions to be modified.

Part 7: Associations

Section 100: Application of this Part

Effect

326. This section provides that this Part of the Act, which prohibits discrimination, harassment and victimisation by associations, does not make it unlawful for an association to discriminate against or harass people because of marriage or civil partnership.

327. It also provides that, if an act of discrimination, harassment or victimisation is made unlawful by the Parts of the Act covering services and public functions, premises, work or education, then those provisions, rather than the provisions in this Part, apply.

Background

328. This section is designed to replicate the position in previous legislation.

Section 101: Members and associates

Effect

329. This section makes it unlawful for an association to discriminate against, harass or victimise an existing or potential member, or an associate. This means that an association cannot refuse membership to a potential member or grant it on less favourable terms because of a protected characteristic. It does not, however, prevent associations restricting their membership to people who share a protected characteristic (see Schedule 16). It also means that an association cannot, among other things, refuse an existing member or associate access to a benefit or deprive him or her of membership or rights as an associate respectively because of a protected characteristic covered by this Part.

Background

330. Previous legislation provided protection from discrimination, harassment and victimisation by associations against existing or potential members and associates because of race, disability and sexual orientation. This section is designed to replicate the effect of the provisions in previous legislation, and to extend protection to the characteristics of gender, age, religion or belief, pregnancy and maternity, and gender reassignment.

Examples

- A gentlemen's club refuses to accept a man's application for membership or charges him a higher subscription rate because he is Muslim. This would be direct discrimination.
- A private members' golf club, which has members of both sexes, requires its female members to play only on certain days while allowing male members to play at all times. This would be direct discrimination.

Section 102: Guests

Effect

331. This section makes it unlawful for an association to discriminate against, harass or victimise existing or potential guests. In particular, an association cannot refuse to invite a person as a guest because of a particular characteristic or invite that person on certain conditions which the association would not apply to other would-be guests. Equally, a

guest cannot be refused access to a benefit or subjected to any other detriment simply because of a protected characteristic.

Background

332. Previous legislation provided protection to existing and potential guests of associations because of disability only. This section extends similar protection to all protected characteristics covered by this Part.

Example

- An association refuses to invite the disabled wife of a member to attend an annual dinner, which is open to all members' partners, simply because she is a wheelchair user. This would be direct discrimination.

Section 103: Sections 101 and 102: further provision

Effect

333. This section imposes on associations the duty to make reasonable adjustments for disabled members and guests.

334. This section also provides that the Act does not prohibit harassment of members, potential members, associates, guests and potential guests because of religion or belief or sexual orientation.

Section 104: Selection of candidates

Effect

335. This section allows registered political parties to make arrangements in relation to the selection of election candidates to address the under-representation of people with particular protected characteristics in elected bodies.

336. These arrangements can include single-sex shortlists for election candidates, but not shortlists restricted to people with other protected characteristics. With the exception of single-sex shortlists, arrangements made under this section must be a proportionate means of reducing under-representation.

337. This provision applies to the selection of candidates in relation to elections to Parliament, local government, the European Parliament, the Scottish Parliament and the National Assembly for Wales.

Background

338. For sex, the section replicates the effect of similar provisions contained in the Sex Discrimination Act 1975, as amended by the Sex Discrimination (Election Candidates) Act 2002, relating to the selection of candidates. For the other protected characteristics this section introduces new provisions allowing political parties to take action in their selection arrangements in order to address under-representation in elected bodies (apart from shortlists restricted to people with a particular protected characteristic) where this would be proportionate. This will, for instance, allow political parties to reserve places on relevant electoral shortlists for people with a specific protected characteristic such as race, disability etc.

Examples

- A political party can have a women-only shortlist of potential candidates to represent a particular constituency in Parliament, provided women remain under-represented in the party's Members of Parliament.

- A political party cannot shortlist only black or Asian candidates for a local government by-election. However, if Asians are under-represented amongst a party's elected councillors on a particular Council, the party could choose to reserve a specific number of seats for Asian candidates on a by-election shortlist.

Section 105: Time-limited provision

Effect

339. This section is linked to the provisions in section 104 relating to the selection of candidates by registered political parties. It provides that the provision in section 104(7) which permits single-sex shortlists for election candidates in order to address under-representation in elected bodies will be repealed automatically at the end of 2030 unless an order is made by a Minister of the Crown to extend it beyond that date.

340. This section also extends the expiry date for the similar provisions in the Sex Discrimination (Election Candidates) Act 2002 until 2030, so far as they apply to Northern Ireland.

Background

341. The section replicates similar provisions in the Sex Discrimination (Election Candidates) Act 2002, but extends the expiry date for those provisions to 2030.

Section 106: Information about diversity in range of candidates, etc.

Effect

342. This section gives a Minister of the Crown power to make regulations requiring registered political parties to publish data relating to the diversity of party candidates seeking selection. The power to make regulations is subject to the affirmative resolution procedure. It can be used to prescribe, among other things, which political parties the duty to publish data will apply to, what data should be published, and when. The requirement to publish could apply to diversity data related to some or all of the protected characteristics of age, disability, gender reassignment, race, sex, sexual orientation and religion or belief. It will be for the Equality and Human Rights Commission to enforce the publication requirement, and the provision inserted into the Equality Act 2006 by paragraph 13 of Schedule 26 to the Act makes clear that it can use its existing powers to do so.

343. Candidates will be free to refuse to disclose any or all the information requested by the party. Data will be published in an anonymous form.

Background

344. This is a new provision which responds to a recommendation, made by the Speaker's Conference on parliamentary representation, that registered political parties be required to publish anonymised information on the diversity of their candidate selections, as a means of encouraging broader representation and increasing involvement of all groups in the democratic process.

Example

- Regulations might require political parties fielding more than a specified number of candidates to publish, six months after a general election, anonymised diversity data relating to gender and race of all candidates who stood at that election.

Section 107: Interpretation and exceptions

Effect

345. This section explains what is meant by terms used in Part 7 of the Act. It defines an association as a body with 25 or more members where access to membership is controlled by rules and involves a genuine selection process based on personal criteria. It gives a Minister of the Crown power to amend this definition so as to change the number of members required by the definition.

346. It also provides that people who have any kind of membership of a particular association are protected by this Part, as are associates who are not members of an association but have many of the rights of members as a consequence of being a member of another association.

347. The exceptions which apply to this Part of the Act are contained in Schedule 16.

Background

348. The substance of the definition of an association remains unchanged from that which was used in the Race Relations Act 1976.

Examples

- Associations include: private members' golf clubs and gentlemen's clubs where applicants for membership are required to make a personal application, be sponsored by other members and go through some kind of selection process.
- Membership would cover full membership, associate membership, temporary membership and day membership.
- Casinos, nightclubs and gyms, where payment of the requisite "membership" fee is all that is required to secure admittance are not associations for the purposes of this Part. These are covered instead by the provisions in Part 3 concerning services provided to the public.
- A book club run by a group of friends which has no formal rules governing admittance or whose membership is less than 25 is not an association for the purposes of this Part.

Part 8: Prohibited Conduct: Ancillary

Section 108: Relationships that have ended

Effect

349. This section makes it unlawful to discriminate against or harass someone after a relationship covered by the Act has ended.

350. It covers any former relationship in which the Act prohibits one person from discriminating against or harassing another, such as in employment, or in the provision of goods, facilities and services. It is designed to ensure that treatment of the kind made unlawful by the Act which results from, and is closely linked to, the existence of a relationship is still unlawful even though the relationship no longer exists.

351. This provision applies to conduct which takes place after the Act is commenced, whether or not the relationship in question ended before that date. If the conduct occurred before this section was commenced, it would be dealt with under the previous legislation.

352. This section also requires reasonable adjustments to be made for disabled people even after a relationship has ended, if they continue to be at a substantial disadvantage in comparison with people without a disability. A person will be considered to have

discriminated against a disabled person if he or she fails to comply with the duty to make reasonable adjustments.

353. A breach of this section triggers the same enforcement procedures as if the treatment had occurred during the relationship. However, if the treatment which is being challenged constitutes victimisation, it will be dealt with under the victimisation provisions and not under this section.

Background

354. This section replaces similar provisions in previous legislation. It also extends the protection after a relationship has ended to cover discrimination outside the workplace because of religion or belief and sexual orientation. It will provide similar protection against age discrimination and harassment outside the workplace when the age protection provisions are commenced.

Examples

- A school or employer refuses to give a reference to an ex-pupil or ex-employee because of his or her religion or belief. This would be direct discrimination.
- A builder or plumber addresses abusive and hostile remarks to a previous customer because of her sex after their business relationship has ended. This would be harassment. It would not be harassment, however, where the reason for the treatment was not the customer's sex but, for example, a dispute over payment.
- A disabled former employee's benefits include life-time use of the company's in-house gym facilities. The employer or owner of the premises must make reasonable adjustments to enable the former employee to continue using the facilities even after she has retired.

Section 109: Liability of employers and principals

Effect

355. This section makes employers and principals liable for acts of discrimination, harassment and victimisation carried out by their employees in the course of employment or by their agents acting under their authority. It does not matter whether or not the employer or principal knows about or approves of those acts.

356. However, employers who can show that they took all reasonable steps to prevent their employees from acting unlawfully will not be held liable.

357. Employers and principals cannot be held liable for any criminal offences under the Act that are committed by their employees or agents, except for those in the provisions on transport services for disabled people in Part 12 of the Act.

Background

358. This section replaces similar provisions in previous legislation. It is designed to ensure that employers and principals are made responsible for the acts of those over whom they have control. The section works together with the provisions on "Liability of employees and agents" (section 110), "Instructing, causing or inducing contraventions" (section 111), and "Aiding contraventions" (section 112) to ensure that both the person carrying out an unlawful act and any person on whose behalf he or she was acting can be held to account where appropriate.

Examples

- A landlord (the principal) instructs an agent to collect rent at a property. The agent harasses an Asian couple, who bring a claim in which the agent is held to have acted unlawfully.

The principal may be held liable for breaching the harassment provisions even if he or she is unaware of the agent's actions.

- A shop owner becomes aware that her employee is refusing to serve disabled customers. The employer tells the employee to treat disabled customers in the same way as other customers and sends the employee on a diversity training course. However, the employee continues to treat disabled customers less favourably. One such customer brings a claim against both the employee and the employer. The employer may avoid liability by showing that she took all reasonable steps to stop the employee from acting in a discriminatory way.

Section 110: ***Liability of employees and agents***

Effect

359. This section makes an employee personally liable for unlawful acts committed in the course of employment where, because of section 109, the employer is also liable - or would be but for the defence of having taken all reasonable steps to prevent the employee from doing the relevant thing. An agent would be personally liable under this section for any unlawful acts committed under a principal's authority. However, an employee or agent will not be liable if he or she has been told by the employer or principal that the act is lawful and he or she reasonably believes this to be true.

360. Subsections (4) and (5) make it an offence, punishable by a fine of (currently) up to £5,000, if an employer or principal knowingly or recklessly makes a false statement about the lawfulness of doing something under the Act.

361. This section does not apply to discriminatory acts done by an employee or agent because of disability in relation to schools, because claims for disability discrimination in schools cannot be enforced against individuals.

Background

362. This section incorporates some of the elements in the "Aiding unlawful acts" provisions in previous discrimination legislation. It takes a more direct approach and unlike the previous provisions it is not necessary to show that the employee or agent knew that the act was unlawful.

Examples

- A factory worker racially harasses her colleague. The factory owner would be liable for the worker's actions, but is able to show that he took all reasonable steps to stop the harassment. The colleague can still bring a claim against the factory worker in an employment tribunal.
- A principal instructs an agent to sell products on her behalf. The agent discriminates against a disabled customer. Both the principal and the agent are liable, but the courts are able to determine that evidence provided by the principal indicate the authority given to the agent did not extend to carrying out an authorised act in a discriminatory manner. The disabled customer can still bring a claim against the agent.

Section 111: ***Instructing, causing or inducing contraventions***

Effect

363. This section makes it unlawful for a person to instruct, cause or induce someone to discriminate against, harass or victimise another person, or to attempt to do so.

364. It provides a remedy for both the recipient of the instruction and the intended victim, whether or not the instruction is carried out, provided the recipient or intended victim suffers a detriment as a result.

365. However, the section only applies where the person giving the instruction is in a relationship with the recipient of the instruction in which discrimination, harassment or victimisation is prohibited.

366. The Equality and Human Rights Commission can enforce this section using its statutory powers under the Equality Act 2006. Equally, both the recipient of the instruction and the intended victim can bring individual claims for breach of this section against the person giving the instructions, so long as they have suffered a detriment as a result. A claim brought by the recipient of the instruction will be dealt with in the same forum (employment tribunal or county courts) as a direct claim for discrimination, harassment or victimisation against the person giving the instruction would be. A claim brought by the intended victim against the person giving the instruction will be dealt with in the same forum as a claim for discrimination, harassment or victimisation against the person carrying out the instruction would be.

Background

367. This section replaces provisions in previous legislation in relation to race, sex, gender reassignment, pregnancy and maternity, age (within the workplace) disability (within the workplace), religion or belief (outside the workplace) and sexual orientation (outside the workplace). It extends protection to all protected characteristics in all areas covered by the Act and allows the Equality and Human Rights Commission to bring enforcement proceedings in relation to any action in breach of the section. (Previously, the Equality and Human Rights Commission's enforcement powers were not uniform even between the protected characteristics and fields where there were provisions on instructions to discriminate.) The provision expressly allowing persons instructed to bring proceedings is new (other than in relation to age within the workplace where such provision already exists), and is designed to codify the current position in common law (see *Weathersfield v Sargent* [1999] IRLR 94). The provision expressly allowing the intended victim to bring proceedings, even where the instruction is not carried out, is also new and is designed to ensure greater clarity about the protection than under previous legislation.

Example

- A GP instructs his receptionist not to register anyone with an Asian name. The receptionist would have a claim against the GP if subjected to a detriment for not doing so. A potential patient would also have a claim against the GP if she discovered the instruction had been given and was put off applying to register. The receptionist's claim against the GP would be brought before the employment tribunal as it relates to employment, while the potential patient's claim would be brought in the county court as it relates to services.

Section 112: Aiding contraventions

Effect

368. This section makes it unlawful for a person to help someone carry out an act which he or she knows is unlawful under the Act. However, this is not unlawful if the person giving assistance has been told that the act is lawful and he or she reasonably believes this to be true.

369. It makes it an offence, punishable by a fine of (currently) up to £5,000, knowingly or recklessly to make a false statement about the lawfulness of doing something under the Act.

370. For the purposes of enforcement, breaches of the prohibition on aiding contraventions are dealt with under the same procedures in the Act as the contraventions themselves.

Background

371. This section is designed to replicate the effect of similar provisions in previous legislation. It ensures that a person who helps another to do something which he or she knows to be prohibited by the Act is liable in his or her own right. Taken together with the provisions on "Liability of employers and principals" (section 109), "Liability of employees and agents" (section 110) and "Instructing, causing or inducing contraventions" (section 111) this section is designed to ensure that both the person carrying out an unlawful act and any person on whose behalf or with whose help he or she was acting can be held to account where appropriate.

Example

- On finding out that a new tenant is gay, a landlord discriminates against him by refusing him access to certain facilities, claiming that they are not part of the tenancy agreement. Another tenant knows this to be false but joins in with the landlord in refusing the new tenant access to the facilities in question. The new tenant can bring a discrimination claim against both the landlord and the tenant who helped him.

Part 9: Enforcement

Chapter 1: Introductory

Section 113: Proceedings

Effect

372. This section applies the provisions of Part 9 to claims made under the Act. These claims must be brought either in a county court (sheriff court in Scotland) or in an employment tribunal. Sections 114 and 120 set out which claims should be brought in the civil courts and which in tribunals.

373. This section does not affect the enforcement powers of the Equality and Human Rights Commission which are in Part 1 of the Equality Act 2006. Nor does it prevent judicial review proceedings (or the equivalent in Scotland) or certain immigration proceedings related to compliance with the Act's provisions.

Background

374. This provision replaces similar provisions in the previous legislation.

Chapter 2: Civil courts

Section 114: Jurisdiction

Effect

375. This section sets out what types of claims under the Act a county court or (in Scotland) the sheriff court has jurisdiction to hear. These are claims related to provision of services, the exercise of public functions, disposal and management of premises, education (other than in relation to disability), and associations.

376. There is a presumption that a judge or sheriff will appoint an assessor to assist the court when hearing discrimination cases. However, an assessor need not be appointed where there are good reasons not to (for example, after an assessment of the judge's own level of experience, the nature of the case and the wishes of the claimant).

Background

377. This section is designed to replicate the effect of provisions in previous legislation. However, for the first time the Act enables disability discrimination in schools cases in Scotland to be heard in the Additional Support Needs Tribunals (Scotland) rather than the sheriff courts, where they were previously heard.

378. Previously, two assessors would sit with judges in cases involving race and sex discrimination only. This section extends the requirement to have assessors for cases of discrimination based on any protected characteristic, such as sexual orientation or religion or belief, but reduces the number of assessors used in each case to one.

Examples

- A woman has joined a golf club but because she is a woman she is allowed to play golf only on Tuesday afternoons and is not allowed access to the club bar. She could bring a discrimination claim in the county or (if the golf course is in Scotland) sheriff court.
- A gay man applies for residential housing in a local authority area, but is told that he can choose from only three housing blocks because all homosexual people are housed together. He could bring a discrimination claim in the county or sheriff court.

*Section 115: **Immigration cases***

Effect

379. This section sets out which claims under the Act are outside the jurisdiction of the county or sheriff courts because they are being dealt with in immigration proceedings. These are claims in relation to decisions on whether a person may enter or remain in the UK and claims where the question of whether there has been a breach of Part 3 of the Act (dealing with services and public functions) has either been raised in immigration proceedings and rejected, or could be raised on appeal.

Background

380. This provision is designed to replicate the effect of provisions in previous legislation.

*Section 116: **Education cases***

Effect

381. This section sets out which education-related claims under the Act are outside the jurisdiction of the county and sheriff courts. These are claims about discrimination because of disability in schools which should be brought instead in specialist tribunals (there is a separate tribunal for England and Wales and for Scotland).

Background

382. The position for England and Wales remains unchanged. As noted in relation to section 114, the Act for the first time enables disability discrimination in schools cases in Scotland to be heard in the Additional Support Needs Tribunals (Scotland) rather than the sheriff courts, where they were previously heard.

*Section 117: **National security***

Effect

383. A county or sheriff court may need to take various steps during proceedings in order to safeguard national security. This section enables the Civil Procedure Rules Committee (for England and Wales) and the Sheriff Court Rules Council (for Scotland) to make rules of court to enable the court to exclude a claimant, representative or assessor from

part or all of the proceedings; permit a claimant or representative who has been excluded to make a statement before the proceedings begin; and ensure that part or all of the reasons for a decision on the merits of the case are kept secret. Where the claimant or his or her representative is excluded from proceedings, a special advocate can be appointed to represent the claimant's interests.

Background

384. This provision is designed to replicate and extend powers in previous legislation. The previous powers applied in relation to some discrimination proceedings but not to those involving sexual orientation and age. This provision extends the power so that it applies across all the protected characteristics.

Section 118: Time limits

Effect

385. A person must bring a claim under the Act in the county and sheriff courts within six months of the alleged unlawful act taking place. If a person wants to make a claim after that period it is at the court's discretion whether it grants permission to allow this. The test applied by the court is what is "just and equitable" in the circumstances.

386. The exception to this rule is for claims which have been referred to a student complaints scheme within six months or to the Equality and Human Rights Commission for conciliation. In these instances the time limit for bringing a claim is increased to nine months. The six month period will only begin, in a claim involving a decision of an immigration body, when that body has ruled that there is a breach of Part 3 and that ruling can no longer be appealed.

387. Where the conduct in respect of which a claim under the Act might arise continues over a period of time, the time limit starts to run at the end of that period. Where it consists of a failure to do something, the time limit starts to run when the person decides not to do the thing in question. In the absence of evidence to the contrary, this is either when the person does something which conflicts with doing the act in question; or at the end of the time when it would have been reasonable for them to do the thing.

Background

388. This section is designed to replicate the effect of provisions in the previous legislation, except that the provision allowing a longer time limit in respect of complaints referred to the student complaints scheme and for conciliation by the Equality and Human Rights Commission is new.

Section 119: Remedies

Effect

389. This section gives powers to county and sheriff courts hearing claims under the Act to grant any remedy that the High Court or Court of Session in Scotland can grant in proceedings in tort or in a claim for judicial review. The main remedies available are damages (including compensation for injuries to feelings), an injunction and a declaration. In cases based on indirect discrimination, if the respondent proves that he or she did not intend to treat the claimant unfavourably then the award of damages cannot be considered until a court has looked at the other remedies available to it.

390. A court cannot grant some remedies, such as an injunction, if doing so would prejudice a criminal investigation or proceedings.

Background

391. This provision is designed to replicate the effect of provisions in the previous legislation.

Chapter 3: Employment tribunals

Section 120: Jurisdiction

Effect

392. This section sets out what types of claims under the Act the employment tribunals have jurisdiction to hear. These are cases involving discrimination in a work context (which includes contract workers, partners, office-holders and barristers and advocates). Their jurisdiction also includes cases about the terms of collective agreements (which can cover any of the terms of employment) and rules of undertakings which are unenforceable under section 145 because they provide for treatment which is prohibited by the Act. This is made clear in section 145 of the Act.

393. It also gives jurisdiction to employment tribunals to hear complaints relating to breaches of a non-discrimination rule. Jurisdiction for hearing a complaint regarding a breach of an equality clause or an equality rule is set out in section 127. An employment tribunal can also make a ruling on an application made by a responsible person in relation to an occupational pension scheme (as defined in section 61(4)) for a declaration about his or her rights and those of a worker or member or prospective member of the scheme.

Background

394. This section is designed to replicate the effect of provisions in the previous legislation.

Examples

- A worker is racially abused by a co-worker. She could bring a discrimination claim in the employment tribunal.
- A gay man has applied to become a partner in a firm of accountants but because he is gay he has not been invited for an interview despite being equally or better qualified than other candidates who were invited for an interview. He could bring a discrimination claim in the employment tribunal.

Section 121: Armed forces cases

Effect

395. This section establishes that, before bringing a claim under the work provisions of the Act to an employment tribunal, a member of the armed forces must raise his or her complaint through the armed services internal complaints procedure and not withdraw that complaint. If the complainant fails properly to progress his or her internal complaint then it may, in certain circumstances, be treated as if it had been withdrawn. The internal service complaint procedures do not have to be concluded before the complainant brings a claim to an employment tribunal.

Background

396. This section is designed to replicate the effect of provisions in the previous legislation.

Example

- A black soldier who thinks he has been discriminated against by being passed over for promotion would have to make an internal service complaint before bringing his claim to an employment tribunal.

Section 122: ***References by court to tribunal, etc.***

Effect

397. The Act does not prevent the civil courts from considering a claim that a pension scheme operates in a discriminatory manner. This section enables a court to strike out such a claim if it would be more convenient for an employment tribunal to deal with it, or to refer an issue relating to such a claim to an employment tribunal.

Background

398. Employment tribunals have the specialist knowledge and procedures to handle claims relating to discrimination in the work context and this section gives a court power to refer such issues to a tribunal. This section reflects similar provisions in previous legislation.

Example

- An employee who is a member of a pension scheme sues his employer in court alleging the employer operates the scheme in a discriminatory manner. The court decides to refer the issue to an employment tribunal and postpones the case until the tribunal's decision.

Section 123: ***Time limits***

Effect

399. This section deals with time limits for cases in the employment tribunals. A person must bring a claim within three months of the alleged conduct taking place. The exception to that rule is a case involving an armed forces complaint, which must be brought within six months. If a person wants to make a claim after that period it is at the tribunals' discretion whether they grant permission to allow them to do so. The test applied by the tribunals is what is "just and equitable" in the circumstances.

400. Where the conduct in respect of which a claim under the Act might arise continues over a period of time, the time limit starts to run at the end of that period. Where it consists of a failure to do something, the time limit starts to run when the person decides not to do the thing in question. In the absence of evidence to the contrary, this is either when the person does something which conflicts with doing the act in question; or at the end of the time when it would have been reasonable for them to do the thing. This section does not apply to a breach of an equality clause or an equality rule, which is covered by section 129.

Background

401. This section is designed to replicate the effect of provisions in previous legislation.

Section 124: ***Remedies: general***

Effect

402. This section sets out the remedies available to employment tribunals hearing cases under the Act. It does not however apply to a breach of an equality clause or an equality rule, which is dealt with in sections 132, 133 and 134.

403. An employment tribunal can make a declaration regarding the rights of the complainant and/or the respondent; order compensation to be paid, including damages for injury to feelings; and make an appropriate recommendation. The measure of compensation is that which applies in tort claims, for example claims of negligence, where the compensation puts the claimant in the same position, as far as possible, as he or she would have been in if the unlawful act had not taken place.

404. Where a tribunal makes a recommendation it does not have to be aimed only at reducing the negative impact on the individual claimant(s) of the respondent's actions which gave rise to the successful claim, but can be aimed at reducing that impact on the wider workforce. The recommendation must state that the respondent should take specific action within a specified period of time. A tribunal has the power in any case where a recommendation made for the benefit of the individual claimant only is not complied with, to award compensation or increase any award already made.

405. In a case of indirect discrimination where the respondent proves that there was no intention to treat the claimant unfavourably, a tribunal cannot award damages to a claimant unless it has first considered making either a declaration or recommendation.

Background

406. This section is designed generally to replicate the effect of provisions in previous legislation, under which employment tribunals could make a declaration, order compensation to be paid and make recommendations. However, under that legislation the recommendations that they could make could only be for the benefit of the individual claimant(s). The Act extends the recommendations power so that employment tribunals can make recommendations which benefit persons other than the claimant.

Example

- A tribunal could recommend that the respondent:
    - introduces an equal opportunities policy;
    - ensures its harassment policy is more effectively implemented;
    - sets up a review panel to deal with equal opportunities and harassment/grievance procedures;
    - re-trains staff; or
    - makes public the selection criteria used for transfer or promotion of staff.

Section 125: ***Remedies: national security***

Effect

407. This section sets out the restrictions on the types of remedies available to an employment tribunal in cases which have been designated as "national security proceedings". National security proceedings are those where an order has been made under various provisions of the Employment Tribunals Act 1996 or regulations made under that Act.

408. In national security proceedings a recommendation must not be made for the benefit of the respondent's wider workforce, if the recommendation would affect anything done by the Security Service, the Secret Intelligence Service, the Government Communications Headquarters or a part of the armed forces which assists the Government Communications Headquarters. In such cases the tribunal is limited to making recommendations for the benefit of the individual claimant or claimants.

Background

409. Because the Act extends the recommendations power to benefit persons other than the claimant, this provision is necessary to ensure that such recommendations do not affect national security.

Section 126: Remedies: occupational pension schemes

Effect

410. This section sets out the additional remedies available to employment tribunals in cases involving occupational pension schemes. These are cases in which the respondent is an employer, or the trustee or manager of the pension scheme; and the complaint relates to the terms on which membership is offered to a pension scheme or how members of an existing scheme are treated. In these cases the tribunal can, in addition to the remedies of declaration, compensation and recommendation, also make a declaration about the terms on which a person should be admitted as a member to that scheme or a declaration about the rights of an existing member of that scheme not to be discriminated against.

411. However, a tribunal can award compensation only for injured feelings or for failure to comply with a recommendation; it cannot compensate the claimant for loss caused by the unlawful discrimination.

Background

412. This provision is designed to replicate the effect of provisions in previous legislation.

Chapter 4: Equality of terms

Section 127: Jurisdiction

Effect

413. This section sets out the types of cases relating to equality of terms which employment tribunals have jurisdiction to hear. Tribunals may hear and decide claims (including those referred to them by courts) involving equality in the rules of occupational pension schemes and claims relating to an equality clause, including claims relating to pregnancy and maternity equality.

414. A responsible person (as defined in section 80, such as an employer, or a pension scheme trustee or manager) can also ask a tribunal for a declaration of each party's rights in relation to a dispute or claim about an equality clause or rule.

415. Members of the armed forces must bring a complaint under service complaints procedures before they can bring a claim to a tribunal.

416. This section does not alter any jurisdiction the courts or the sheriff have in relation to an equality clause or rule.

Background

417. This section is designed to replicate the effect of provisions in previous legislation.

Example

- An employment tribunal can hear claims brought by an employee, office-holder or member of the armed forces in relation to a breach of an equality clause and in relation to breach of an equality rule concerning a pension scheme.

Section 128: References by court to tribunal, etc.

Effect

418. The Act does not prevent the civil courts from considering a contractual claim relating to an equality clause or rule. However, this section gives a court the power to strike out such a claim if it would be more convenient for a tribunal to deal with it, or to refer an issue relating to such a claim to an employment tribunal.

Background

419. Employment tribunals have the specialist knowledge and procedures to handle claims relating to equality of terms and this section gives a court power to refer such issues to a tribunal. This section replaces similar provisions in previous legislation.

Example

- An employer sues an employee in a civil court for breach of her employment contract. In response, the employee counterclaims for breach of an equality clause. The court decides to refer the counterclaim to an employment tribunal and postpones the case until the tribunal's decision.

Section 129: Time limits

Effect

420. A person who wishes to bring a claim for breach of an equality clause or rule or to apply for a declaration about the effect of such a clause or rule must normally do so within six months of the end of the employment contract. In certain circumstances, this section gives a claimant more time to make a claim. This applies where the employer conceals certain information from the claimant or where the claimant has an incapacity (as defined in section 141). Members of the armed forces have an additional three months in which to bring a claim because they must first make a complaint under the service complaint procedures.

Background

421. This section replaces similar provisions in previous legislation. Time limits provide certainty by requiring claims to be brought within specified periods and also take into account factors which may affect a claimant's ability to assert his or her claim.

Example

- A former member of the armed forces wishes to bring a claim about her terms of service. She first makes a service complaint and then brings a claim for breach of an equality clause in an employment tribunal. The claim for breach of an equality clause must be brought in an employment tribunal within nine months after her period of service ended.

Section 130: Section 129: supplementary

Effect

422. Under section 129, the time limit for bringing a claim for breach of an equality clause is six months (nine months for members of the armed forces) from the date on which employment ended in a standard case. Different time limits apply to non-standard cases. This section defines what is not a standard case.

423. In a stable work case, a series of fixed- or short-term contracts and breaks between contracts is treated as a continuing single contract. In a standard case, the time limit would start at the end of the contract of employment. In a stable work case, the time limit only begins to run when the stable working relationship ends.

424. In a concealment case, the employer deliberately conceals relevant information from the employee. The time limit starts to run when the employee discovers, or could reasonably have discovered, the information.

425. In an incapacity case, the appropriate time limit will start to run when the incapacity ends. Section 141 sets out when a person has an incapacity.

426. The section makes similar provisions for claims by members of the armed forces and in relation to occupational pension schemes.

Background

427. This provision replaces similar provisions in the previous legislation.

Examples

- A woman's employment ends due to mental health problems which result in her temporary loss of capacity to make decisions for herself. She could make a claim for breach of an equality clause to an employment tribunal but is not well enough to do so. The six month time limit will start when she recovers sufficiently to make a claim.
- A woman suspects that her male colleagues who do the same work are better paid. Her employer reassures her that she and her colleagues get the same salary but he deliberately does not tell her that the men also receive performance bonuses under their contracts. Her male colleagues refuse to discuss their pay with her. The woman only discovers the discrepancy between her pay and the men's when one of the men tells her 18 months after she ceases employment. Within six months, she makes an equal pay claim to a tribunal based on the value of the bonus payments she would have received if her contract had provided for them. Although the woman's claim is made more than six months after her employment ends, she shows that her employer deliberately misled her into believing that her salary was the same as the men's. She had no way of discovering the truth earlier. Her claim can proceed as a concealment case.

Section 131: Assessment of whether work is of equal value

Effect

428. Where an employment tribunal has to decide if the work of a claimant and comparator are of equal value, this section gives it the power to require an independent expert, designated by the Advisory, Conciliation and Arbitration Service, to prepare a report on the matter.

429. Unless the tribunal withdraws its request for a report (in which case it can ask the expert to give it any documents or other information the expert has to help it make a decision) it must wait for the expert's report before deciding whether the work is of equal value.

430. If there has been a job evaluation study in relation to the work involved and the study finds that the claimant's work is not of equal value to the work of the comparator, the tribunal is required to come to the same decision unless it has a good reason to suspect that the study is discriminatory or unreliable.

Background

431. This provision replaces similar provisions in previous legislation.

Example

- A woman claims that her job is of equal value to that of a male comparator. The employer produces a job evaluation study to the tribunal in which the woman's job is rated below her comparator's job. The employer asks the tribunal to dismiss the woman's claim but the woman is able to show that the study is unreliable because it is out of date and does not take account of changes in the jobs resulting from new technology. The tribunal can disregard the study's conclusion and can proceed to decide if the work of the claimant and the work of the comparator are of equal value.

Section 132: Remedies in non-pensions cases

Effect

432. If a claim for breach of an equality clause (other than in relation to a pension scheme) succeeds, the court or employment tribunal can make a declaration clarifying what the rights of the parties to the claim are.

433. The court or tribunal can also order the employer to pay the claimant arrears of pay or damages. The period used for calculating arrears depends on the type of case. There are different periods for claims brought in England and Wales and in Scotland. The basic period in relation to England and Wales is six years from the date a claim is made. In relation to Scotland, the period is five years. Special provision is made for claims involving concealment and/or incapacity (as set out in section 135).

Background

434. This provision replaces similar provisions in previous legislation.

Example

- A woman successfully establishes that her work is the same as her male comparator's and that in addition to a discrepancy between her pay and that of her male comparator, she has been denied access to the benefit of a company car. The claimant is entitled to claim the difference in pay going back up to six years from the date of the claim. She is also entitled to monetary compensation for not having had the use of a company car.

Section 133: Remedies in pensions cases

Effect

435. This section allows an employment tribunal to declare that in cases where an equality rule or equality clause has been breached in relation to:

    - scheme membership, the complainant is entitled to be admitted to the scheme from a date specified by the tribunal, although the date cannot be earlier than 8 April 1976;
    - scheme rights, the complainant is entitled to have any rights which would have accrued under the scheme secured from a date specified by the tribunal, although the date cannot be earlier than 17 May 1990.

436. However, the section prevents a tribunal ordering an award of compensation to the complainant.

Background

437. This section replicates requirements in the Equal Pay Act 1970, as modified by the Occupational Pension Schemes (Equal Treatment) Regulations 1995.

438. The restrictions on dates derive from judgments of the European Court:

    - for scheme membership: 8 April 1976, the date of the Court's judgment in *Defrenne v Sabena ((C 43/75) [1981]1 All ER 122; [1976] ECR 455)*. The Court, in holding that the principle of equal pay was directly effective, held that what was Article 119 of the Treaty of Rome (now Article 157 of the Treaty on the Functioning of the European Union) should not be applied to periods of service before the judgment.
    - for scheme rights: 17 May 1990, the date of the Court's judgment in *Barber v Guardian Royal Exchange Assurance Group ((C 262/88)[1991] 1 QB 344; [1990] ECR I-1889)*, which established that occupational pensions were pay for the purposes of what was Article 119 of the Treaty of Rome.

Section 134: Remedies in claims for arrears brought by pensioner members

Effect

439. This section allows a court or an employment tribunal to require compensation to be paid to a pensioner member for a breach of an equality clause or rule in relation to an occupational pension scheme and sets out the period for which arrears may be awarded for different types of cases. In a standard case in England and Wales, the period is six years before the date when a claim is made. Different periods apply to cases brought in England and Wales and to cases brought in Scotland. Special provision is made for claims involving concealment and/or incapacity (as set out in section 135).

Background

440. This section replicates requirements previously in the Equal Pay Act 1970, as modified by the Occupational Pension Schemes (Equal Treatment) Regulations 1995.

Section 135: Supplementary

Effect

441. The amount an employment tribunal can award a successful claimant is affected by how far back in time it can go in making its calculation. The type of case which is before the tribunal determines this period. This section defines the different types of cases.

Background

442. This section replicates the effect of similar provisions in previous legislation.

Chapter 5: Miscellaneous

Section 136: Burden of proof

Effect

443. This section provides that, in any claim where a person alleges discrimination, harassment or victimisation under the Act, the burden of proving his or her case starts with the claimant. Once the claimant has established sufficient facts, which in the absence of any other explanation point to a breach having occurred, the burden shifts to the respondent to show that he or she did not breach the provisions of the Act. The exception to this rule is if the proceedings relate to a criminal offence under this Act.

Background

444. Under previous legislation, in most cases the burden of proof was reversed once the claimant had established a case to an initial level. However, the burden of proof was not previously reversed in race discrimination claims brought because of colour and nationality; claims of victimisation which related to race discrimination; non-work disability discrimination claims; and sex discrimination claims which related to the exercise of public functions. In these areas the burden of proof is now reversed once the claimant establishes his or her case to an initial level.

Example

- A man of Chinese ethnic origin applies for a promotion at work but is not given an interview for the job. He finds that a number of white colleagues were given interviews despite having less experience and fewer qualifications. He brings a case for race discrimination before the employment tribunal and provides sufficient evidence to show that he had been treated less favourably because of his ethnic origin. It would then be up to his employer to prove that she had not discriminated against him in the promotion process.

Section 137: Previous findings

Effect

445. This section provides that if a person has brought a case under any of the previous legislation listed in this section (which this Act replaces), and a finding by a tribunal or court has been finalised, the issues decided in that case cannot be re-opened and litigated again under the provisions in this Act.

Background

446. This provision is necessary because the Act replaces many of the provisions in the legislation listed at subsection (2). It would not be appropriate for the Act to allow the re-opening of issues which have been decided in proceedings under the previous legislation.

Section 138: Obtaining information, etc.

Effect

447. This section provides a mechanism for a person who thinks that he or she may have been unlawfully discriminated against, harassed or victimised to obtain information from the person he or she thinks has acted unlawfully against him or her (that is to say, the potential respondent or defendant). The person may ask questions either on a form prescribed by order by a Minister of the Crown or in some other form.

448. The questions and the answers are admissible as evidence in a case brought under the Act and the court or tribunal may draw inferences from a failure by the respondent to answer the questions posed within eight weeks or from evasive or equivocal answers.

449. However, the court or tribunal cannot draw such inferences in certain specified circumstances. These are if the respondent says that to answer differently would have prejudiced criminal proceedings or revealed the reason for criminal proceedings being withdrawn or not being brought and this is reasonable. The section contains a power for a Minister of the Crown to specify by order additional circumstances where such inferences may not be drawn.

Background

450. This provision is designed to replicate the effect of provisions in previous legislation.

Section 139: Interest

Effect

451. This section enables a Minister of the Crown to make regulations enabling an employment tribunal to add interest payments to any award of compensation made to a claimant as a result of a discrimination case brought under this Act. The regulations can set out how the tribunal should calculate how much interest should be paid.

452. The regulations may provide that interest is to be calculated in a different way in discrimination proceedings from how it is in other cases before the employment tribunals, so they can modify the effect of an order made under the Employment Tribunals Act 1996 about interest calculations which applies to employment cases more generally.

Background

453. This replicates powers contained in previous legislation.

Example

- A claimant is awarded compensation for being discriminated against by his employer. Regulations made under this section may provide that if the award is not settled by the respondent within 14 days of the employment tribunal's decision then interest is to accrue on this award. The current regulations specify that the rate of interest applied to unpaid awards is fixed at 8%. A different rate can be applied if this is provided in regulations.

Section 140: Conduct giving rise to separate proceedings

Effect

454. This section enables an employment tribunal to transfer a case to a county or sheriff court, or a court to transfer a case to an employment tribunal, if it is based on the same conduct as one or more separate cases and one of the claims relates to instructing, causing or inducing a person to discriminate against, harass or victimise another person. It also provides that an employment tribunal or court cannot make a decision about such a case which is inconsistent with an earlier decision about the same conduct.

Background

455. This is a new provision which will allow for the transfer of certain types of connected cases between the tribunals and courts.

Example

- An employer instructs an employee to discriminate against a customer. The customer brings a case against the employer or an employee in a county court. The employee brings a case against the employer in an employment tribunal. These claims both arise out of the same conduct and so the court and the tribunal can transfer one set of proceedings so that they can be dealt with together as this is a better way of managing the cases.

Section 141: Interpretation, etc.

Effect

456. This section explains the meaning of various terms used in this Part.

Part 10: Contracts, Etc.

Section 142: Unenforceable terms

Effect

457. This section makes terms of contracts which discriminate against a person or would otherwise lead to conduct prohibited by the Act unenforceable in that respect. But a person who would have been disadvantaged by any such term will still be able to rely on it so as to obtain any benefit to which it entitles him.

458. For disability alone, this section also applies to terms of non-contractual agreements relating to the provision of employment services (within section 56(2)(a) to (e)) or group insurance arrangements for employees. These terms are referred to in the section as "relevant non-contractual terms".

459. This section does not apply to a term of contract modified by an equality clause under Part 5, Chapter 3, because once the term is modified it is no longer discriminatory. Nor, as a result of section 148, does it deal with contractual terms which may breach the public sector equality duty (Part 11, Chapter 1) or the public sector duty regarding socio-economic inequalities (Part 1), to which different enforcement mechanisms apply.

Background

460. The section replaces provisions in previous legislation which had a similar effect including the specific protection for certain non-contractual provisions in the Disability Discrimination Act 1995.

Example

- A term in a franchise agreement which included a requirement that the franchisee should only employ Asian people (which would be unlawful direct discrimination because of race unless an exception applied) could not be enforced by the franchisor. But the franchisee could still obtain any benefit he is due under the term, for example he could continue operating the franchise. However, if the franchisee complied with the discriminatory term, a person discriminated against under it could make a claim against the franchisee for unlawful discrimination under other provisions in the Act.

*Section 143: **Removal or modification of unenforceable terms***

Effect

461. This section allows a county court (or a sheriff court in Scotland) to modify or remove a contractual (or relevant non-contractual) term which is made unenforceable under section 142, when asked to do so by a person who has an interest in the contract (which includes anyone affected by it). The court may also decide that the term is to be treated as having been removed or modified during the period prior to the making of the order.

462. The court must first ensure that anyone who would be affected has been told of the proceedings and given an opportunity to make his or her views known. Rules of court determine what the court must do to meet this obligation.

Background

463. This section replaces similar provisions in previous legislation.

Example

- A person renting an office in a serviced office block could ask for a term in the rental contract to be amended if the term discriminated indirectly, for example by including an unjustified requirement that people entering the premises remove any facial covering (thus discriminating against Muslim women). The term could be adjusted by the court or sheriff to allow special arrangements to be made to satisfy both genuine security needs of other users and the religious needs of Muslim women visiting the claimant.

*Section 144: **Contracting out***

Effect

464. Under this section, contractual and relevant non-contractual terms which try to exclude or limit the operation of any provision in the Act (which includes those dealing with equality of terms) or a provision of secondary legislation made under the Act (for example regulations made under section 81 (ships and hovercraft)) are unenforceable by the person in whose favour the term operates. There are exceptions to this to allow negotiated settlement of claims in the following circumstances:

    - a contract settling a claim in an employment tribunal (including an agreement settling a claim for a breach of an equality clause) that has been negotiated with the help of a conciliation officer or which meets the standards set out in section 147 (meaning of qualifying compromise contract). This includes an arbitration agreement made in accordance with a scheme under section 212A of the Trade Union and Labour Relations (Consolidation) Act 1992 (where the parties agree to submit a dispute to arbitration);

- a contract settling a county or sheriff court claim.

Background

465. This section replaces similar provisions in previous legislation.

Examples

- A woman who thinks she may have a claim for unlawful discrimination upon being made redundant may give up any right to pursue the claim under the Act in return for payment. She will not then be able to ask a court to modify or remove that term so as to pursue the claim at a later date.
- However, if the agreement was not reached with the assistance of a conciliation officer or was not a qualifying compromise agreement, it would be unenforceable (and thus would not prevent the claimant pursuing the claim before an employment tribunal).

Section 145: Void and unenforceable terms

Effect

466. This section deals with collective agreements (which are defined in the Trade Union and Labour Relations (Consolidation) Act 1992).

467. It also deals with rules of undertakings of employers, trade organisations and qualifications bodies (which are defined in Part 5).

468. Any term of a collective agreement is rendered void to the extent that it discriminates against a person or would otherwise lead to conduct prohibited by the Act. Terms of collective agreements are made void rather than unenforceable because making them unenforceable would be of no help to those affected, since they are unenforceable in any case unless incorporated into a contract. The term is therefore made of no effect at all, leaving the interested parties to renegotiate.

469. A rule of an undertaking which discriminates against a person or would otherwise lead to conduct prohibited by the Act is made unenforceable. A rule of an undertaking is defined in section 148 as a rule made by a qualifications body or trade organisation in relation to membership or conferral of a qualification, or a rule made by an employer for application to employees and prospective employees.

Background

470. This section replaces similar provisions in previous legislation.

Examples

- A collective agreement which required jobs in a particular part of a factory to be given only to men would be void, so a woman who applied could not be refused on those grounds.
- An indirectly discriminatory rule of a qualifications body (providing for example a professional qualification for plumbers) which required that applicants must have two years' previous experience with a British firm would be unenforceable against a person who had the equivalent experience with a foreign firm. It would still be enforceable against a person who did not have the required experience at all (provided it was justified).

Section 146: Declaration in respect of void term, etc.

Effect

471. This section enables an employment tribunal to declare a term of a collective agreement void, or a rule of an undertaking unenforceable, as set out in section 142, when a person thinks that it might in the future have the effect of discriminating against him or her. Because collective agreements apply to many people in many (possibly varying) situations, it is not appropriate for a tribunal to modify them and so they are made void, rather than subject to modification or amendment, and the parties are left to renegotiate, bearing all those potentially affected in mind.

472. The section sets out who can make a complaint in each instance. Terms of discriminatory collective agreements can be challenged by employees or prospective employees. Rules of undertakings of employers can be challenged by employees or prospective employees; those of trade organisations by members or prospective members; and those of qualifications bodies by persons seeking or holding relevant qualifications (as defined in section 54).

Background

473. This section replaces similar provisions in previous legislation.

Example

- A person who is studying for an engineering qualification who is told he will only be eligible for it if he passes a test of his ability to write English can ask a tribunal to declare that the rule requiring the test is indirectly discriminatory and therefore, if unjustified, unenforceable.

Section 147: Meaning of "qualifying compromise contract"

Effect

474. This section sets the conditions under which a compromise contract settling a case can be lawful, even though it seeks to limit the application of the Act under section 144.

475. It must be a written contract which meets each of the following conditions: the contract must be tailored to the circumstances of the claim, the complainant must have received independent advice from a named person who is insured or indemnified against the risk of a claim against him arising from that advice, and the contract must state that the conditions about independent advice and insurance have been met.

476. The section describes who can be an independent adviser and includes a power to add new descriptions of people who may be independent advisers in the future. It makes clear that a conflict of interest prevents a person being an independent adviser.

Background

477. The section replaces provisions in previous legislation which had the same purpose. The power to add to the kinds of person who may be independent advisers could be used to add, for example, Fellows of the Institute of Legal Executives employed by a solicitors' practice.

Examples

- An employee who settled a claim at an employment tribunal on the advice of a lawyer who works for the employer he was seeking to sue would still be able to pursue the claim (assuming a conciliation officer was not involved in the settlement). The settlement agreement would be unenforceable because the lawyer had a conflict of interest and therefore the agreement would not be a qualifying compromise contract.

- An employee who settled a claim of harassment in a contract which also provides that she will forego all other claims arising under the Act in exchange for a fixed sum would still be able to pursue a claim for damages because of a discriminatory failure to promote her. The term of the contract precluding all claims would be unenforceable in respect of the discrimination claim because it is insufficiently tailored to the circumstances of the claim and therefore is not a qualifying compromise contract in respect of it.

Section 148: Interpretation

Effect

478. This section explains what is meant by various terms used in this Part of the Act, or applies definitions provided elsewhere. These are referred to in the notes on earlier sections.

Part 11: Advancement of Equality

Chapter 1: Public sector equality duty

Section 149: Public sector equality duty

Effect

479. This section imposes a duty, known as the public sector equality duty, on the public bodies listed in Schedule 19 to have due regard to three specified matters when exercising their functions. The three matters are:

- eliminating conduct that is prohibited by the Act, including breaches of non-discrimination rules in occupational pension schemes and equality clauses or rules which are read, respectively into a person's terms of work and into occupational pension schemes;
- advancing equality of opportunity between people who share a protected characteristic and people who do not share it; and
- fostering good relations between people who share a protected characteristic and people who do not share it.

480. The second and third matters apply to the protected characteristics of age, disability, gender reassignment, pregnancy and maternity, race, religion or belief, sex and sexual orientation. They do not apply to the protected characteristic of marriage and civil partnership.

481. As well as the public bodies listed in Schedule 19, the section also imposes the public sector equality duty on others that exercise public functions, but only in respect of their public functions. Section 150 explains what is meant by "public function".

482. Subsections (3), (4) and (5) expand on what it means to have due regard to the need to advance equality of opportunity and foster good relations. In particular, subsection (4) makes clear that having due regard to the need to advance equality of opportunity between disabled people and non-disabled people includes consideration of the need to take steps to take account of disabled people's disabilities. Subsection (6) makes clear that complying with the duty might mean treating some people more favourably than others, where doing so is allowed by the Act. This includes treating disabled people more favourably than non-disabled people and making reasonable adjustments for them, making use of exceptions which permit different treatment, and using the positive action provisions in Chapter 2 of this Part where they are available.

483. Schedule 18 sets out persons and functions to which the equality duty does not apply.

Background

484. This section replaces section 71 of the Race Relations Act 1976, section 49A of the Disability Discrimination Act 1995 and section 76A of the Sex Discrimination Act 1975. These provisions imposed similar public sector equality duties in relation to race, disability and gender (including pregnancy and maternity as an implicit part of gender, and partly covering gender reassignment) respectively. There were no equivalent public sector equality duties for age, religion or belief or sexual orientation in previous legislation. The section extends the new public sector equality duty to cover gender reassignment in full, age, religion or belief and sexual orientation.

Examples

- The duty could lead a police authority to review its recruitment procedures to ensure they do not unintentionally deter applicants from ethnic minorities, with the aim of eliminating unlawful discrimination.
- The duty could lead a local authority to target training and mentoring schemes at disabled people to enable them to stand as local councillors, with the aim of advancing equality of opportunity for different groups of people who have the same disability, and in particular encouraging their participation in public life.
- The duty could lead a local authority to provide funding for a black women's refuge for victims of domestic violence, with the aim of advancing equality of opportunity for women, and in particular meeting the different needs of women from different racial groups.
- The duty could lead a large government department, in its capacity as an employer, to provide staff with education and guidance, with the aim of fostering good relations between its transsexual staff and its non-transsexual staff.
- The duty could lead a local authority to review its use of internet-only access to council services; or focus "Introduction to Information Technology" adult learning courses on older people, with the aim of advancing equality of opportunity, in particular meeting different needs, for older people.
- The duty could lead a school to review its anti-bullying strategy to ensure that it addresses the issue of homophobic bullying, with the aim of fostering good relations, and in particular tackling prejudice against gay and lesbian people.
- The duty could lead a local authority to introduce measures to facilitate understanding and conciliation between Sunni and Shi'a Muslims living in a particular area, with the aim of fostering good relations between people of different religious beliefs.

Section 150: Public authorities and public functions

Effect

485. This section supplements section 149. It introduces Schedule 19 which lists the public bodies that are subject to the public sector equality duty and provides for them to be subject to this duty in respect of all of their functions unless such a body is listed only in respect of some of its functions, in which case the duty only applies to those specified functions.

486. "Public function" is given the same meaning as it has in the Human Rights Act 1998. This term is used in subsection (2) of section 149, which extends the public sector equality duty to persons not listed in Schedule 19 but who exercise public functions.

Background

487. The public sector equality duties in previous legislation specified which bodies were subject to the duties in different ways. The Race Relations Act 1976 used a list, while

the Disability Discrimination Act 1995 and the Sex Discrimination Act 1975 applied the disability equality duty and the gender equality duty to those who have "functions of a public nature". The Act combines the two approaches by including a list of public bodies subject to the duty, to provide legal certainty, and in addition applying the duty to anyone else who is exercising public functions, in respect of those functions (see subsection (2) of section 149).

Section 151: Power to specify public authorities

Effect

488. Schedule 19, which lists public bodies subject to the public sector equality duty, comprises three Parts. This section enables a Minister of the Crown to make an order amending any of those Parts. The changes might consist in adding a new body or removing an existing body, or moving a body from one Part of the Schedule to another. It also enables the Welsh Ministers and the Scottish Ministers, with the consent of a Minister of the Crown, to amend Parts 2 and 3 of the Schedule respectively, which list relevant Welsh and Scottish bodies subject to the duty.

489. Relevant Welsh and Scottish bodies (as defined in section 157) cannot be added to Part 1 of the Schedule. They must be included in Parts 2 and 3 respectively. Nor can cross-border Welsh and Scottish bodies (as defined in section 157) be added to Part 1. Only a Minister of the Crown has the power to amend the Schedule in relation to cross-border Welsh and Scottish bodies. They must be added to what will become a new Part 4, which will be created when the first cross-border body is added to the Schedule.

490. The power to add to the Schedule can only be used where the person exercising the power considers that the person being added is exercising at least one public function. This means that a wholly private company could not be added unless it were carrying out what the person exercising the power considered to be a public function. Orders cannot be made under this section to apply the duty to those functions and people who are excluded from application of the duty by the provisions of Schedule 18 that relate to judicial functions, Parliament, the Scottish Parliament, the National Assembly for Wales and the General Synod.

Examples

- A Minister of the Crown may decide that a new public body which has just been created should be included in the Schedule, and add it to the appropriate Part.
- A public body might cease its devolved activities, and so a Minister of the Crown might move it to Part 1 of the Schedule from another Part of the Schedule.

Section 152: Power to specify public authorities: consultation and consent

Effect

491. This section sets out whom a Minister of the Crown must consult before exercising a power under section 151 to amend Schedule 19. On each occasion the Minister must consult the Equality and Human Rights Commission. If the Minister is modifying the Schedule in respect of a relevant Welsh body, or a cross-border Welsh body, then he or she must also consult the Welsh Ministers. And similarly, if the amendment relates to a relevant Scottish body or a cross-border Scottish body, there is a requirement to consult the Scottish Ministers.

492. The section also provides that, before the Welsh Ministers amend Part 2 of the Schedule with respect to relevant Welsh bodies, they must first consult the Equality and Human Rights Commission and obtain the consent of a Minister of the Crown. The same requirements apply to Scottish Ministers with respect to Part 3 of the Schedule and relevant Scottish bodies.

Background

493. The Race Relations Act 1976 did not contain a requirement for the Lord Privy Seal to consult before amending the Schedule of bodies subject to the general race equality duty. Neither the Scottish Ministers nor the Welsh Ministers had the power to amend the Schedule. Neither the Disability Discrimination Act 1995 nor the Sex Discrimination Act 1975 adopted a list-based approach to the general duty.

Section 153: Power to impose specific duties

Effect

494. This section enables a Minister of the Crown to make regulations imposing specific duties on public bodies listed in Part 1 of Schedule 19 to enable them to carry out the public sector equality duty more effectively. The Welsh Ministers can similarly impose specific duties on relevant Welsh bodies listed in Part 2 of the Schedule, and the Scottish Ministers can impose specific duties on relevant Scottish bodies listed in Part 3 of the Schedule.

495. Section 154 deals with the imposition of specific duties on public bodies listed in Part 4 of the Schedule (cross-border authorities).

496. The Equality and Human Rights Commission must be consulted before specific duties are imposed.

Background

497. This section replaces similar provisions in previous legislation for the Lord Privy Seal and the Scottish Ministers to impose specific duties for the race and gender public sector equality duties, and for the Secretary of State and the Scottish Ministers to impose specific duties for the disability public sector equality duty. The Welsh Ministers previously did not have the power to impose specific duties on Welsh bodies.

498. The pre-existing provisions have in the past been used to require listed public bodies to prepare and publish race, disability and gender equality schemes, for example.

Section 154: Power to impose specific duties: cross-border authorities

Effect

499. This section sets out the process for determining who imposes specific duties on any cross-border Welsh and Scottish bodies that may in time be added to Part 4 of the Schedule.

500. Whenever a body is listed in Part 4 of the Schedule, beside its entry will appear a letter corresponding to the procedure to be followed.

501. For all the procedures, the person imposing the specific duties must consult the Equality and Human Rights Commission.

Background

502. In respect of the previous race and gender public sector equality duties the Scottish Ministers had the power to impose specific duties on the devolved functions of cross-border Scottish bodies, subject to consultation with the Lord Privy Seal or, in the case of the disability public sector equality duty, the Secretary of State. The Lord Privy Seal in relation to the race and gender public sector equality duties, or the Secretary of State in relation to the disability public sector equality duty, had the power to impose specific duties on the non-devolved, or reserved, functions of those cross-border Scottish bodies, again subject to consultation with the Scottish Ministers. Before imposing specific duties in respect of the previous race, disability and gender public sector equality duties

which related to functions in Wales exercisable by a person who was not a Welsh public body, the Lord Privy Seal or the Secretary of State as the case may be had to consult the Welsh Ministers.

Section 155: Power to impose specific duties: supplementary

Effect

503. This section provides that a specific duty imposed using the powers in sections 153 and 154 may require public bodies to consider matters set out elsewhere by a Minister of the Crown, or the Welsh or Scottish Ministers.

504. This section also makes clear that a Minister of the Crown or the Welsh or Scottish Ministers may impose specific duties on public bodies listed in Schedule 19 that are also contracting authorities for public procurement purposes in relation to their public procurement functions, for example when buying goods and services from private firms. "Public procurement functions" are those activities that fall within the European law public procurement regime. The provisions on public procurement do not affect the extent of any other provision that may be made using the powers in sections 153 and 154 outside this field.

505. This section also provides that a Minister of the Crown and the Welsh and Scottish Ministers may modify or remove duties that they have imposed. A duty imposed by one Minister of the Crown may be modified by a different Minister of the Crown.

Background

506. The previous public sector equality duties did not provide for the imposition of specific duties which required public bodies to take into account matters set out elsewhere. It was inherent, but not explicit, in those duties that duties could be imposed which apply to a body's public procurement functions.

Examples

- A person exercising the power may decide to impose a specific duty that requires specified public bodies to take into account particular national priorities set out in a Public Service Agreement when setting their equality objectives.
- A person exercising the power may decide to impose a specific duty which requires contracting authorities to set out how they will use their procurement functions to better meet the requirements of the public sector equality duty.

Section 156: Enforcement

Effect

507. This section is designed to make it clear that the duties imposed by or under Chapter 1 of Part 11 do not create any private law rights for individuals. These duties are, however, enforceable by way of judicial review.

Background

508. This section is new, but it reflects the position under previous legislation.

Example

- A local council fails to give due regard to the requirements of the public sector equality duty when deciding to stop funding a local women's refuge. An individual would not be able to sue the local council as a result and claim compensation. She would need to consider whether to pursue judicial review proceedings.

Section 157: Interpretation

Effect

509. This section defines the terms used in this Chapter to refer to devolved issues.

510. The other sections in this Chapter refer to relevant Welsh and Scottish bodies, cross-border Welsh and Scottish bodies and devolved Welsh and Scottish functions. This section explains what all those terms mean.

Chapter 2: Positive action

Section 158: Positive action: general

Effect

511. This section provides that the Act does not prohibit the use of positive action measures to alleviate disadvantage experienced by people who share a protected characteristic, reduce their under-representation in relation to particular activities, and meet their particular needs. It will, for example, allow measures to be targeted to particular groups, including training to enable them to gain employment, or health services to address their needs. Any such measures must be a proportionate way of achieving the relevant aim.

512. The extent to which it is proportionate to take positive action measures which may result in people not having the relevant characteristic being treated less favourably will depend, among other things, on the seriousness of the relevant disadvantage, the extremity of need or under-representation and the availability of other means of countering them. This provision will need to be interpreted in accordance with European law which limits the extent to which the kind of action it permits will be allowed.

513. To provide greater legal certainty about what action is proportionate in particular circumstances, the section contains a power to make regulations setting out action which is not permitted under it.

514. If positive action measures are taken in recruitment or promotion under section 159(3) or the selection of political candidates under section 104, those provisions will apply rather than this section.

515. Should the provision allowing single-sex shortlists for the selection of political candidates (section 104(7)) be repealed, this section will not permit action to be taken similar to that permissible under that provision.

516. This section does not allow any action to be taken that would be prohibited by other legislation.

Background

517. This section is new. There were positive action provisions in previous legislation, but these applied to different protected characteristics in different ways and in some cases were specific about the types of action they permitted. This section extends what is possible to the extent permitted by European law, and applies in relation to all protected characteristics.

Examples

- Having identified that its white male pupils are underperforming at maths, a school could run supplementary maths classes exclusively for them.
- An NHS Primary Care Trust identifies that lesbians are less likely to be aware that they are at risk of cervical cancer and less likely to access health services such as national screening programmes. It is also aware that those who do not have children do not know that they

are at an increased risk of breast cancer. Knowing this it could decide to establish local awareness campaigns for lesbians on the importance of cancer screening.

Section 159: Positive action: recruitment and promotion

Effect

518. This section permits an employer to take a protected characteristic into consideration when deciding whom to recruit or promote, where people having the protected characteristic are at a disadvantage or are under-represented. This can be done only where the candidates are as qualified as each other. The question of whether one person is as qualified as another is not a matter only of academic qualification, but rather a judgement based on the criteria the employer uses to establish who is best for the job which could include matters such as suitability, competence and professional performance. The section does not allow employers to have a policy or practice of automatically treating people who share a protected characteristic more favourably than those who do not have it in these circumstances; each case must be considered on its merits. Any action taken must be a proportionate means of addressing such disadvantage or under-representation.

519. The section defines recruitment broadly, so that for example offers of partnership or pupillage, or tenancy in barristers' chambers, are included.

520. The section is intended to allow the maximum extent of flexibility to address disadvantage and under-representation where candidates are as good as each other, within the confines of European law.

Background

521. This section is new. While previous legislation allowed employers to undertake a variety of positive action measures, for instance offering training and encouragement for certain forms of work, it did not allow employers to take any form of positive action at the actual point of recruitment or promotion. This section extends what is possible to the extent permitted by European law, and applies in relation to all protected characteristics.

Examples

- A police service which employs disproportionately low numbers of people from an ethnic minority background identifies a number of candidates who are as qualified as each other for recruitment to a post, including a candidate from an under-represented ethnic minority background. It would not be unlawful to give preferential treatment to that candidate, provided the comparative merits of other candidates were also taken into consideration.
- An employer offers a job to a woman on the basis that women are under-represented in the company's workforce when there was a male candidate who was more qualified. This would be unlawful direct discrimination.

Part 12: Disabled Persons: Transport

Chapter 1: Taxis, etc.

Section 160: Taxi accessibility regulations

Effect

522. This section contains a power for the Secretary of State to make regulations (in relation to England and Wales) specifying the technical standards applying to licensed taxis and imposing requirements on taxi drivers, to enable disabled people to access taxis safely, even when seated in a wheelchair, and to be carried in safety and reasonable comfort.

It makes it an offence, punishable by a fine of (currently) up to £1,000, for a driver of a regulated taxi to fail to comply with the requirements of the regulations.

Background

523. This section replicates provisions the effect of conditions in section 32 of the Disability Discrimination Act 1995.

524. These conditions do not apply to taxis which are drawn by horses or other animals.

Examples

- It is an offence for a taxi driver not to comply with a requirement to have a ramp or other device to enable a disabled person in a wheelchair to access the taxi in safety.
- It is an offence for a taxi driver not to comply with a requirement to ensure the correct position of a wheelchair in the taxi so as to ensure the disabled person can travel in safety.

Section 161: Control of numbers of licensed taxis: exception

Effect

525. A licensing authority (in England or Wales) cannot refuse to license a wheelchair-accessible vehicle on the grounds of controlling taxi numbers, if the proportion of wheelchair-accessible vehicles operating in the area is smaller than the proportion prescribed in regulations by the Secretary of State.

Background

526. This is a new provision. Section 16 of the Transport Act 1985 permits licensing authorities to control the number of taxis operating in their areas by refusing licences, if satisfied that there is no unmet demand for taxis in the area.

527. Section 161 is intended to ensure that licensing authorities in England or Wales with few, or even no, wheelchair-accessible taxis operating in their areas cannot refuse licences to wheelchair-accessible vehicles on the grounds of controlling taxi numbers.

Examples

- Owing to a large number of taxis operating in the area, a licensing authority has decided not to license any more taxis. However, of the licensed taxis, only a few are wheelchair-accessible. The owner of a wheelchair-accessible vehicle applies for a taxi licence. Since the proportion of wheelchair-accessible vehicles in the area is below the level prescribed by the Secretary of State, the licensing authority cannot refuse to issue a taxi licence for the vehicle for the purposes of controlling taxi numbers.
- Another owner of a wheelchair-accessible vehicle also applies for a taxi licence at the same licensing authority. However, the vehicle does not meet the licensing authority's other requirements, as it is too old. The licensing authority is therefore able to refuse the licence on the grounds that the vehicle is too old.

Section 162: Designated transport facilities

Effect

528. This section enables the Secretary of State in England and Wales, or Scottish Ministers in Scotland, to make regulations applying taxi provisions contained in or made under Chapter 1 of Part 12 of the Act or under section 20(2A) of the Civic Government (Scotland) Act 1982 to private hire vehicles used in the provision of services under a franchise agreement.

Background

529. This section replicates similar provisions in section 33 of the Disability Discrimination Act 1995.

530. Franchise agreements exist between operators of transport facilities (premises which form part of railway stations, airports, ports and bus stations) and operators of private hire cars, in order to provide services to members of the public so that they can travel from, for example, the mainline station to their destination. This section allows requirements to be placed on vehicles used under a franchise agreement and their drivers to ensure accessibility for disabled people.

Example

- Regulations could require that the vehicles entering, and for use in, an airport to fulfil the terms of a franchise agreement must be accessible to wheelchair users.

Section 163: Taxi licence conditional on compliance with taxi accessibility regulations

Effect

531. This section prevents a licensing authority from granting a licence for a taxi to ply for hire unless the vehicle complies with the regulations made under section 160, so as to ensure that licensed taxis in use are accessible by disabled passengers. The provisions do not apply if a licence has been in force in respect of the taxi in the preceding 28 days, so that existing vehicles can continue to be used even if they do not meet the accessibility requirements.

Background

532. This section replicates similar provisions in section 34 of the Disability Discrimination Act 1995.

Examples

- Someone making an application for a taxi licence will need to ensure the taxi will be accessible by disabled people.
- A driver renewing the licence for a taxi will not need to show that the vehicle meets the accessibility requirements as long as it was licensed in the 28 days preceding the grant of the new licence.

Section 164: Exemption from taxi accessibility regulations

Effect

533. This section contains a power for the Secretary of State to make regulations allowing a licensing authority to apply for an order exempting it from the requirements of section 163 if it has undertaken a consultation, published the outcome and taken into account any representations. A licensing authority may only apply for an exemption order if applying section 163 would reduce the number of taxis in the area to an unacceptable level.

534. The Secretary of State may grant or refuse such an order but, before deciding whether or not to do so, is required to consult the Disabled Persons Transport Advisory Committee and any other appropriate persons. In granting an exemption order, the Secretary of State may impose certain conditions. Where exemption is given from the full accessibility requirements, taxis may instead be required to be fitted with swivel seats and to conform to any safety conditions when such seats are in use.

Background

535. This section replicates provisions in section 35 of the Disability Discrimination Act 1995.

Example

- A particular licensing authority can apply for an exemption order if it considers that requiring all taxis to comply with the accessibility requirements would mean that licensed taxi drivers in the area would transfer from being hackney carriage drivers to private hire vehicle drivers, because the cost of purchasing accessible taxis would make their business unprofitable. The Secretary of State can agree to make an exemption order but, in doing so, can require a certain number of accessible taxis to be available in the area.

Section 165: Passengers in wheelchairs

Effect

536. This section places duties on drivers of designated taxis and private hire vehicles to carry a disabled passenger while in a wheelchair; to not make an additional charge; if the passenger chooses to sit in a passenger seat, to carry the passenger's wheelchair; to carry the passenger in safety and in reasonable comfort; and to provide reasonable assistance to enable the passenger to use the taxi. A taxi or private hire vehicle is designated if it appears on a list maintained by the local licensing authority under section 167.

537. A driver of a designated taxi or private hire vehicle who refuses to carry a wheelchair user commits an offence punishable by a fine of (currently) up to £1,000.

Background

538. This section has its basis in section 36 (as amended by the Local Transport Act 2008) of the Disability Discrimination Act 1995. The previous legislation applied the provisions of this section to regulated taxis. The provisions in this section now apply just to the drivers of designated, rather than regulated, taxis and private hire vehicles. Further explanation of provisions regarding the designation of wheelchair accessible vehicles is provided in the notes on section 167.

Examples

- A person in a wheelchair hires a wheelchair-accessible taxi or private hire vehicle. The driver must help the passenger into and out of the vehicle by using a ramp or lift and helping the passenger onto the lift or up the ramp. The driver must ensure the wheelchair is correctly positioned in the vehicle and secured so that the passenger travels safely and in reasonable comfort.
- If a passenger in a wheelchair wishes to travel in a passenger seat, the driver must assist the passenger into and out of the vehicle and transport the wheelchair.
- A driver must load a disabled passenger's luggage into and out of the taxi.
- A driver cannot charge a person in a wheelchair more than any other passenger.

Section 166: Passengers in wheelchairs: exemption certificates

Effect

539. The Secretary of State may make regulations which allow a licensing authority to exempt a driver from the duties contained in section 165 if it is satisfied that the driver cannot provide assistance due to a medical or physical condition.

540. The exemption certificate must be displayed in the vehicle.

Background

541. This section has its basis in section 36 of the Disability Discrimination Act 1995, but it extends further, as described in relation to section 165 above.

Example

- A driver is not required to provide physical assistance to help a passenger in a wheelchair into and out of a vehicle if he is medically unfit to do so.

Section 167: Lists of wheelchair-accessible vehicles

Effect

542. This section permits a licensing authority to maintain a list of wheelchair-accessible taxis and private hire vehicles operating in its area. If it so wishes, a licensing authority may decide to list just those vehicles that also hold a special licence to operate a local bus service, and not list wheelchair-accessible vehicles that hold only a conventional licence.

543. The duties contained in section 165 will apply to drivers of the vehicles that appear on the list of designated wheelchair-accessible vehicles.

544. The section permits the Secretary of State to issue guidance to licensing authorities and the licensing authority must have regard to any guidance issued.

Background

545. This section has its basis in section 36A of the Disability Discrimination Act 1995, which allowed licensing authorities to maintain lists of wheelchair-accessible vehicles with special licences to operate a local bus service. However, provisions in this section now extend further to allow licensing authorities to also include wheelchair-accessible vehicles that hold only conventional licences.

Examples

- A licensing authority maintains a list of the wheelchair-accessible taxis and private hire vehicles operating in its area. The drivers of the vehicles on that list are required to perform the duties to assist passengers in wheelchairs contained in section 165.
- The driver of a vehicle that is included on the list will provide assistance to passengers in wheelchairs and will not charge them an additional fare.

Section 168: Assistance dogs in taxis

Effect

546. This section places duties on drivers of taxis in England and Wales to transport a disabled person's assistance dog, for example, a blind person's guide dog, and allow it to stay with the passenger without making any additional charge. Under section 20 of the Civic Government (Scotland) Act 1982, regulations may make provision corresponding to sections 168 and 169 for Scotland.

547. A driver of a taxi who refuses to carry an assistance dog commits an offence that is punishable by a fine of (currently) up to £1,000.

Background

548. This section replicates the main provision contained in section 37 of the Disability Discrimination Act 1995.

Example

- A person with an assistance dog hails a taxi. The driver must not refuse to transport the assistance dog and must let it accompany the passenger in the taxi.

Section 169: Assistance dogs in taxis: exemption certificates

Effect

549. This section permits a licensing authority in England and Wales to exempt a driver of a taxi from the duties contained in section 168 if it is satisfied that the driver cannot carry an assistance dog on medical grounds, or that the vehicle is not suitable for the carriage of assistance dogs.

550. The exemption certificate must be displayed on the taxi.

Background

551. This section is designed to replicate the exemption provision that was contained in section 37 of the Disability Discrimination Act 1995. However the definition of "licensing authority" in relation to London now means "Transport for London" as it is this body that exercises functions relating to taxi licensing.

Example

- A driver who has a medically certified allergy to dogs is not required to carry an assistance dog, as long as she displays an exemption certificate on her taxi.

Section 170: Assistance dogs in private hire vehicles

Effect

552. This section places duties on operators and drivers of private hire vehicles in England and Wales to transport a disabled person's assistance dog and allow it to stay with the passenger without making any additional charge. Under section 20 of the Civic Government (Scotland) Act 1982, regulations may make provision corresponding to section 170 for Scotland.

553. An operator or driver of a private hire vehicle who refuses to carry an assistance dog commits an offence that is punishable by a fine of (currently) up to £1,000.

Background

554. This section is replicates the main provision contained in section 37A of the Disability Discrimination Act 1995.

Examples

- A driver of a private hire vehicle cannot impose an additional charge for carrying an assistance dog.
- An operator of a fleet of private hire vehicles accepts a booking from a passenger with an assistance dog. The driver cannot refuse to carry the assistance dog.

Section 171: Assistance dogs in private hire vehicles: exemption certificates

Effect

555. This section permits a licensing authority in England and Wales to exempt a driver of a private hire vehicle from the duties contained in section 170 if it is satisfied that the

driver cannot carry an assistance dog because of a medical condition, or that the vehicle is not suitable for the carriage of assistance dogs.

556. The exemption certificate must be displayed on the private hire vehicle.

Background

557. This section is designed to replicate the exemption provision that was contained in section 37A of the Disability Discrimination Act 1995.

Example

- A driver is not required to carry an assistance dog if he has a medically certified allergy to dogs and displays his exemption certificate in his vehicle.

Section 172: Appeals

Effect

558. In England and Wales, if a taxi or a private hire vehicle driver is refused a certificate exempting him or her from the requirements to assist disabled passengers in wheelchairs or to carry assistance dogs, this section gives a right of appeal to a magistrates' court, within 28 days of being refused.

559. In Scotland, if a taxi or private hire vehicle driver is refused a certificate exempting him or her from the requirements to assist disabled passengers in wheelchairs, this section gives a right to appeal to the sheriff, within 28 days of being refused.

560. The owner of a taxi or private hire vehicle may appeal, to the magistrates' court in England and Wales, or the sheriff in Scotland, against a licensing authority's decision to include his or her vehicle on a designated list of wheelchair-accessible vehicles held by the licensing authority under section 167.

Background

561. Section 172 is designed to replicate the provisions of section 38 of the Disability Discrimination Act 1995. However this section also reflects the extension of provisions in section 167 to drivers of designated taxis and private hire vehicles when not providing a local bus service (i.e. when providing a conventional service).

Examples

- A taxi driver applies for a certificate exempting him from the requirement to assist disabled passengers in wheelchairs because he has a bad back. His application is refused by the licensing authority but the driver believes insufficient consideration was given to the medical information supporting his application, so he lodges an appeal within 28 days of the decision. The appeal is successful and the court directs the licensing authority to issue an exemption certificate to the driver.
- A licensing authority lists a taxi or private hire vehicle as being accessible for passengers in wheelchairs, meaning the driver is required to assist disabled passengers in wheelchairs. The owner of the vehicle, who considers that it is not accessible, can appeal the decision to be listed.

Section 173: Interpretation

Effect

562. This section explains the meaning of the terms, "accessibility requirements", "assistance dog", "taxi" and "taxi accessibility regulations".

Chapter 2: Public service vehicles

Section 174: PSV accessibility regulations

Effect

563. This section enables the Secretary of State to make public service vehicle accessibility regulations specifying the technical standards applying to buses and coaches, to provide greater accessibility to disabled passengers including when seated in a wheelchair. The requirements can relate to the construction, use and maintenance of the vehicle, to the design and carriage of equipment, and to wheelchair restraints and wheelchair position.

Background

564. This section replicates the provisions of section 40 of the Disability Discrimination Act 1995.

Example

- Buses and coaches must meet certain technical standards in respect of equipment and design to ensure accessibility by disabled passengers. If accessibility features, such as handrails or other aids, were present when the vehicle was approved but have subsequently been removed, the bus must not be used on the road.

Section 175: Offence of contravening PSV accessibility regulations

Effect

565. This section makes it an offence to fail to comply with the requirements of the regulations or to use or allow to be used on the road a public service vehicle which does not meet the requirements of the regulations. If an offence is found to have been committed by or with the consent of a responsible person, such as a director, manager or company secretary, that individual, as well as the company, is guilty of the offence.

566. The offence is punishable by a fine of (currently up) to £2,500.

Background

567. This section replicates the offence provisions of section 40 of the Disability Discrimination Act 1995.

Example

- A bus has an accessibility feature removed and is subsequently used on a registered service. By using, or permitting the vehicle to be used in this condition, an offence is committed and may lead to the driver and the operator being convicted of the offence and a fine of up to £2,500 being imposed.

Section 176: Accessibility certificates

Effect

568. This section requires a regulated public service vehicle to have an accessibility certificate to demonstrate that it meets the requirements of the public service vehicle accessibility regulations (see section 174), or an approval certificate (see section 177), before it can be used on a road. It also allows the Secretary of State to make regulations relating to applications and the issue (or copies) of accessibility certificates and providing for vehicle examinations.

Background

569. This section replicates the provisions contained in section 41 of the Disability Discrimination Act 1995.

Example

- A bus must have an accessibility certificate showing that it conforms to requirements about accessibility features, for example, ramps, handrails and wheelchair spaces. The certificate shows that the bus meets the minimum acceptable standard to enable disabled passengers to get on and off it and be carried on it in reasonable safety and comfort.

Section 177: Approval certificates

Effect

570. This section allows the Secretary of State to approve a public service vehicle as a "type vehicle" if the relevant technical requirements are met, and the issue of an approval certificate if a particular vehicle conforms with a "type vehicle". This allows a design of vehicle to be approved as meeting the technical and accessibility requirements. It also contains a power for the Secretary of State to make regulations relating to applications and the issue (or copies) of approval certificates and providing for vehicle examinations.

571. The Secretary of State can withdraw approval for a "type vehicle" at any time. When this happens, no further approval certificates may be issued. The certificates issued prior to withdrawal remain valid.

Background

572. This section replicates the provisions contained in section 42 of the Disability Discrimination Act 1995.

Example

- A particular bus manufacturer's chassis in combination with a body is approved as a "type vehicle", and approval certificates are issued in respect of buses conforming to this design. Modifications are subsequently made to the "type vehicle" which mean that it no longer meets the technical requirements, so its approval as a "type vehicle" is withdrawn and no approval certificates will be issued in respect of buses conforming to the modified design.

Section 178: Special authorisations

Effect

573. This section contains a power for the Secretary of State to authorise the use of a public service vehicle in certain circumstances where such a vehicle may not meet the requirements of regulations under section 174. It also allows restrictions or conditions to be placed on the use of such vehicles.

Background

574. This section replicates the provisions contained in section 43 of the Disability Discrimination Act 1995.

Example

- A new design of vehicle, which does not conform to the current accessibility regulations, is to be trialled. The Secretary of State makes an order allowing the use of the vehicle in a restricted environment, specifying the permitted areas and times of operation, so that its performance can be tested.

Section 179: Reviews and appeals

Effect

575. If the Secretary of State refuses to approve a vehicle as a "type vehicle", this section allows the applicant to ask the Secretary of State to review of the decision on payment of a fee. It also gives a right of appeal to the Secretary of State against any refusal to issue an accessibility or approval certificate. It also allows the Secretary of State to set out the appeals procedure in regulations.

Background

576. This section replicates the provisions contained in section 44 of the Disability Discrimination Act 1995.

Example

- A vehicle manufacturer is refused approval of a new bus design as a "type vehicle". The manufacturer asks the Secretary of State to review the decision and pays the required fee. The Secretary of State must review the decision and any supporting written evidence or representations, and can confirm, vary or reverse the original decision.

Section 180: Fees

Effect

577. This section contains a power for the Secretary of State make fees regulations and to charge fees in accordance with them for processing applications for approval as a "type vehicle", processing accessibility and approval certificates, issuing duplicate certificates and conducting reviews and appeals. Fees are not likely to be greater than the amount needed to cover costs. The section allows provision for repaying fees in whole or part in certain circumstances, for example, on a successful appeal.

Background

578. This section replicates the provisions contained in section 45 of the Disability Discrimination Act 1995.

Example

- An applicant may have to pay a fee for accessibility and approval certificates for a public service vehicle, to cover the cost of dealing with the application and inspection process.

Section 181: Interpretation

Effect

579. This section explains the meaning of the terms, "accessibility certificate", "approval certificate", "PSV accessibility regulations" and "regulated public service vehicle".

Chapter 3: Rail vehicles

Section 182: Rail vehicle accessibility regulations

Effect

580. This section includes powers for the Secretary of State to make regulations to ensure that trains, trams and certain other guided transport systems are accessible to disabled people including wheelchair users.

581. However, due to the limited definition of "rail vehicle" used in this section, its scope is restricted to rail vehicles which do not operate on the "interoperable rail system". Regulations made under this section could therefore only be applicable for the most part to light rail vehicles (those used on metro, underground and tram systems and prescribed modes of guided transport).

582. All rail vehicles must comply with accessibility standards, or have an appropriate exemption in place, by no later than 1 January 2020.

583. Before making any regulations under this section, the Secretary of State must first consult the Disabled Persons Transport Advisory Committee and other representative organisations.

Background

584. This section replicates the provisions of section 46 of the Disability Discrimination Act 1995 as amended by the Disability Discrimination Act 2005.

Example

- All new rail vehicles introduced on metro, underground or tram systems, or prescribed modes of guided transport, will need to be fully accessible or seek an exemption (under section 183) if there are compelling circumstances which mean they cannot comply.

*Section 183: **Exemptions from rail vehicle accessibility regulations***

Effect

585. This section contains a power for the Secretary of State to make orders ("exemption orders") authorising a regulated rail vehicle to be used in passenger service even though it does not comply with accessibility standards, or the way it is to be used would not comply with such standards.

586. It provides for regulations to specify who may apply for an exemption order, what information needs to be supplied, how the exemption regime will operate, how long an exemption order can apply and measures for revocation. This list is not exhaustive.

587. Before granting an exemption order, the Secretary of State must first consult the Disabled Persons Transport Advisory Committee and such other persons as considered appropriate.

Background

588. This section replicates the provisions of section 47 of the Disability Discrimination Act 1995 as amended by the Disability Discrimination Act 2005.

Example

- The exemption power can be used to exempt a specified rail vehicle, or a rail vehicle of a specified description or the use of such a vehicle in specified circumstances. So, for example, all the vehicles used on a particular network (such as a heritage or tourist railway or tramway) could be exempted.

*Section 184: **Procedure for making exemption orders***

Effect

589. This section provides that exemption orders made under section 183 may, at the discretion of the Secretary of State, be subject to either the draft affirmative resolution or the negative resolution procedure. It sets out the procedure for the exercise of this

discretion and enables regulations to be made setting out the criteria under which a decision will be made.

590. The Secretary of State is required to consult the Disabled Persons Transport Advisory Committee, and other appropriate persons, before making such regulations, which are themselves subject to the draft affirmative resolution procedure.

Background

591. This section replicates sections 67(5A) and 67A of the Disability Discrimination Act 1995 as inserted by the Disability Discrimination Act 2005.

Section 185: Annual report on exemption orders

Effect

592. This section requires the Secretary of State to produce an annual report ("the report") on the use of powers to exempt regulated rail vehicles from accessibility requirements. The report will be produced for each calendar year and must contain details of all exemption orders made under section 183. It must also contain information about the consultation on both applications for exemption orders and the exercise of discretion under section 184. The report must be laid before both Houses of Parliament.

Background

593. This section replicates the provisions of section 67B of the Disability Discrimination Act 1995 as inserted by the Disability Discrimination Act 2005.

Section 186: Rail vehicle accessibility: compliance

Effect

594. This section relates to the provisions of Schedule 20 which contain powers to introduce compliance certification and a civil enforcement regime with associated penalties.

595. Commencement of subsection (1) would bring Schedule 20 into effect. However, subsection (2) provides that, if not commenced (either fully or to any extent) before the end of 2010, this section and Schedule 20 would be automatically repealed.

Background

596. Schedule 20 replicates the provisions of the Disability Discrimination Act 1995 section s 47A to 47M as inserted by the Disability Discrimination Act 2005 (but not yet in force). More detail on the reasons why this section has been included in the Act can be found in paragraphs 923-965

Section 187: Interpretation

Effect

597. This section includes cross references to explanations of what is meant by the terms "rail vehicle", "regulated rail vehicle" and "rail vehicle accessibility regulations" used throughout this Chapter of the Act. It also explains what is meant by use "for carriage".

Background

598. This section replicates certain provisions of the Disability Discrimination Act 1995 as amended by the Disability Discrimination Act 2005.

Chapter 4: Supplementary

Section 188: Forgery, etc.

Effect

599. This section makes it a criminal offence for a person to forge, alter, use, lend, or allow another person to use a public service vehicle accessibility certificate, public service vehicle "type" certificate or any exemption certificate issued in respect of assisting disabled passengers in taxis or carriage of assistance dogs, or to make or have in his possession a document which resembles such a certificate, with intent to deceive. It is also an offence to knowingly make a false statement in order to obtain any of these certificates.

Background

600. This section replicates the effect of provisions in the Disability Discrimination Act 1995.

Part 13: Disability: Miscellaneous

Section 189: Reasonable adjustments

Effect

601. This section applies the supplementary provisions on reasonable adjustments set out in Schedule 21 to the fields of services, premises, work, education and associations where a person providing a service or delivering functions, an employer or an education provider, or an association is required to consider reasonable adjustments to premises which it rents and would require the landlord's consent to proceed.

Section 190: Improvements to let dwelling houses

Effect

602. This section provides a procedure for a disabled tenant or occupier of rented residential premises to seek consent to make a disability-related improvement to the premises where the lease allows a tenant to make an improvement only with the consent of the landlord. The landlord may not unreasonably withhold consent, but may place reasonable conditions on the consent. A landlord who refuses consent must set out the reasons for that refusal. In deciding whether a refusal or condition is unreasonable, the onus is on the landlord to show that it is not. This section applies to all leases of residential property used as the occupier's or tenant's only or main residence, other than a protected tenancy, a statutory tenancy or a secure tenancy. That is because similar rights already apply in respect of those tenancies under the Housing Acts 1980 and 1985.

603. This section applies only in England and Wales.

Background

604. This section replaces similar provisions in the Disability Discrimination Act 1995.

Examples

- A disabled tenant who has mobility problems asks her landlord to consent to the installation of a walk-in shower and a grab rail to help her use the lavatory. Her landlord refuses consent. It would be for the landlord to give reasons for the refusal, and to show that it was not unreasonable.

- The landlord consents to the fitting of the grab rail and shower, on condition that their colour matches the other bathroom fittings, and that they must be removed if the disabled person moves out of the property. These might be reasonable conditions, but it is for the landlord to show that they are.

Part 14: General Exceptions

Section 191: Statutory provisions

Effect

605. This section gives effect to Schedule 22, which allows differential treatment which would otherwise be made unlawful by specific parts of the Act, where that is required by law. It also allows differential treatment of pregnant women for their own protection, and allows people of particular religions or beliefs to be appointed to specified educational posts. It also allows rules about Crown employment to provide for differential treatment on the basis of nationality.

Section 192: National security

Effect

606. This section ensures that the Act does not make it unlawful to do anything which is proportionate in order to safeguard national security.

Background

607. The section replaces similar exceptions in previous legislation, narrowing those which excuse disability discrimination in some areas or sex discrimination. For the first time, it provides a national security exception in relation to age and sexual orientation discrimination outside work.

Example

- Denying people of a particular nationality access to sensitive information is not unlawful race discrimination under the Act if it is proportionate in order to guard against terrorist attacks.

Section 193: Charities

Effect

608. This section allows charities to provide benefits only to people who share the same protected characteristic (for example sex, sexual orientation or disability), if this is in line with their charitable instrument and if it is objectively justified or to prevent or compensate for disadvantage. It remains unlawful for them to limit their beneficiaries by reference to their colour – and if they do their charitable instrument will be applied as if that limitation did not exist.

609. Charities must not restrict benefits consisting of employment, contract work or vocational training to people who share a protected characteristic, except that the section does allow people to provide, and the Government to agree, arrangements for supported employment only for people with the same disability, or disabilities of a description to be set out in regulations.

610. The section also allows certain charities to make acceptance of a religion or belief a condition of membership, and to refuse members access to benefits if they do not accept a religion or belief where membership itself is not subject to such a condition, if they have done so since before 18 May 2005. It also allows single-sex activities for the purpose of promoting or supporting a charity (such as women-only fun-runs), and

allows the charity regulators to exercise their functions in a charity's interests, taking account of what is said in its charitable instrument, without contravening the Act.

Background

611. This section replaces and harmonises separate exceptions in previous legislation allowing charities to benefit only people of the same sex, racial group, religion or belief or sexual orientation, and creates new exceptions along these lines for charities benefiting only people of the same age group or with the same disability. This section also replicates the effect of other exceptions for charities in previous discrimination law, and creates a new exception in subsection (7) allowing participation in activities to promote or support charities to be restricted to men or women.

Examples

- It is lawful for the Women's Institute to provide educational opportunities only to women.
- It is lawful for the RNIB to employ, or provide special facilities for, visually impaired people in preference to other disabled people.
- A charitable instrument enabling the provision of benefits to black members of a community actually enables the benefits to be provided to all members of that community.
- It is lawful for the Scout Association to require children joining the Scouts to promise to do their best to do their duty to God.
- Race for Life, a women-only event which raises money for Cancer Research UK, is lawful.

Section 194: Charities: supplementary

Effect

612. This section makes it clear that section 193 does not allow charities to restrict their benefits to people because of colour.

613. It explains what is meant by "charity" and related expressions used in section 193.

Section 195: Sport

Effect

614. This section allows separate sporting competitions to continue to be organised for men and women where physical strength, stamina or physique are major factors in determining success or failure, and in which one sex is generally at a disadvantage in comparison with the other. It also makes it lawful to restrict participation of transsexual people in such competitions if this is necessary to uphold fair or safe competition, but not otherwise.

615. In addition, this section allows the existing selection arrangements of national sports teams, regional or local clubs or related associations to continue. It also protects "closed" competitions where participation is limited to people who meet a requirement relating to nationality, place of birth or residence.

Background

616. This section replaces similar provisions in previous legislation.

Examples

- It would be lawful to have men and women, though not necessarily younger boys and girls, compete in separate 100 metre races.

- It would be lawful to require participants in a county tennis championship to have been born in that county or to have lived there for a minimum period prior to the event.

Section 196: General

Effect

617. This section gives effect to Schedule 23, which contains a number of general exceptions to the prohibitions against discrimination and harassment, covering acts authorised by statute or the Government, organisations relating to religion or belief, communal accommodation and training provided to people who are not resident in the European Economic Area.

Section 197: Age

Effect

618. This section enables a Minister of the Crown to make orders setting out exceptions to the prohibition on discriminating against people because of age, except in relation to work and further and higher education. These exceptions can relate to particular conduct or practices, or things done for particular purposes, or things done under particular arrangements, as set out in any order made under this power. Orders can provide for a Minister of the Crown or the Treasury to issue guidance, for consultation about the guidance, and for the imposition of requirements that refer to the guidance. Any guidance will come into force at a date specified in a further order subject to the negative procedure so that Parliament has the opportunity to consider the particular use of the guidance power

Background

619. This is a new provision designed to allow exceptions to be made from the new prohibitions on age discrimination in the provision of services and the exercise of public functions.

Examples

620. Appropriate age-based treatment may include the following:

    - concessionary travel for older and young people;
    - disease prevention programmes such as cancer screening targeted at people in particular age groups on the basis of clinical evidence;
    - age differences in the calculation of annuities and insurance programmes which are reasonable and based on adequate evidence of the underlying difference in risk;
    - holidays for particular age groups.

Part 15: Family Property

Section 198: Abolition of husband's duty to maintain wife

Effect

621. This section abolishes the common law duty of a husband to maintain his wife.

Background

622. The husband's common law duty to provide his wife with the necessities of life was a consequence of now obsolete rules of law which prevented the wife from having capacity to hold property and to enter into contracts. There is no equivalent common

law duty for a wife to maintain her husband. There are, however, now adequate statutory provisions requiring both spouses to maintain each other. The common law duty to maintain has little if any practical application.

Example

- Either party to a marriage can apply to the court for a financial provision order against the other party under the Domestic Proceedings and Magistrates' Courts Act 1978 or the Matrimonial Causes Act 1973 on the grounds that his or her spouse has failed to provide reasonable maintenance for them or for any child of the family. There will no longer be any additional common law requirement for a husband to maintain his wife.

*Section 199: **Abolition of presumption of advancement***

Effect

623. This section abolishes the common law presumption of advancement. The abolition does not affect any transfer made before the provision comes into force.

Background

624. The presumption of advancement was a presumption that a man who transfers property to his wife, child or fiancée is making the recipient a gift of that property, unless there was evidence to the contrary. This presumption acted as an exception to the normal rule – that where one person transfers property to another without gaining anything in return, the recipient is presumed to be holding the property on trust for the transferor unless there is evidence that a gift was intended.

625. The presumption of advancement did not apply where a woman transferred property to her husband, child or fiancé.

Example

- A husband transfers property to his wife. It is presumed that she is to hold the property on trust for her husband, unless there is evidence that a gift was intended.

*Section 200: **Amendment of Married Women's Property Act 1964***

Effect

626. This section amends section 1 of the Married Women's Property Act 1964 so that money and property derived from a housekeeping allowance will, in the absence of an agreement to the contrary, be owned by the husband and wife in equal shares regardless of who paid or received the allowance. The provision does not apply to any allowance paid before it comes into force.

Background

627. Under the Married Women's Property Act 1964, if a husband paid a housekeeping allowance to his wife, any money or property derived from the allowance (in the absence of an agreement to the contrary) was treated as belonging to the husband and wife in equal shares. But the 1964 Act was silent on housekeeping allowances paid by a wife to her husband.

Example

- A wife pays her husband a housekeeping allowance. Unless they agree otherwise, the allowance and any property bought from it will be shared equally.

Section 201: Civil partners: housekeeping allowance

Effect

628. This section inserts a new section 70A into the Civil Partnership Act 2004. The new section applies section 1 of the Married Women's Property Act 1964 (as amended by this Act) to allowances paid by civil partners so that money and property derived from a housekeeping allowance is to be treated as belonging to both civil partners in equal shares.

Background

629. The Civil Partnership Act 2004 replicates most of the legal provisions relating to husbands and wives. However, as long as the provisions of section 1 of the Married Women's Property Act 1964 were gender specific, in that they only dealt with housekeeping allowances made by a husband to his wife and not allowances made by either spouse, it was not possible to replicate them for civil partners.

Example

- A woman pays her civil partner a housekeeping allowance. Unless they agree otherwise, the allowance and any property bought from it will be shared equally.

Part 16: General and Miscellaneous

Section 202: Civil partnerships on religious premises

Effect

630. 1. This section amends section 6 of the Civil Partnership Act 2004, by repealing the prohibition on civil partnerships being registered in religious premises in England and Wales and repealing the definition of "religious premises".

631. 2. This section also amends section 6A of the Civil Partnership Act 2004, which contains a power to make regulations about the approval of premises for the registration of civil partnerships, by making clear that such regulations may provide for different premises to be approved for registration of civil partnerships from those approved for registration of civil marriages, and for different provision to be made for different kinds of premises. In particular it enables the regulations to set out, in relation to particular denominations, who has the authority to decide whether civil partnerships can be registered on any of their premises, and makes clear that nothing in the Civil Partnership Act 2004 obliges any religious organisation to host civil partnerships if they do not wish to.

632. 3. It also inserts into section 6A definitions of "civil marriage" and "religious premises". Both definitions are the same as existing definitions in the Civil Partnership Act 2004.

Background

633. 4. The Civil Partnership Act 2004 included an express prohibition on civil partnership registrations taking place in religious premises. The regulations governing the approval of premises for the registration of civil partnerships are the Marriages and Civil Partnerships (Approved Premises) Regulations 2005. They currently align provision for civil partnerships with that for civil marriage.

Examples

- Regulations under section 6A could provide that, for example, Church of England premises may be approved for the registration of civil partnerships only with the consent of the General Synod of the Church of England.
- A couple seeking to register their civil partnership in a church that had not been approved for that purpose could not require those responsible for the church to allow them to hold the registration there. Nor could they require the denomination responsible for the church to seek approval to enable this.

Section 203: Harmonisation

Effect

634. This section enables a Minister of the Crown by order to amend the Act and the Equality Act 2006, to ensure consistency across the legislation where changes required by European law would otherwise result in inconsistent provision. Section 2(2)(a) of the European Communities Act 1972 allows a Minister by regulations or order to give effect to a right or obligation arising out of an EU law provision. Where provisions of this Act and equality law of the UK more generally deal with a sector on a single basis some of the matters covered may not be within the reach of EU law and so outside section 2(2)(a). This arises for instance in the case of nationality and colour which are not dealt with under the EU law provisions on race discrimination but are covered by the UK provisions. Section 2(2)(b) of the European Communities Act 1972 would not allow amendment of all relevant parts of the legislation in these circumstances, because the change required in respect of, say nationality or colour, would not be consequential on or arising out of the EU obligation. In order to retain the unitary approach to discrimination law it is necessary to have a power such as this so that in appropriate cases amendments can also be made to those areas of the Act unaffected by new EU law obligations.

635. A Minister may use this power only after consulting interested parties on the Government's proposals; and where the consultation prompts the Minister to consider changes to those proposals, these changes must be the subject of such further consultation as the Minister considers appropriate. Following the consultation, the Minister must act in accordance with the requirements in section 204.

636. A Minister must report to Parliament every two years on the use of this power.

Background

637. This is a new provision designed to ensure that the areas of the Act that are covered by European law and those that are domestic in origin do not get out of step, as was the case with the previous legislation.

Example

- A future European Court of Justice judgement on the Race Directive requires an amendment to alter the definition of indirect discrimination. This power could be used to ensure that any such amendment applies to the "colour and nationality" elements of race in the Act, as well as those in relation to which EU law applies.

Section 204: Harmonisation: procedure

Effect

638. This section sets out the procedure to be followed by a Minister following a consultation under section 203.

639. The Minister must lay an explanatory report on the consultation findings alongside any draft order being laid before each House of Parliament for debate and approval. The explanatory report must include the reasons for making harmonising provision, and why the conditions for using the power in section 203 are satisfied. It must also set out details of the consultation, the responses and any changes that were made in response to them. This section also provides protection against disclosure of information in representations provided on a confidential basis.

640. A Minister must not lay any instrument before Parliament until the minimum consultation period of 12 weeks has expired.

*Section 205: **Crown application***

Effect

641. This section sets out how the Act applies to Ministers, government departments and certain statutory bodies – collectively known as the Crown. The section does not affect the Sovereign in her private capacity.

Background

642. This section replicates the effect of similar provisions in previous legislation. The principle is that the machinery of government, both elected and administrative, should be subject to the Act in the same way as everybody else, unless there are good reasons for it not being. The section also replicates the arrangements in the previous discrimination legislation for taking proceedings against the Crown.

Example

- A government department as employer must not discriminate against an employee because of race; just as any other employer is prohibited from doing so under the Act.

*Section 206: **Information society services***

Effect

643. This section gives effect to Schedule 25, which applies the Act to information society service providers established in Great Britain (see the explanatory notes to Schedule 25).

Background

644. The provisions in Schedule 25 are new.

*Section 207: **Exercise of power***

Effect

645. This section makes provision for the powers to make secondary legislation under the Act. Unless it is stated otherwise, they will be exercised by a Minister of the Crown and be statutory instruments. It also provides that orders and regulations may deal with different situations differently and include consequential and other provisions dealing with transition to the new provisions.

646. In some cases, the power to make consequential provision can be exercised to amend an enactment, including in relation to section 197 (age) and section 216 (commencement) of this Act. For example, this power would enable a consequential amendment to be made to this Act where it is necessary to update a reference to other legislation that has been passed since this Act received Royal Assent but before it comes into force.

647. The section also enables matters that need to be dealt with on commencement of a particular section, such as transitional provisions and consequential amendments, to be dealt with in more than one order and, if necessary, at different times and by different procedures. For example, it would enable consequential amendments to primary legislation, which require an affirmative resolution, to be dealt with in a separate commencement order or orders from other provisions which do not require a parliamentary procedure.

648. This section also provides that the negative parliamentary procedure applies to an Order in Council made under section 82.

Background

649. As with any Act delegating the power to legislate, this section is needed to set out the arrangements for how Ministers are to exercise such delegated power. This is a large Act with a number of provisions that confer power to amend primary legislation. Much of the Act involves consolidation and harmonisation of previous legislation, so that the range of possible consequential amendments is likely to be limited. It is thought convenient to specify in one place those powers to amend primary legislation that include a power to make consequential amendments to primary legislation. It is also thought that having a general broad power of the kind often found in other legislation would create duplication in those cases where it is considered that power to make consequential amendments is required and might raise doubt in those cases where it is not. The power in the form used in this Act allows for separate orders for consequential amendments and will in practice produce the same result as a general consequential power of the usual kind would.

Section 208: Ministers of the Crown, etc.

Effect

650. This section establishes which parliamentary procedures apply to the regulations and orders which can be made by Ministers of the Crown or the Treasury under the Act.

Background

651. In common with any Act containing powers to make secondary legislation, this section is needed to set out the arrangements for how Parliament is to control the use of powers in the Act. It provides for any instrument amending any Act of Parliament (including this Act), any Act of the Scottish Parliament or Act or Measure of the Welsh Assembly to be made only using the affirmative resolution procedure. There are some exceptions. In a few other cases (for example, where regulations under section 78 are made to introduce a requirement on employers to publish their gender pay gap), the affirmative resolution procedure must also be used and the relevant order or regulations must be approved by both Houses of Parliament before they can come into force.

Section 209: The Welsh Ministers

Effect

652. This section establishes the parliamentary procedures that apply to regulations and orders under the Act made by Welsh Ministers.

653. A few instruments, including those which impose the socio-economic duty or the public sector equality specific duties on public authorities or cross-border authorities, must be considered by the National Assembly for Wales before they can come into force. The rest do not automatically need to be considered by the Assembly but in most cases they can be opposed, in which case a debate may be held.

Background

654. In common with any Act containing powers to make secondary legislation, this section is needed to set out who is to make regulations and orders (usually a Minister), how their effect may vary according to particular circumstances and the arrangements for Assembly control over their exercise.

Section 210: The Scottish Ministers

Effect

655. This section establishes the parliamentary procedures that apply to regulations and orders under the Act made by Scottish Ministers.

656. A few instruments, including those which impose the socio-economic duty or public sector equality specific duties on public authorities or cross-border authorities, must be debated by the Scottish Parliament before they can come into force. The rest do not automatically need to be debated by the Scottish Parliament but in most cases they can be opposed, in which case a debate may be held.

Background

657. In common with any Act containing powers to make secondary legislation, this section is needed to set out who is to make regulations and orders (usually a Minister), how their effect may vary according to particular circumstances and the arrangements for parliamentary control over their exercise.

Section 211: Amendments, repeals and revocations

Effect

658. This section gives effect to Schedules 26 and 27. Schedule 26 contains amendments to other primary legislation which are necessary as a consequence of the Act's provisions. Schedule 27 lists the provisions in previous legislation which will cease to have effect when the relevant provisions of the Act are brought into force.

Section 212: General interpretation

Effect

659. This section explains what is meant by various words and phrases which appear in more than one Part of the Act.

Background

660. While a key objective of the Act is to present discrimination law in plain language and most words used in the Act have an ordinarily obvious meaning, it is sometimes necessary to make clear the specific legal meaning of some words and phrases that are used several times in the Act.

661. Subsection (5), which expands the meaning of "detriment" in subsection (1), makes clear that although the express prohibition of sexual orientation harassment does not apply for example to schools, a pupil who is bullied by a school employee as a result of his or her sexual orientation may nevertheless bring a claim of direct discrimination if the bullying caused the pupil to suffer a "detriment".

662. Other important words and phrases appear in only one Part or Chapter of the Act. Where necessary these are defined in the Part or Chapter where they appear. Others are not defined at all, either because they are clear, or because they are to be interpreted in accordance with the Interpretation Act 1978.

Section 213: References to maternity leave, etc.

Effect

663. This section explains what is meant by the different periods of maternity leave which are referred to in the Act.

Background

664. The rights of female employees to statutory maternity leave are provided for in the Employment Rights Act 1996. Compulsory maternity leave, ordinary maternity leave and additional maternity leave are the three types of maternity leave provided for in sections 72(1), 71(1) and 73(1) of that Act respectively.

Section 214: Index of defined expressions

Effect

665. This section gives effect to Schedule 28, which provides an index of the expressions that are defined in the Act.

Section 215: Money

Effect

666. This section is included to comply with rules of procedure on financial matters. It does not, of itself, authorise expenditure that is not covered elsewhere in the Act.

Section 216: Commencement

Effect

667. This section sets out when provisions of the Act come into effect. Certain provisions came into force automatically on the day on which the Act received Royal Assent, for example the sections relating to commencement, short title, subordinate legislation and interpretation. The rest of the Act will be brought into force by commencement orders made by a Minister of the Crown with the exception of the sections related to family property (Part 15) which will be brought into force by a commencement order made by the Lord Chancellor. The orders will set out the date on which specific provisions start to have legal effect.

Section 217: Extent

Effect

668. This section explains that all of the provisions of the Act are part of the law of England and Wales.

669. All of the provisions of the Act, except for section 190 (improvements to let dwelling houses) and Part 15 (family property), are also part of the law of Scotland.

670. In relation to Northern Ireland, the Act is not part of Northern Ireland's law, except for the following:

- Section 82 (offshore work);
- Section 105(3) and (4) (expiry of Sex Discrimination (Election Candidates), Act 2002);
- Section 199 (abolition of presumption of advancement).

Section 218: Short title

Effect

671. This section sets out the short title of the Act.

Schedule 1: Disability: supplementary provision

Effect

672. Part 1 of this Schedule clarifies the definition of disability in section 6 and provides a number of regulation-making powers to enable the definition to be amended at a later date if required.

673. Part 2 describes what can be included in guidance about the definition of disability and prescribes adjudicating bodies which are obliged to take account of guidance, the role of Ministers in developing and publishing guidance and the associated parliamentary procedures.

Background

674. This Schedule replaces similar provisions in the Disability Discrimination Act 1995. However, the Act introduces one change by removing a requirement to consider a list of eight capacities, such as mobility or speech, hearing or eyesight, when considering whether or not a person is disabled. This change will make it easier for some people to demonstrate that they meet the definition of a disabled person. It will assist those who currently find it difficult to show that their impairment adversely affects their ability to carry out a normal day-to-day activity which involves one of these capacities.

Example

675. A man with depression finds even the simplest of tasks or decisions difficult, for example getting up in the morning and getting washed and dressed. He is also forgetful and can't plan ahead. Together, these amount to a "substantial adverse effect" on his ability to carry out normal day-to-day activities. The man has experienced a number of separate periods of this depression over a period of two years, which have been diagnosed as part of an underlying mental health condition. The impairment is therefore considered to be "long-term" and he is a disabled person for the purposes of the Act.

Schedule 2: Services and public functions: reasonable adjustments

Effect

676. This Schedule explains how the duty to make reasonable adjustments in section 20 applies to a service provider or person exercising a public function where a disabled person is placed at a substantial disadvantage. It includes definitions of "substantial disadvantage" and "physical features" and stipulates that the duty does not require fundamental changes to the nature of the service. As the duty is owed to disabled persons generally, it is an anticipatory duty which means service providers and people exercising public functions must anticipate the needs of disabled people and make appropriate reasonable adjustments.

677. This Schedule also explains how the duty to make reasonable adjustments in section 20 applies to operators of transport vehicles. It specifies that the duty applies in different ways to different types of vehicle. It provides that a transport service provider is not required to make adjustments to the physical features of vehicles or to whether vehicles are provided, except in specified circumstances. It provides a power to make regulations to allow further amendments to be made to this paragraph in the future.

Background

678. This Schedule replaces similar provisions in the Disability Discrimination Act 1995.

Examples

- The manager of a large shop in a national chain installs a ramp, automatic entry doors, hearing induction loops and waives the "no dogs policy" in respect of assistance dogs, to comply with the duty to make reasonable adjustments.
- A police officer is carrying out a public function when interviewing a witness who is deaf. Arranging a British Sign Language / English interpreter for the interview might be a reasonable adjustment to make.
- It might be a reasonable adjustment for a rail service provider to arrange an alternative catering service for disabled people who cannot get to the buffet or dining car, or to provide assistance from staff where passengers have a sensory or physical impairment.

Schedule 3: Services and public functions: exceptions

679. This Schedule sets out exceptions from the prohibitions on discriminating against, harassing or victimising a person when providing services or exercising a public function set out in section 29 of the Act.

Part 1: Constitutional matters: paragraphs 1-5

Effect

680. Part 1 of this Schedule provides that the prohibitions do not apply to:

- the exercise of parliamentary functions and functions linked to the undertaking of parliamentary business;
- preparing, making, approving or considering primary legislation or particular forms of secondary legislation, including legislation of the Scottish Parliament and the National Assembly for Wales;
- exercising judicial functions or deciding not to commence or continue criminal proceedings.

681. Part 1 also provides that the prohibition on discriminating against a person when exercising a public function does not apply to the armed forces in respect of the protected characteristics of age, disability, gender reassignment and sex when the reason for such acts is to ensure combat effectiveness.

682. It also provides that the prohibitions on discriminating against, harassing or victimising a person when providing a service or exercising a public function do not apply to the Security Service, the Security Intelligence Service, the Government Communications Headquarters (GCHQ) or any part of the armed forces assisting GCHQ.

Background

683. Part 1 of this Schedule is designed to replicate the effect of exceptions contained in previous legislation where discrimination, harassment and victimisation in the exercise of a public function are already prohibited, and apply the exception to relevant protected characteristics.

Examples

- Activity related to the preparation and making of primary legislation, such as this Act, would be excepted from the prohibition on discrimination. However, activity related to the making of a bye-law by a local authority would not be within the exceptions in this Schedule.

- A decision of a judge on the merits of a case would be within the exceptions in this Schedule. An administrative decision of court staff, about which contractor to use to carry out maintenance jobs or which supplier to use when ordering stationery would not be.

Part 2: Education

Education: paragraph 6

Effect

684. Paragraph 6 provides that the prohibitions on discrimination in Part 3 do not, so far as they relate to age, or religion or belief, apply to a local authority performing its function under sections 13 and 14 of the Education Act 1996, which relate to providing primary and secondary schools for children in a given catchment area.

Background

685. Similar exceptions for religion or belief were in the Equality Act 2006. The age exceptions are new because of the extension of age discrimination law in this Act.

686. The reason for the provision in paragraph 6 is to prevent a local authority being bound to provide schools for pupils of different faiths, or no faith, or for particular age groups, in every catchment area.

Examples

- Catholic parents will not be able to claim that their local authority is discriminating unlawfully if there is no Catholic school in their catchment area, or if there are fewer places in Catholic schools than in Church of England schools.
- Parents of secondary age children will not be able to claim that it is age discrimination if their children have to travel further than younger ones to reach their school.

Education: paragraph 7

Effect

687. Paragraph 7 makes similar provision for Scotland as is made by paragraph 6 for England and Wales.

Education: paragraph 8

Effect

688. This paragraph provides an exception from the prohibition on sex discrimination in Part 3 in relation only to the establishment of a school. A local authority will not be prevented from establishing single-sex schools, but must provide similar numbers of places for boys and girls.

Background

689. This provision is designed to replicate the effect of provisions in the Sex Discrimination Act 1975.

Education: paragraph 9

Effect

690. Paragraph 9 excepts from the prohibition on age discrimination in Part 3 (to the extent that it is not excepted elsewhere), the exercise by any public authority of functions in a number of areas that relate to schools.

Background

691. These exceptions ensure that policies and practices which relate to things which schools are allowed to do under the Act do not become unlawful when carried out by public authorities.

Examples

- School admissions policies can continue to be based on the ages of prospective pupils.
- School transport can be provided for children of a particular age only.

Education: paragraph 10

Effect

692. Paragraph 10 provides an exception for local authorities from the provisions requiring reasonable adjustments in Part 3, in respect of their activities in relation to school education, from the requirement to alter physical features of premises when making reasonable adjustments for disabled people.

Background

693. These exceptions are designed to replicate the effect of provisions in the Disability Discrimination Act 1995 and ensure that local authorities, when carrying out their education functions, do not have to take account of altering physical features since such things will fall within the requirements on them to produce accessibility strategies as set out in Schedule 12. This mirrors the requirements placed on schools themselves.

Education: paragraph 11

Effect

694. Paragraph 11 provides an exception from the prohibition on religious or belief-related discrimination in Part 3 (to the extent that it is not excepted elsewhere), in relation to the exercise by any public body of functions in a number of areas that relate to faith and non-faith educational institutions. In relation to all schools those areas are the curriculum, collective worship, school transport and the establishment, alteration and closure of schools; and in relation to schools which have a religious ethos the exception also applies to admission of pupils and the responsible body of such a school.

Background

695. This provision is designed to replicate the effect of provisions in Part 2 of the Equality Act 2006. It ensures that policies and practices which relate to things which schools are allowed to do under the Act do not become unlawful when carried out by public authorities.

Examples

- A public body will not be open to claims of religious discrimination as a result of its decision to establish, alter or close a faith school.
- A local authority can select a person of a particular religion or belief to be a governor of a school with a religious ethos.

Part 3: Health and care

Blood services: paragraph 13

Effect

696. Paragraph 13 provides that it is not unlawful for a person operating a blood service to refuse to accept someone's donation of blood provided they have reliable evidence that accepting it would put the public or the individual donor at risk and that such a refusal would not be unreasonable.

697. A blood service is a service that collects donations of human blood and blood components to use for medical purposes, for example the NHS Blood and Transplant Special Health Authority.

698. "Blood" includes components, for instance plasma or red blood cells.

Background

699. This provision is designed to replicate the effect of Regulation 28 of the Equality Act (Sexual Orientation) Regulations 2007, and extend the exception to the other protected characteristics. It also provides that a refusal to allow somebody to donate blood or blood components because of a risk to the donor's own health would not be unlawful.

Examples

- If there is evidence that people who have been sexually active in a particular country are more likely to be infected with HIV, the operator of the blood service can refuse to accept donations of blood or blood components from people who have been sexually active there, even if that disproportionately affects members of a particular nationality and so might otherwise be unlawful indirect discrimination because of race.
- If there is evidence that women who have recently given birth are likely to suffer detrimental effects from giving blood or blood components, then a blood service can refuse to accept donations from them. This would not be unlawful direct discrimination because of maternity.

Health and safety: paragraph 14

Effect

700. Paragraph 14 provides that it is not unlawful for a person to discriminate against a pregnant woman by refusing to provide her with a service or only providing the service to her on certain conditions if he or she reasonably believes that to do otherwise would create a risk to her health or safety and he or she would take similar measures in respect of persons with other physical conditions.

Background

701. Provisions making it unlawful for a person to discriminate against a pregnant woman in the provision of services were introduced into the Sex Discrimination Act 1975 by the Sex Discrimination Act 1975 (Amendment) Regulations 2008. Those provisions contained an equivalent exception on health and safety grounds.

Examples

- A leisure centre could refuse to allow a pregnant woman to use certain gym equipment (for example, a rowing machine) after a certain point in her pregnancy if it reasonably believed that allowing her to use the equipment would create a risk to her health and safety and it would also refuse, for example, to allow a man with a serious heart condition to use the equipment.
- An airline could refuse to allow a pregnant woman to travel beyond her 35th week of pregnancy if it reasonably believed that allowing her to travel would create a risk to her health and safety and it would also refuse people with other physical conditions that affect their health and safety to travel.

Care within the family: paragraph 15

Effect

702. Paragraph 15 is designed to ensure that people who provide foster care, or other similar forms of care, in their own home are not subject to the prohibitions on discriminating against, harassing or victimising a person in the provision of services while providing that care.

703. It applies irrespective of whether or not the person is paid for providing the care service.

Background

704. Similar provisions existed in previous legislation for race, religion or belief and sexual orientation. This provision extends the exception to all of the protected characteristics.

Examples

- A Muslim family could choose to foster only a Muslim child. This would not constitute discrimination against a non-Muslim child.
- A woman who is the main carer for her mother decides to provide care for another person too, and decides to restrict any offer of care to another woman. This would not constitute discrimination against a man who needed similar care.

Part 4: Immigration

Disability: paragraph 16

Effect

705. Paragraph 16 provides an exception from the prohibition on discriminating against a person when providing a service or exercising a public function because he or she has a disability, in relation to certain immigration decisions, including making a decision not to allow someone to enter the country or a decision not to allow him or her to remain in the country. However, this exception only applies where the decision is necessary for the public good.

Background

706. This is a new exception. An express exception was not previously needed since the Disability Discrimination Act 1995 did not prohibit direct disability discrimination in the provision of services or exercise of a public function and because disability-related discrimination, which did apply to the provision of services or exercise of a public function, could be justified if it was necessary for a number of reasons, including not to endanger the health or safety of any person.

Nationality and ethnic or national origins: paragraph 17

Effect

707. Paragraph 17 provides an exception from the prohibition on discriminating against a person in the provision of services or the exercise of a public function because of his or her ethnic or national origins or nationality, in relation to the exercise of immigration functions.

Background

708. This is designed to replicate the effect of a provision in the Race Relations Act 1976.

Examples

- Different visa requirements for nationals of different countries, which arise for a variety of historical and political reasons, do not constitute unlawful race discrimination.
- Granting asylum to members of a minority ethnic group being targeted by the majority ethnic group in a country would similarly not be unlawful discrimination.

Religion or belief: paragraph 18

Effect

709. Paragraph 18 provides an exception from the prohibition on discriminating against a person in the provision of services or the exercise of a public function because of their religion or belief in relation to decisions not to allow someone to enter the country or to remove someone from the country, if that decision is made on the grounds that it

is conducive to the public good to exclude that person from the country or it is not desirable to permit the person to remain in United Kingdom.

710. It also provides an exception for decisions relating to an application for entry clearance or leave to enter to cover people entering the country to provide services in connection with religion or belief, such as a Minister or clergyman.

Background

711. This is designed to replicate the effect of provisions in the Equality Act 2006.

Examples

- The immigration services may differentiate between certain religious groups in order to allow a person such as a minister of religion to enter the UK to provide essential pastoral services, without being challenged by groups which could operate against the public interest, but which might also claim to represent a religion.
- A decision to prevent a person who holds extreme religious views from entering or remaining in the country if his or her presence is not conducive to the public good, for example, preachers who use the pulpit to incite violence, would not constitute unlawful discrimination because of religion or belief.

Part 5: Insurance, etc.

Services arranged by employer: paragraph 20

Effect

- Paragraph 20 provides an exception to section 29 (provision of services, etc) for group insurance schemes and group personal pensions ("group schemes"). As group schemes are offered to employees as part of the employment relationship:
- the employer is responsible for ensuring that the provision of benefits under group schemes complies with the requirements of Part 5 (work); and
- the insurer or pension provider is not responsible for ensuring that the provision of benefits complies with the requirements of Part 3 (services and public functions).

Background

712. Group policies and schemes are arrangements between an employer and an insurer for the benefit of the employees, their partners and their dependants. They are entered into not on the basis of the individual characteristics of each employee but on the basis of the employer's business and the profile of the employees. Employees can sign up to the benefits under such policies on standard terms that are the same for all employees. This is a new provision but one that reflects current practice.

Example

713. An employer enters into a contract with an insurer for the provision of health insurance to employees. As the health insurance is part of the package of benefits provided by the employer to the employee, the employer must ensure that the provision complies with Part 5. So, if benefits under the health insurance policy differ between men and women, the employer may have to justify the difference by reference to paragraph 20 of Schedule 9 (insurance contracts, etc.).

Disability: paragraph 21

Effect

714. Paragraph 21 provides an exception from the prohibition on discriminating against disabled people in the provision of services connected with insurance business (as defined) where the decision in question is based on relevant and reliable information. It

enables insurance providers to offer different premiums and benefits to disabled people where it is reasonable to do so.

Background

715. These provisions are designed to replicate the effect of provisions in the Disability Discrimination (Service Providers and Public Authorities Carrying Out Functions) Regulations 2005. This exception has been carried forward into the Act because it is recognised that insurers may need to distinguish between people on the basis of the risks against which they are insuring. The consensus is that it works well.

Examples

- A disabled person with cancer applies for a life insurance policy. The insurance company refuses to provide life insurance cover based on a medical report from the person's doctor which provides a prognosis on the person's condition.
- An insurer charges higher premiums for travel insurance for a person with a particular disability because actuarial evidence suggests that people with this disability are at increased risk of having a heart attack.

Sex, gender reassignment, pregnancy and maternity: paragraph 22

716. Paragraph 22 provides exceptions to allow insurers to calculate different premiums and benefits for men and women, relating to pregnancy and maternity or gender reassignment on the basis of actuarial data.

717. Sub-paragraph (1) provides an exception for an annuity, life assurance policy, accident insurance policy or similar matter which involves the assessment of risk. Under this exception, the difference in treatment must be done by reference to actuarial or other reliable data, and must be reasonable in all the circumstances. Sub-paragraph (2) applies to a contract of insurance, or for related financial services, entered into before 6 April 2008. In such a case, the exception only applies in relation to differences in premiums and benefits applicable to a person under that contract.

718. Sub-paragraph (3) applies sub-paragraph (1) to contracts of insurance, or for related financial services, entered into on or after 6 April 2008. It permits differences in treatment which are proportionate having regard to relevant and accurate data, which the insurance industry has compiled, published and updated in accordance with Treasury guidance. For contracts entered into on or after 22 December 2008, the differences must not result from costs related to a woman's pregnancy or her having given birth within the previous 26 weeks.

719. Insurers must calculate premiums and benefits based on the sex of the person seeking such services (sub-paragraph (5)).

Background

720. This paragraph is designed to replicate the effect of section 45 of the Sex Discrimination Act 1975 in respect of insurance and financial services. Services relating to premises or education are dealt with under Parts 4 and 6 of the Act.

Example

- An insurer can lawfully quote higher motor insurance premiums for young men if this is based on actuarial and statistical up-to-date data that is published so that customers can see the information that justifies proportionate differences in male and female premiums and benefits.

Existing insurance policies: paragraph 23

Effect

721. Paragraph 23 provides an exception so that insurers will not be discriminating unlawfully if they continue to apply terms of insurance policies entered into before the date on which this paragraph comes into force. Where pre-existing policies are renewed,

or have their terms reviewed, on or after the date this paragraph comes into force, the exception no longer applies to them.

Background

722. This paragraph provides an exception for existing insurance policies, which may not comply with subsequently altered discrimination law. But where such a policy is renewed or reviewed, it would need to be amended to meet the requirements of this Act.

Examples

- An existing life insurance policy which was taken out in 1989, and has not been subsequently renewed or reviewed, continues to be lawful and does not have to be altered to comply with current relevant discrimination law.
- A company has a death in service benefit insurance policy for its employees which has been in place for many years and whose terms have not been reviewed. It benefits from the exception unless and until the policy is reviewed or renewed.

Part 6: Marriage

Gender reassignment: England and Wales: paragraph 24

Effect

723. Paragraph 24 contains exceptions from the general prohibition of gender reassignment discrimination in section 29 of the Act for the religious solemnisation of marriages.

724. A person with a full Gender Recognition Certificate acquired under the Gender Recognition Act 2004 is able to marry someone of the opposite gender to his or her acquired gender. The Marriage Act 1949 imposes an obligation on a clergyman in the Church of England or a clerk in Holy Orders of the Church in Wales to marry anyone residing in his or her parish, or who fits other stated connection criteria. However, section 5B of that Act contains an exception where the clergyman or clerk reasonably believes one of the parties' gender is acquired under the Gender Recognition Act. The legislation that preceded this Act did not prohibit discrimination because of gender reassignment in the field of public functions. As this Act now prohibits this, paragraph 24 provides an exception for Anglican clergy in England and Wales, as well as those of other faiths in England and Wales whose consent is required to conduct marriages in religious premises registered under the Marriage Act, and others who may solemnise marriages.

Background

725. This paragraph is new. There was previously no prohibition on discriminating against people because of gender reassignment in the exercise of public functions, hence there was no exception in relation to solemnising marriages.

Example

- A clergyman in the Church of England advises an engaged couple that he will not solemnise their marriage as he reasonably believes that one of the couple has acquired his or her gender under the Gender Recognition Act 2004. This would not be unlawful discrimination because of gender reassignment.

Gender reassignment: Scotland: paragraph 25

Effect

726. Paragraph 25, which applies to Scotland, contains a similar exception to paragraph 24.

727. An "approved celebrant" is not obliged to marry a person if he or she reasonably believes the person to have acquired his or her gender under the Gender Recognition

Act 2004. An "approved celebrant" is a person defined in the Marriage (Scotland) Act 1977 as a person entitled under that Act to solemnise religious marriages.

Background

728. This paragraph is new. There is currently no prohibition on discriminating against people because of gender reassignment in the exercise of public functions, hence there is no exception in relation to solemnising marriages.

Example

- A Roman Catholic priest, who is recognised as an "approved celebrant" in Scotland, advises an engaged couple that he will not solemnise their marriage as he reasonably believes that one of the couple has acquired his or her legal gender under the Gender Recognition Act 2004. This would not be unlawful discrimination because of gender reassignment.

Part 7: Separate and single services

Separate services for the sexes: paragraph 26

Effect

729. This paragraph contains exceptions to the general prohibition of sex discrimination which allow the provision of separate services for men and women.

730. A provider can deliver separate services for men and women where providing a combined service would not be as effective. A provider can deliver separate services for men and women in different ways or to a different extent where providing a combined service would not be as effective and it would not be reasonably practicable to provide the service otherwise than as a separate service provided differently for each sex. In each case such provision has to be justified.

731. The exceptions also cover the exercise of public functions in respect of the "back-room" managerial, administrative and finance decisions which allow separate services to be provided.

Background

732. This paragraph replaces similar provisions in the Sex Discrimination Act 1975 that only cover public functions. The exceptions have been extended to cover all services, whether privately or publicly provided.

Example

- It would not be unlawful for a charity to set up separate hostels, one for homeless men and one for homeless women, where the hostels provide the same level of service to men and women because the level of need is the same but a unisex hostel would not be as effective.

Single-sex services: paragraph 27

Effect

733. This paragraph contains exceptions to the general prohibition of sex discrimination to allow the provision of single-sex services.

734. Single sex services are permitted where:

    - only people of that sex require it;
    - there is joint provision for both sexes but that is not sufficient on its own;
    - if the service were provided for men and women jointly, it would not be as effective and it is not reasonably practicable to provide separate services for each sex;

- they are provided in a hospital or other place where users need special attention (or in parts of such an establishment);
- they may be used by more than one person and a woman might object to the presence of a man (or vice versa); or
- they may involve physical contact between a user and someone else and that other person may reasonably object if the user is of the opposite sex.

735. In each case, the separate provision has to be objectively justified.

736. These exceptions also cover public functions in respect of the "back-room" managerial, administrative and finance decisions which allow such single-sex services to be provided.

Background

737. This paragraph replaces some similar provisions that only covered public functions and some that applied to services in the Sex Discrimination Act 1975. These exceptions have been extended to cover both services and public functions.

Examples

738. These exceptions would allow:

- a cervical cancer screening service to be provided to women only, as only women need the service;
- a fathers' support group to be set up by a private nursery as there is insufficient attendance by men at the parents' group;
- a domestic violence support unit to be set up by a local authority for women only but there is no men-only unit because of insufficient demand;
- separate male and female wards to be provided in a hospital;
- separate male and female changing rooms to be provided in a department store;
- a massage service to be provided to women only by a female massage therapist with her own business operating in her clients' homes because she would feel uncomfortable massaging men in that environment.

Gender reassignment: paragraph 28

Effect

739. This paragraph contains an exception to the general prohibition of gender reassignment discrimination in relation to the provision of separate- and single-sex services. Such treatment by a provider has to be objectively justified.

Background

740. This paragraph replaces a similar provision in the Sex Discrimination Act 1975.

Example

- A group counselling session is provided for female victims of sexual assault. The organisers do not allow transsexual people to attend as they judge that the clients who attend the group session are unlikely to do so if a male-to-female transsexual person was also there. This would be lawful.

Services relating to religion: paragraph 29

Effect

741. This paragraph contains an exception to the general prohibition of sex discrimination to allow ministers of religion to provide separate and single-sex services.

742. The minister can provide such services so long as this is done for religious purposes, at a place occupied or used for those purposes and it is either necessary to comply with the tenets of the religion or for the purpose of avoiding conflict with the strongly held religious views of a significant number of the religion's followers. This does not apply to acts of worship (which are not themselves "services" within the meaning of the Act so no exception is required).

Background

743. This paragraph replaces a similar provision in the Sex Discrimination Act 1975. The requirement regarding avoiding conflict with the religion's followers has been altered in order to give consistency within the Act and some explanatory provisions have been added for the same reason.

Example

- A synagogue can have separate seating for men and women at a reception following a religious service.

Services generally provided only for persons who share a protected characteristic: paragraph 30

Effect

744. Paragraph 30 provides that a service provider does not breach the requirement in section 29 not to discriminate in the provision of a service if he or she supplies the service in such a way that it is commonly only used by people with a particular protected characteristic (for example, women or people of Afro-Caribbean descent) and he or she continues to provide that service in that way. If it is impracticable to provide the service to someone who does not share that particular characteristic, a service provider can refuse to provide the service to that person.

Background

745. This is designed to replicate the effect of provisions previously contained in the Sex Discrimination Act 1975 and the Equality Act 2006, and extends the clarification they provide across all other protected characteristics for the first time.

Examples

- A hairdresser who provides Afro-Caribbean hairdressing services would not be required to provide European hairdressing services as well. However, if a white English person wanted his hair braided and there was no technical difficulty to prevent that, it would be unlawful for the hairdresser to refuse to provide her services to him.
- A butcher who sells halal meat is not required also to sell non-halal meat or kosher meat. However, if a non-Muslim customer wanted to purchase the meat that was on offer, he could not refuse to sell it to her.

Part 8: Television, radio and on-line broadcasting and distribution

Paragraph 31

Effect

746. Paragraph 31 makes it clear that claims for discrimination, harassment and victimisation cannot be brought in relation to broadcasting and distribution of content, as defined in the Communications Act 2003. This would include, for example, editorial decisions on the content of a television programme or the distribution of on-line content.

747. This paragraph does not, however, extend to the provision of an electronic communications network, service or associated facility, which are also defined in the Communications Act 2003. This will ensure that the act of sending signals is not excluded by the exception in sub-paragraph (1), only the content of what is broadcast.

Background

748. This provision is new and is intended to safeguard the editorial independence of broadcasters when broadcasting or distributing content, whether on television, radio or on-line.

Examples

- An aggrieved person is not entitled to bring a claim for discrimination against a broadcaster in relation to an editorial decision about what programmes to commission; on what day a specific programme should be shown; or who should appear in a particular programme.
- An aggrieved person is, however, entitled to bring a claim for discrimination against a broadcaster in relation to a decision to refuse to send a signal to his house purely on the basis that he has a particular protected characteristic.

Part 9: Transport

Application to disability: paragraph 32

Effect

749. Paragraph 32 applies the exceptions listed in paragraphs 33 and 34 in relation to disability, thereby stipulating the extent to which providers of transport services are bound by the disability provisions of the Act.

Background

750. These provisions replicate the effect of provisions contained in the Disability Discrimination Act 1995.

Transport by air: paragraph 33

Effect

751. Paragraph 33(1) provides an exception to the prohibition of discrimination, so far as it relates to disability, in respect of the provision of services in connection with air transport.

752. Paragraph 33(2) ensures that there is no duplication where there would otherwise be an overlap between the disability provisions of the Act and Regulation (EC) No1107/2006 of the European Parliament and of the Council of 5 July 2006 concerning the rights of disabled persons and persons with reduced mobility when travelling by air ("EC Regulation 1107/2006").

Background

753. These provisions replicate the effect of provisions in the Disability Discrimination Act 1995.

Examples

- An airline is required to make reasonable adjustments to its booking services to ensure that they are accessible to disabled people. It is not required to make any structural adjustments to the cabin environment inside an aircraft by reason of the derogation in Article 4(1)(a) of EC Regulation 1107/2006.
- An airport owner charges a disabled person for wheelchair assistance to board an aircraft. This would be a breach of EC Regulation 1107/2006, so section 29 of the Act would not apply. However, if the same airport owner fails to make adjustments to allow disabled people to access car parks at the airport, this would fall within the scope of the Act.

Transport by land: paragraph 34

Effect

754. Paragraph 34 provides an exception from section 29 for all services of transporting people by land, except those listed. The definitions of the vehicles listed are contained in paragraph 4 of Schedule 2.

Background

755. This paragraph replicates the effect of provisions in the Disability Discrimination Act 1995.

Example

- A train operating company is required to provide a reasonable alternative when a disabled person is unable to access the buffet car due to his or her disability.

Part 10: Supplementary

Power to amend: paragraph 35

Effect

756. Paragraph 35 contains a power for a Minister of the Crown to add, vary, or remove exceptions in this Schedule relating to both services and public functions in respect of disability, religion or belief and sexual orientation. It allows a Minister of the Crown also to add, vary or remove the exceptions that relate to the provision of public functions only, in relation to gender reassignment, pregnancy and maternity, race, religion or belief, sex and sexual orientation.

757. This power cannot, however, be used to omit or reduce the scope of the exceptions in respect of the functions of Parliament; the preparation, making, consideration or approval of legislation; and the functions of the courts which are set out in paragraphs 1 to 3 of this Schedule.

758. In relation to transport by air, a Minister of the Crown can also vary, remove or add exceptions in relation to the provision of services and the exercise of public functions for disability only. For these purposes, it does not matter where the transport in fact takes place.

759. The Minister must consult the Equality and Human Rights Commission before exercising the power under this paragraph.

Background

760. This paragraph broadly reflects the substance of powers contained in previous legislation.

Schedule 4: Premises: reasonable adjustments

Effect

761. This Schedule explains how the duty to make reasonable adjustments in section 20 applies to a controller of "let" premises or of premises "to let" and to the commonhold association where a disabled tenant (or prospective tenant) or unit-holder in commonhold land or the disabled person legally occupying the property is placed at a substantial disadvantage, so that the disabled person can enjoy the premises or make use of them. It stipulates that the duty does not require the removal or alteration of a physical feature, and makes clear what are not "physical features" for these purposes. The duty only applies if a request for an adjustment is made by or on behalf of a disabled person.

762. This Schedule also explains how the duty to make reasonable adjustments in section 20 applies in relation to "common parts", for example an entrance hall in a block of flats. These provisions relate specifically to physical features and set out the process that must be followed by the person responsible for the common parts (for example in England and Wales either a landlord or, in the case of commonhold land, the

commonhold association) if a disabled tenant or someone on his or her behalf requests an adjustment. This includes a consultation process with others affected which must be carried out within a reasonable period of the request being made. If the responsible person decides to make an adjustment to avoid the disadvantage to the disabled person, a written agreement must be entered into between them setting out their rights and responsibilities. Section 37 provides the corresponding process for common parts in Scotland.

763. The Schedule also makes it unlawful for a controller or responsible person to victimise a disabled tenant because costs have been incurred in making a reasonable adjustment.

Background

764. This Schedule partly replaces similar provisions in the Disability Discrimination Act 1995. However, the Act introduces a new requirement for disability-related alterations to the physical features of the common parts of let residential premises or premises owned on a commonhold basis.

Examples

- A landlord has a normal practice of notifying all tenants of any rent arrears in writing with a follow-up visit if the arrears are not reduced. A learning- disabled person explains to the landlord that he cannot read standard English so would not be aware that he was in arrears. He asks to be notified of any arrears in person or by telephone. The landlord arranges to visit or telephone the learning-disabled person to explain when he has any arrears of rent. This personal contact may be a reasonable adjustment for the landlord to make.
- A landlord is asked by a disabled tenant to install a ramp to give her easier access to the communal entrance door. The landlord must consult all people he thinks would be affected by the ramp and, if he believes that it is reasonable to provide it, he must enter into a written agreement with the disabled person setting out matters such as responsibility for payment for the ramp. The landlord can insist the tenant pays for the cost of making the alteration.

*Schedule 5: **Premises: exceptions***

Effect

765. This Schedule sets out limited exceptions to the prohibitions on discrimination and harassment contained in the premises provisions in Part 4 of the Act.

766. The first exception applies where a person who owns and lives in a property disposes of all or part of it privately (for example by selling, letting or subletting) without using the services of an estate agent, or publishing an advertisement.

767. This exception does not apply to race discrimination in disposing of premises. It only applies to discrimination in relation to permission to dispose of premises where it is based on religion or belief or sexual orientation.

768. This exception also exempts a controller of leasehold premises (as defined in section 36) from the duty to make reasonable adjustments provided that:

- where the premises have been let, the premises are (or have been) the controller's main or only home and he or she has not used the services of a manager since letting the premises (paragraph 2(1));
- where the premises are to let, they are the controller's main or only home and he or she has not used the service of an estate agent for letting purposes (paragraph 2(3)).

769. The second exception applies to disposal, management or occupation of part of small premises. It applies where a person engaging in the conduct in question, or a relative

of that person, lives in another part of the premises and the premises include facilities shared with other people who are not part of their household.

770. This exception does not apply to race discrimination when disposing of or giving permission for the disposal of premises, or in the management of premises.

771. The small premises exception also exempts a controller of premises or a person responsible in relation to common parts (as defined in section 36) from the duty to make reasonable adjustments where the premises are small, where that person or a relative of that person lives in one part of the premises and residents who are not members of that person's household live in another part of the premises. The definitions of "small premises" and "relative" in paragraph 3 apply.

772. Paragraph 5 contains a power for a Minister of the Crown to amend or repeal the small premises exception.

Background

773. This Schedule replaces similar provisions in previous legislation.

Examples

- A homeowner makes it known that she is preparing to sell her flat privately. A work colleague expresses an interest in buying it but she refuses to sell it to him because he is black. That refusal would not be covered by this exception and so would be unlawful.
- A homeowner makes it known socially that he wants to sell his house privately. Various prospective buyers come forward and the homeowner opts to sell it to a fellow Christian. The other prospective buyers cannot claim that they were discriminated against because the homeowner's actions were covered by this exception.
- A single woman owns a large house in London and lives on the top floor, although the bathroom and toilet facilities are on the first floor. The ground floor is unoccupied and she decides to take in a lodger, sharing the bathroom and toilet facilities. Various prospective tenants apply but she chooses only to let the ground floor to another woman. This would be permissible under this exception.
- A Jewish family own a large house but only live in part of it. They decide to let out an unoccupied floor but any new tenant will have to share kitchen and cooking facilities. The family choose only to let the unoccupied floor to practising Jews as they are concerned that otherwise their facilities for keeping their food kosher may be compromised. This would be permissible under this exception.

Schedule 6: Office-holders: excluded offices

Effect

774. This Schedule provides that an office or post is not treated as a personal or public office in the Act in circumstances where the office-holder is protected by one of the other forms of protection given in Part 5 of the Act – employment, contract work, employment services (as they relate to work experience), partnerships, limited liability partnerships, barristers and advocates. It also provides that political offices, life peerages, and any other dignity or honour conferred by the Crown are not personal or public offices for the purposes of the Act.

Background

775. The Schedule replaces similar provisions in previous legislation. The conferral of honours and dignities is treated as a public function for the purposes of the Act, and the specific provisions formerly found in the Race Relations Act 1976 alone are not

replicated. Public bodies' activities in relation to honours and dignities will also be subject to the public sector equality duty.

Example

- A person appointed as a commissioner of a public body may be both an employee and an office-holder. Such a person will be protected under the employment provisions in section 39 as against his employer, and under the office-holder provisions in sections 49 or 50 and 51 as against the person who appointed him and/or any relevant person.

Schedule 7: Equality of terms: exceptions

Part 1: Terms of work

Compliance with laws regulating employment of women, etc.

776. Part 1 of this Schedule sets out exceptions to the operation of a sex equality clause or a maternity equality clause. It provides that such clauses will not have effect on any terms of employment, appointment or service that are governed by laws regulating employment of women. A few of these remain, mainly for health and safety purposes. A sex equality clause will also have no effect on terms giving special treatment to women in connection with pregnancy or childbirth.

Background

777. This Schedule replaces similar provisions in the Equal Pay Act 1970.

Part 2: Occupational pension schemes

Effect

778. Part 2 of this Schedule sets out certain circumstances where a sex equality rule does not have effect in relation to occupational pension schemes.

779. It allows payments of different amounts for comparable men and women, in prescribed circumstances, if the difference is only because of differences in retirement benefits to which men and women are entitled. It permits payment of different amounts where those differences result from the application of prescribed actuarial factors to the calculation of the employer's contributions to an occupational pension scheme. It also permits payment of different amounts where actuarial factors are applied to the determination of certain prescribed benefits.

780. It also contains a regulation-making power to vary or add to these circumstances. The regulations may make provision for past periods, but not for pensionable service before 17 May 1990.

Background

781. This replaces similar provisions in section 64 of the Pensions Act 1995.

Schedule 8: Work: reasonable adjustments

Effect

782. This Schedule explains how the duty to make reasonable adjustments in section 20 applies to an employer or other persons under Part 5 of the Act. It sets out the three requirements of the duty which apply where an "interested" disabled employee or job applicant is placed at a substantial disadvantage compared with non-disabled employees or applicants. As the duty is owed to an "interested" disabled employee or job applicant, it is not an anticipatory duty which means that an employer is not required to anticipate

the needs of potential disabled employees or job applicants and make reasonable adjustments in advance of their having an actual disabled employee or job applicant.

783. The tables set out who is an interested disabled person in relation to different categories of "relevant matters" and the circumstances in which the duty applies in each case. These tables capture how the duty applies in a number of areas related to work, for example to qualifications bodies and to trade organisations and there is a regulation-making power to enable further detail to be set out about how the duty applies to local authorities in respect of disabled members.

784. The Schedule also sets out the circumstances in which lack of knowledge of the person's disability or that a disabled person may be an applicant for a job means that the duty does not apply.

Background

785. This Schedule replaces similar provisions in the Disability Discrimination Act 1995. The Schedule provides greater clarity than in the previous legislation that a duty to make reasonable adjustments includes a requirement to provide an auxiliary aid if this would overcome the substantial disadvantage to the disabled person.

Examples

- An employer provides specially adapted furniture for a new employee with restricted movement in his upper limbs. This is likely to be a reasonable adjustment for the employer to make.
- A large employer is recruiting for posts which routinely attract a high number of applications. He arranges for large-print application forms to be available for any visually impaired people applying for a job. This is likely to be a reasonable adjustment for the employer to make.

Schedule 9: Work: exceptions

Part 1: Occupational requirements

786. Part 1 of this Schedule concerns requirements for particular kinds of work.

General: paragraph 1

Effect

787. This paragraph provides a general exception to what would otherwise be unlawful direct discrimination in relation to work. The exception applies where being of a particular sex, race, disability, religion or belief, sexual orientation or age – or not being a transsexual person, married or a civil partner – is a requirement for the work, and the person whom it is applied to does not meet it (or, except in the case of sex, does not meet it to the reasonable satisfaction of the person who applied it). The requirement must be crucial to the post, and not merely one of several important factors. It also must not be a sham or pretext. In addition, applying the requirement must be proportionate so as to achieve a legitimate aim.

788. The exception can be used by employers, principals (as defined in section 41) in relation to contract work, partners, members of limited liability partnerships and those with the power to appoint or remove office-holders, or to recommend an appointment to a public office.

Background

789. This paragraph replicates the effect of exceptions for occupational requirements in current discrimination legislation, and creates new exceptions in relation to disability and to replace the existing exceptions for occupational qualifications in relation to sex, gender reassignment, colour and nationality. It differs from the existing exceptions for

occupational requirements in that it makes clear that the requirement must pursue a legitimate aim and that the burden of showing that the exception applies rests on those seeking to rely on it.

Examples

- The need for authenticity or realism might require someone of a particular race, sex or age for acting roles (for example, a black man to play the part of Othello) or modelling jobs.
- Considerations of privacy or decency might require a public changing room or lavatory attendant to be of the same sex as those using the facilities.
- An organisation for deaf people might legitimately employ a deaf person who uses British Sign Language to work as a counsellor to other deaf people whose first or preferred language is BSL.
- Unemployed Muslim women might not take advantage of the services of an outreach worker to help them find employment if they were provided by a man.
- A counsellor working with victims of rape might have to be a woman and not a transsexual person, even if she has a Gender Recognition Certificate, in order to avoid causing them further distress.

Religious requirements relating to sex, marriage etc., sexual orientation: paragraph 2

Effect

790. This specific exception applies to employment for the purposes of an organised religion, which is intended to cover a very narrow range of employment: ministers of religion and a small number of lay posts, including those that exist to promote and represent religion. Where employment is for the purposes of an organised religion, this paragraph allows the employer to apply a requirement to be of a particular sex or not to be a transsexual person, or to make a requirement related to the employee's marriage or civil partnership status or sexual orientation, but only if –

   - appointing a person who meets the requirement in question is a proportionate way of complying with the doctrines of the religion; or,
   - because of the nature or context of the employment, employing a person who meets the requirement is a proportionate way of avoiding conflict with a significant number of the religion's followers' strongly held religious convictions.

791. The requirement must be crucial to the post, and not merely one of several important factors. It also must not be a sham or pretext. Applying the requirement must be a proportionate way of meeting either of the two criteria described in paragraph 790 above.

792. The requirement can also be applied by a qualifications body in relation to a relevant qualification (within the meaning of section 54), if the qualification is for employment for the purposes of an organised religion and either of the criteria described in paragraph 790 above is met.

Background

793. This exception replaces and harmonises exceptions contained in previous discrimination law.

Examples

- This exception would apply to a requirement that a Catholic priest be a man and unmarried.
- This exception is unlikely to permit a requirement that a church youth worker who primarily organises sporting activities is celibate if he is gay, but it may apply if the youth worker mainly teaches Bible classes.

- This exception would not apply to a requirement that a church accountant be celibate if he is gay.

Other requirements relating to religion or belief: paragraph 3

Effect

794. This paragraph allows an employer with an ethos based on religion or belief to discriminate in relation to work by applying a requirement to be of a particular religion or belief, but only if, having regard to that ethos:

    - being of that religion or belief is a requirement for the work (this requirement must not be a sham or pretext); and
    - applying the requirement is proportionate so as to achieve a legitimate aim.

795. It is for an employer to show that it has an ethos based on religion or belief by reference to such evidence as the organisation's founding constitution.

Background

796. This paragraph is designed to replicate the effect of provisions in current legislation.

Example

- A religious organisation may wish to restrict applicants for the post of head of its organisation to those people that adhere to that faith. This is because to represent the views of that organisation accurately it is felt that the person in charge of that organisation must have an in-depth understanding of the religion's doctrines. This type of discrimination could be lawful. However, other posts that do not require this kind of in-depth understanding, such as administrative posts, should be open to all people regardless of their religion or belief.

Armed forces: paragraph 4

Effect

797. This paragraph allows women and transsexual people to be excluded from service in the armed forces if this is a proportionate way to ensure the combat effectiveness of the armed forces.

798. It also exempts the armed forces from the work provisions of the Act relating to disability and age.

Background

799. This paragraph replicates the effects of exemptions for the armed forces in previous legislation, but narrows the scope of the former combat effectiveness exception so that this applies only to direct discrimination in relation to recruitment and access to training, promotion and transfer opportunities.

Example

- Only ground close-combat roles requiring Service personnel to deliberately close with and kill the enemy face-to-face are confined to men. Women and transsexual people are, therefore, currently excluded from the Royal Marines General Service, the Household Cavalry and Royal Armoured Corps, the Infantry and the Royal Air Force Regiment only.

Employment services: paragraph 5

Effect

800. This paragraph makes it lawful for an employment service-provider to restrict a service to people with a particular protected characteristic if the treatment relates either to work for which having that characteristic is an occupational requirement, or to training for such work.

801. The service-provider can rely on the exception by showing that he or she reasonably relied on a statement from a person who could offer the work in question that having the particular characteristic was an occupational requirement. It is, however, a criminal

offence for such a person to make a statement of that kind which they know to be false or misleading.

Background

802. This paragraph is designed to replicate the effect of provisions in previous legislation.

Example

- The provider of a Catholic theological training course required exclusively for those training to be Catholic priests may limit access to the course to Catholics because the training relates to work the offer of which can be limited to Catholics by virtue of an occupational requirement.

Interpretation: paragraph 6

Effect

803. This paragraph defines "work" for the purposes of Part 1 of the Schedule and provides that the exceptions in this Part are available in respect of direct discrimination in recruitment, access to promotion, transfer or training, or (except in the case of sex discrimination) dismissal only. None of these exceptions can be used to justify indirect discrimination or harassment.

Part 2: Exceptions relating to age

Retirement: paragraph 8

Effect

804. This paragraph allows employers to dismiss on the grounds of retirement employees at the age of 65 or over without this being regarded as age discrimination and/or unfair dismissal. However, where an employee has a normal retirement age which is applicable to him or her which exceeds the age of 65, if the employee is dismissed on the grounds of retirement before he or she has reached that normal retirement age, this is capable of amounting to age discrimination and/or unfair dismissal.

805. This exception applies only to employees within the meaning of section 230(1) of the Employment Rights Act 1996, those in Crown employment, and House of Lords and House of Commons staff. This paragraph needs to be read closely with the amendments to the unfair dismissals provisions of Part 10 of the Employment Rights Act 1996, which were amended by Schedule 8 to the Employment Equality (Age) Regulations 2006 (S.I. 2006/1031) ("the 2006 Regulations") and which amendments remain in place when this paragraph is commenced.

806. Under paragraph 8(3) retirement is a reason for dismissal only if it is a reason for dismissal by virtue of Part 10 of the Employment Rights Act 1996. Schedule 6 to the 2006 Regulations (which remains in place) sets out the procedures that need to be followed by an employer in order for the reason for the dismissal to be retirement under the sections inserted into Part 10 of the Employment Rights Act 1996 by Schedule 8 to the 2006 Regulations, and in order for the dismissal to be fair.

Background

807. Paragraph 8 preserves the exception for retirement previously provided for by regulation 30 of the 2006 Regulations, and accompanying provisions at Schedule 6 and Schedule 8 to the 2006 Regulations.

808. Before the coming into force of the 2006 Regulations, the concept of retirement was not legally defined. Where an employee was either over 65 or the employer's normal retirement age, the employee did not have the right to claim unfair dismissal. The employee could be compulsorily retired once he had reached the employer's normal

retirement age, or 65. The removal of this age cap on the right to claim unfair dismissal was removed by the 2006 Regulations.

809. Compulsory retirement ages are a form of direct age discrimination. Where the retirement age is below the age of 65 (or the employer's normal retirement age if over the age 65) it needs to be objectively justified.

810. The Government considers this exception for retirement ages of 65 and over to be within the exemption contained in article 6(1) of the Council Directive 2000/78/EC ("the Directive") as being justified by reference to a legitimate aim of social policy.

811. This provision is being reviewed during 2010. It is intended that any changes resulting from the review will be implemented during 2011.

Examples

- An employee has reached the age of 65. His employer has followed the correct procedure for the reason for dismissal to be deemed retirement. He is dismissed by reason of retirement. This is not direct age discrimination.
- An employer dismisses an employee on her 65th birthday by giving her notice, but does not follow the correct procedure. This is direct age discrimination.

Applicants at or approaching retirement age: paragraph 9

Effect

812. As a result of this paragraph it is not unlawful discrimination for an employer to decide not to offer employment to a person where, at the time of the person's application to the employer, he or she is over the employer's normal retirement age or he or she is over the age of 65 if the employer has no normal retirement age.

813. It is also not unlawful to refuse to offer employment where the applicant will reach the employer's normal retirement age or the age of 65 (if the employer has no normal retirement age) within six months of the application for employment.

814. For these purposes, the employer's normal retirement age must be 65 or over and has the same meaning as is given in section 98ZH of the Employment Rights Act 1996 (as inserted by Schedule 8 to the 2006 Regulations).

815. The employees to which paragraph 9 applies are the same group of employees to which paragraph 8 (exception for retirement) applies: that is to say, employees within the meaning of section 230(1) of the Employment Rights Act 1996, Crown employees, House of Lords staff and House of Commons staff.

Background

816. Paragraph 9 preserves the exception previously provided for at regulation 7(4) of the 2006 Regulations.

817. The rationale for this exclusion from the requirement not to discriminate flows from the rationale for paragraph 8 (exception for retirement). There is little point in requiring an employer not to discriminate at the point of receiving an application from a prospective employee when, if he or she were to employ the person, that person could be retired (without it amounting to discrimination to do so) within six months of their appointment.

818. The appointment provisions are also being reviewed during 2010. It is intended that any changes resulting from the review will be implemented in 2011.

Examples

- An applicant is 66 years old at the time of applying for a job to work in an organisation where there is no normal retirement age. It is lawful for the employer to refuse her application simply on the basis of the applicant's age.

- An applicant is 69 years and 8 months old at the time of making an application to work in an organisation that has a normal retirement age of 70. Because the applicant will reach the age of 70 within 6 months, it is lawful for the employer to refuse his application.

Benefits based on length of service: paragraph 10

Effect

819. This paragraph ensures that an employer does not have to justify paying or providing fewer benefits to a worker with less service than a comparator, should such a practice constitute indirect discrimination because of age. The employer can rely on the exception as an absolute defence where the benefit in question was awarded in relation to service of five years or less.

820. If the length of service exceeds five years, the exception applies only if it reasonably appears to an employer that the way in which he uses length of service to award benefits will fulfil a business need of his undertaking. For example, by encouraging the loyalty or motivation, or rewarding the experience, of some or all of his workers.

821. Sub-paragraph (6) contains provisions which ensure that in calculating an employee's length of service previous service is taken into account where that is the result of the operation of section 218 of the Employment Rights Act 1996 or any other enactment such as an Order made under section 155 of that Act.

822. Sub-paragraph (7) defines what a benefit is and expressly rules out benefits provided only by virtue of a person's ceasing to work.

Background

823. The intention is to replicate the effect of regulation 32 of the 2006 Regulations (as amended by the Employment Equality (Age) Regulations 2006 (Amendment) Regulations 2008).

824. This paragraph enables employers to continue to effect employment planning, in the sense of being able to attract, retain and reward experienced staff through service-related benefits. This exception cannot be used to justify the level of payments when a worker leaves as service- related termination payments are not a reward for experience from which the employer can benefit. Therefore, redundancy payment is dealt with separately.

Examples

- An employer's pay system includes an annual move up a pay spine, or a requirement that a certain amount of time must elapse before an employee is entitled to be a member of an employee benefits scheme. Provided that the pay spine or time it takes to get the benefit is no longer than five years or can be justified the exception will apply.
- An employer's terms and conditions relating to annual leave entitlement provide that employees are entitled to an additional five days' leave after ten years of service. Such an entitlement needs to be justified as reasonably fulfilling a business need.

The national minimum wage: young workers: paragraph 11

Effect

825. This paragraph allows employers to base their pay structures on the National Minimum Wage Act 1998 and the National Minimum Wage Regulations 1999 ("the 1999 Regulations"). Employers cannot rely on this exception, however, if they do not base their pay structure on the national minimum wage legislation.

826. This will allow employers to continue to use the development bands of the national minimum wage without the threat of legal challenge on the grounds of age discrimination.

Background

827. This paragraph is designed to replicate the effect of the exception in regulation 31 of the 2006 Regulations.

Examples

- It is lawful for an employer to pay 16 to 21 year olds a lower rate of minimum wage than that given to adults, when based on the development bands set out in 1999 Regulations. For example, based on the 2009/10 rates:

  — 16-17 a rate of £3.57 per hour

  — 18-21 a rate of £4.83 per hour

  whereas the national minimum wage for those 22 and over is £5.80.

- Rather than pay the amounts stated by the 1999 Regulations, this paragraph also permits an employer to base its pay scales on the development bands and so, for example, it may pay 16-17 year olds £4 per hour, 18-21 year olds £5 per hour and those over 22 £6 per hour.

The national minimum wage: apprentices: paragraph 12

Effect

828. This paragraph deals with apprentices. It enables an employer to pay an apprentice who is not entitled to the national minimum wage (any apprentice who is under 19 or in the first year of his apprenticeship) less than an apprentice who is entitled to the national minimum wage (any apprentice who is 19 or over and not in the first year of his apprenticeship). Employers cannot rely on this exception, however, if they do not base their pay structure on the national minimum wage legislation.

Background

829. This paragraph is designed to replicate the effect of the exception in regulation 31 of the 2006 Regulations.

Examples

- It is lawful for an employer to pay an apprentice who is under the age of 19 or in the first year of his apprenticeship at a lower rate than an apprentice who is 19 or over and not in the first year of his apprenticeship. For example, based on the 2009/10 rates:

  ○ an 18 year old apprentice is not entitled to the minimum wage;

  ○ a 19 year old apprentice in the first year of his apprenticeship is not entitled to the minimum wage;

  ○ a 19 year old apprentice in his 2nd year of apprenticeship is entitled to £4.83 per hour based on the National Minimum Wage Rate for 18-21 year olds.

- So it is lawful to pay an 18 year old apprentice and a 19 year old apprentice in the first year of her apprenticeship £5 per hour and to pay a 19 year old in the second year of his apprenticeship £5.50 per hour.

Redundancy: paragraph 13

Effect

830. This paragraph permits employers to provide redundancy schemes which mirror the statutory redundancy payments scheme contained in Part 11 of the Employment Rights Act 1996 but offer more generous terms.

831. The statutory redundancy scheme at Part 11 of the Employment Rights Act 1996 ("ERA 1996") requires an employer to make a payment upon redundancy, the amount of which is dependent upon the employee's age, length of service, and weekly pay (subject to a cap: see Schedule 227 to the ERA 1996). The statutory redundancy scheme is lawful under Directive 2000/78/EC as it is objectively justified under Article 6.1 of the Directive.

832. An employer who makes a redundancy payment to an employee in accordance with Part 11 ERA 1996 does not have to justify it. Both the statutory authority exemption (in Schedule 22) and this regulation make it clear that the employer is acting lawfully, even though the payment is calculated using age-related criteria.

833. But this paragraph is not aimed at such employers. The principal object of this provision is to assist those employers who base their redundancy schemes on the statutory scheme but who are more generous than the statutory scheme requires them to be.

Background

834. This exception is designed to replicate the effect of an existing exception in regulation 33 of the 2006 Regulations.

Examples

- An employer may pay qualifying employees an enhanced redundancy payment based on their actual week's pay rather than the maximum amount as specified in section 227 ERA 1996 (currently £380).
- So an employee (P) aged 45 with 18 years continuous employment earning £600 a week would receive one and a half weeks pay for each year of employment in which he was not below the age of 41 and one week's pay for each year of employment in which he was not below the age of 22 so P would receive the following: 3 x (1.5 x £600) + (15 x £600) = £11,700.
- An employer may pay qualifying employees an enhanced redundancy payment calculated in accordance with section 162 of ERA 1996 but after calculating the appropriate amount for each year of employment, the employer may apply a multiple of two rather than one. So the employer could pay P £23,400 rather than £11,700.
- Alternatively, the employer could apply the maximum amount of £380 to P's payment but apply a multiple of 2 and pay P the following: 2 x 3 x (1.5 x £380) + (15 x £380) = 2 x (£1710 + 5700) = £14820.

Life assurance: **paragraph 14**

Effect

835. This paragraph provides an exception for employers who provide life assurance cover to workers who have had to retire early because of ill health.

Background

836. This paragraph is designed to replicate the effect of the exception in regulation 34 of the 2006 Regulations.

837. Life assurance cover is usually provided in respect of people below the age of 65 (or the employer's normal retirement age if different). Such cover is not provided in respect of older people because, as the probability of death increases, it becomes more and more expensive to provide. If employers were no longer able to impose – or had to objectively justify – a "cut off" for the provision of such cover to those who have retired early, there is a real risk they would simply "level down": in other words, they would cease to offer it to anyone. This exception is intended to avoid that happening.

Examples

- An employer who has no normal retirement age provides life assurance cover for an employee who has retired early due to ill health. If the employer then ceases to provide such cover when the employee reaches the age of 65, this is lawful.
- An employer who operates a normal retirement age of 70 provides life assurance cover for an employee who has retired early due to ill health. If the employer then ceases to provide such cover when the employee reaches the age of 70, this is lawful.

Child care: paragraph 15

Effect

838. This paragraph creates an exception from the prohibition of age discrimination in employment and certain other work relationships for benefits which relate to the provision of child care, and to which access is restricted to children of a particular age group. The exception applies not only to natural parents, but also to others with parental responsibility for a child.

839. The exception covers benefits which relate to the provision of care for children aged up to and including 16.

Background

840. This is a new provision. Following the ruling of the European Court of Justice in *Coleman v Attridge Law and another (Case C-303/06) [2008] ECR I-5603)* it could potentially be direct discrimination for an employer to treat an employee less favourably because of the age of an employee's child. There is, therefore, a potential impact on the provision of facilities, such as child care, where access is limited by reference to the child's age.

841. The exception allows employers to continue to offer employees child care facilities based on the age of a child without being open to a challenge of direct discrimination from other employees.

Examples

- An employer may provide a crèche for employees' children aged two and under; or a holiday club open only to employees' children aged between 5 and 9. In each of these examples, the exception allows an employer to discriminate against employees because of their association with a child who does not fall within the specified age groups.
- The exception does not apply to employee benefits which do not have a close relationship with the provision of child care. For example, if an employer offers luncheon vouchers, gym membership or a company car only to those employees with children of a particular age group, the exception does not apply as none of these benefits involves child care.
- Neither does the exception apply to benefits conferred as a result of the employee's employment, but applying directly to the child, where child care is not involved. For example, an employer may offer private healthcare to employees' children up to a certain age, or use of the employer's services (e.g. free train tickets if the employer is a train company) by such children.

Contributions to personal pension schemes: paragraph 16

Effect

842. This paragraph gives a Minister of the Crown the power to specify practices, actions or decisions relating to age in respect of employer contributions to personal pension schemes that an employer can use without breaching a non-discrimination rule.

Background

843. Exceptions to the non-discrimination rule in relation to age in respect of employer contributions to personal pension schemes were previously set out at Schedule 2 to the Employment Equality (Age) Regulations 2006 (S.I. 2006/1031).

Part 3: Other exceptions

Non-contractual payments to women on maternity leave: paragraph 17

Effect

844. This paragraph sets out an exception to the prohibitions on pregnancy and maternity discrimination by employers which allows an employer not to offer an applicant or provide an employee who is on maternity leave the benefits of the non-contractual terms

and conditions of her employment. It also explains what is and is not covered by this exception.

Background

845. This paragraph is designed to replicate the effect of provisions in the Sex Discrimination Act 1975. It does for non-contractual terms and conditions of employment relating to pay what is done for contractual terms in section 74.

Examples

- An employer would not have to pay a woman on maternity leave a discretionary bonus if the only condition of eligibility for the bonus was that the employee must be in active employment at the time of payment.
- If a discretionary bonus amounted to retrospective payment for time worked over a specific period (such as the past year) during which a woman took maternity leave, the employer must include any part of that period the woman spent on compulsory maternity leave in calculating the bonus.

Benefits dependent on marital status: paragraph 18

Effect

846. This paragraph concerns a specific exception to the prohibition of discrimination because of sexual orientation in the field of work. The exception concerns the provision of benefits by reference to marital status in respect of periods of service before 5 December 2005 (the coming into force of the Civil Partnership Act 2004). It also concerns benefits restricted to married persons and civil partners.

Background

847. This exception is intended to preserve the effect of regulation 25 of the Employment Equality (Sexual Orientation) Regulations 2003.

Examples

- An example of an employment benefit provided by reference to marital status is an occupational pension scheme which pays benefits to an employee's spouse on the death of the employee, but does not similarly compensate an unmarried employee's partner.
- A scheme which pays out only to surviving married and civil partners could be indirectly discriminatory because it might disadvantage gay couples, but it is permitted by the exception.
- A scheme which pays out to surviving married partners must also pay out to surviving civil partners in respect of any employee service since 5 December 2005 (when the Civil Partnership Act 2004 came into force). Provided the scheme does that, the exception allows it, even though it may (directly or indirectly) discriminate by paying out only to married partners for service before that date.

Provision of services, etc. to the public: paragraph 19

Effect

848. This paragraph provides that an employer who provides services to the public at large is not liable for claims of discrimination or victimisation by an employee under Part 5 of the Act in relation to those services. Rather, where individuals are discriminated against or victimised in relation to those services, they can make a claim in the county court under Part 3. If on the other hand the service differs from that provided to other employees, is provided under the terms and conditions of employment, or the service is to do with training, the individual can bring a claim in an employment tribunal for breach of the provisions in Part 5. These provisions are also applicable to services provided by principals, firms, limited liability partnerships and relevant persons (in respect of personal or public office-holders).

Background

849. This section is designed to replace similar provisions in previous legislation and has been extended to partnerships.

Examples

- If an employee of a car hire company is denied the hire of one of its cars (on the same terms available to the general public) because he is black, the employee must claim under the "services" section of the Act in the county court, rather than through an employment tribunal under the "work" provisions of the Act.
- If the same employee's employment contract provides that he is allowed to hire the company's cars at a discount (which members of the public would not get), but the employee is refused the discount when he goes to hire one of the firm's cars because he is a Muslim, then the employee would be able to make a discrimination claim under section 39.

Insurance contracts etc.: paragraph 20

Effect

850. This paragraph applies where annuities, life assurance policies, accident insurance policies or similar matters which involve the assessment of risk are provided in the field of employment. It allows for employers to provide for payment of premiums or benefits that differ for men and women, persons who are or are not married or in a civil partnership, pregnancy or maternity or gender reassignment so far as this is reasonable in the light of actuarial or other reliable data.

Background

851. This paragraph is designed to replace a similar exception in the Sex Discrimination Act 1975. It permits differences in treatment for insurance or risk-related matters where the difference is done by reference to reliable actuarial or other data and it is reasonable in all the circumstances.

Example

- An employer makes access to a group insurance policy available as a result of being employed by it. The employer, not the insurer, is responsible for ensuring that the provision of benefits under the policy complies with this Act – see paragraph 20 of Part 5 of Schedule 3. In providing access to these group policies the employer may take advantage of this exception.

Schedule 10: Accessibility for disabled pupils

852. This Schedule provides for accessibility arrangements for pupils in schools as set out in section 88.

Effect

853. Local authorities must prepare written accessibility strategies which will increase disabled pupils' access to the school curriculum, improve the physical environment for such pupils and improve the provision of information to them. Strategies must be implemented by local authorities after taking account of pupils' disabilities and preferences expressed by them and their parents. They should be reviewed regularly, and revised if needed.

854. Local authorities must have regard to the need to allocate adequate resources to implementation of the strategy and use any guidance which may be issued by a Minister of the Crown in England and the Welsh Ministers in Wales.

855. Schools must develop written accessibility plans which will increase the access of disabled pupils to the school curriculum, improve the physical environment for such pupils and improve the provision of information to them. Plans must be implemented by schools after taking account of disabled pupils' disabilities and preferences expressed by them and their parents. They should be reviewed regularly, and revised if needed.

Inspections of schools by OFSTED can look at the performance of these duties by schools.

856. Schools must have regard to the need to allocate adequate resources to the plans.

857. If the Secretary of State in England or the Welsh Ministers in Wales determine that a maintained school or Academy or local authority has failed to discharge these duties, has acted unreasonably in respect of these duties or has failed to comply with an order of the First-tier Tribunal or the Special Educational Needs Tribunal for Wales, they may give directions to the school or local authority about discharging the duty or compliance with the order. However, a Secretary of State in England may not issue directions if the matter has been, or could have been, referred to the Local Commissioner unless, if the matter has been referred to the Local Commissioner, the school has not complied with any recommendation given.

858. Paragraph 6 gives a power, in England to a Minister of the Crown, and in Wales to the Welsh Ministers, to make regulations to say what is, and is not, education and a benefit, facility or service.

Background

859. These provisions are designed to replicate the effect of provisions in the Disability Discrimination Act 1995, and require schools and local authorities to plan to make all aspects of school more accessible to disabled pupils, particularly as the requirement to make reasonable adjustments to physical features of premises does not apply to schools.

Example

- A school discusses with its disabled pupils their needs and requirements in order to help it develop a written accessibility plan. The plan includes a strategy to improve the physical environment of the school by putting in ramps and more easily accessible rooms, putting in hearing loops and producing newsletters in Braille.

Schedule 11: Schools: exceptions

Part 1: Sex discrimination

860. Part 1 of this Schedule makes exceptions from the prohibition on sex discrimination by schools in section 85 to allow for the existence of single-sex schools and for single-sex boarding at schools, and to make transitional provisions for single-sex schools which are turning co-educational.

Background

861. These provisions are designed to replicate the effect of provisions in the Sex Discrimination Act 1975.

Admission to single-sex schools: paragraph 1

Effect

862. This paragraph allows a single-sex school to refuse to admit pupils of the opposite sex. A school is defined as single-sex if it admits pupils of one sex only. This is so even if it admits a small number of pupils of the opposite sex on an exceptional basis or in relation to particular courses or classes only. Limiting those pupils to particular courses or classes is not discrimination. However, other forms of sex discrimination by the school against its opposite-sex pupils would still be unlawful.

Examples

- A school which admits only boys is not discriminating unlawfully against girls.

- If the daughters of certain members of staff at a boys' school are allowed to attend, it is still regarded as a single-sex school.
- A boys' school which admits some girls to the Sixth Form, or which lets girls attend for a particular GCSE course not offered at their own school is still regarded as a single-sex school.
- A boys' school which admits girls to A-level science classes is not discriminating unlawfully if it refuses to admit them to A-level media studies or maths classes.
- A boys' school which admits girls to the Sixth Form but refuses to let them use the same cafeteria or go on the same visits as other Sixth Form pupils would be discriminating unlawfully against them.

Single-sex boarding at schools: paragraph 2
Effect

863. This paragraph provides that a mixed-sex school some of whose pupils are boarders may lawfully admit only pupils of one sex to be boarders. The exception applies even if some members of the other sex are admitted as boarders, so long as their numbers are comparatively small. It allows a school to refuse to admit a pupil to a boarding place at the time he or she initially joins the school, or to provide him or her with boarding facilities at a later stage.

Example

- A mixed-sex school has facilities for female boarders and can lawfully state in its prospectus that males cannot be accepted as boarders.

Single-sex schools turning co-educational: paragraphs 3 and 4
Effect

864. Paragraphs 3 and 4 enable a school which is going through the process of changing from a single-sex to a co-educational institution to apply for a transitional exemption order to enable it to continue to restrict admittance to a single sex until the transition from single-sex is complete.

865. Paragraph 4 sets out the procedures for applying for a transitional exemption order for each type of school.

Examples

If a transitional exemption order is made in accordance with the arrangements in paragraph 4:

- A boys' school which decides to become co-educational by starting to admit girls to Year 7 while keeping upper classes as they are, will not be discriminating unlawfully by refusing to admit girls to other years, until co-educational classes have been phased in throughout the school.
- A girls' school which decides to become co-educational by initially admitting a certain number of boys to each year group will not be discriminating unlawfully by reserving a number of places in each year group for boys.
- A school in the process of becoming co-educational must treat its male and female pupils equally once they have been admitted, since the transitional exemption order only relates to admissions.

Part 2: Religious or belief-related discrimination

866. Part 2 of this Schedule makes some exceptions to the prohibition on discrimination because of religion or belief in relation to schools with a religious character, and to acts of worship or other religious observance in any school.

Background

867. These exceptions, and the amending powers in paragraph 7, are designed to replicate the effect of provisions in Part 2 of the Equality Act 2006.

Schools with religious character, etc.: paragraph 5

Effect

868. This paragraph allows schools which have a religious character or ethos (often referred to as faith schools) to discriminate because of religion or belief in relation to admissions and in access to any benefit, facility or service. It means that faith schools may have admissions criteria which give preference to members of their own religion and it allows them to conduct themselves in a way which is compatible with their religious character or ethos. It does not allow faith schools to discriminate because of any other of the protected characteristics, such as sex, race or sexual orientation. Nor does it allow them to discriminate because of religion in other respects, such as by excluding a pupil or subjecting him to any other detriment.

Examples

- A Muslim school may give priority to Muslim pupils when choosing between applicants for admission (although the Admissions Code will not allow it to refuse to accept pupils of another or no religion unless it is oversubscribed). However, it may not discriminate between pupils because of any other of the protected characteristics, such as by refusing to admit a child of the school's own faith because she is black or a lesbian.
- A Jewish school which provides spiritual instruction or pastoral care from a rabbi is not discriminating unlawfully by not making equivalent provision for pupils from other religious faiths.
- A Roman Catholic school which organises visits for pupils to sites of particular interest to its own faith, such as a cathedral, is not discriminating unlawfully by not arranging trips to sites of significance to the faiths of other pupils.
- A faith school would be acting unlawfully if it sought to penalise or exclude a pupil because he or she had renounced the faith of the school or joined a different religion or denomination.

Curriculum, worship etc.: paragraph 6

Effect

869. This paragraph disapplies the prohibition on religious discrimination from anything done in relation to acts of worship or other religious observance organised by or on behalf of a school, whether or not it is part of the curriculum.

Background

870. This exception applies to any school, not just faith schools, and reflects the need to avoid any conflict with the existing legislative framework in respect of religious worship in schools, which generally requires collective worship to be of a broadly Christian nature. While parents can remove their children from collective worship, and sixth form pupils may decide to withdraw themselves, schools are under no obligation to provide opportunities for separate worship for the different religions and beliefs represented among their pupils. The exception in paragraph 6 maintains that position. It is designed to replicate the position in the Equality Act 2006.

Examples

- Under education law, a school must allow Jewish or Hindu parents to withdraw their children from daily assemblies which include an element of worship of a mainly Christian character, but it will not be discriminating unlawfully against those children by not providing alternative assemblies including Jewish or Hindu worship.

- Schools are free to organise or to participate in ceremonies celebrating any faith, such as Christmas, Diwali, Chanukah or Eid, without being subject to claims of religious discrimination against children of other religions or of none.

Power to amend: paragraph 7
Effect

871. Paragraph 7 provides a power for a Minister of the Crown to add to, amend or repeal these religious discrimination exceptions.

Background

872. This power is designed to replicate the effect of provisions in Part 2 of the Equality Act 2006, which first prohibited religious discrimination in schools. It has not yet been used. Its purpose is to enable a Minister of the Crown to review the working of these provisions once they have been in effect for a sufficient period and make any changes which appear to be necessary in the light of that experience, using secondary legislation.

Part 3: Disability discrimination

Permitted form of selection: paragraph 8

Effect

873. This paragraph provides that schools will not be discriminating against disabled children when applying a permitted form of selection that they are using.

Background

874. This provision is designed to replicate the effect of provisions in the Disability Discrimination Act 1995. Permitted forms of selection are the selective admission arrangements operated by grammar schools, and selection by ability and aptitude in accordance with the School Standards and Framework Act 1998.

Example

- The parents of a disabled pupil cannot claim disability discrimination against a particular school if that pupil fails to meet any educational entry requirements set by the school.

Schedule 12: Further and higher education exceptions

Part 1: Single-sex institutions

Effect

875. Part 1 of this Schedule makes exceptions from the prohibition on sex discrimination by further and higher education institutions to allow for the existence of single-sex colleges and to make transitional provisions for single-sex institutions which are turning co-educational.

Background

876. These provisions are designed to replicate the effect of provisions in the Sex Discrimination Act 1975.

Admission to single-sex institutions: paragraph 1
Effect

877. This paragraph allows a single-sex institution to refuse to admit members of the opposite sex. An institution is defined as single-sex if it admits students of one sex only. An institution which exceptionally admits students of the opposite sex, or which

admits a comparatively small number of opposite-sex students to particular courses or classes only, is still regarded as single-sex. Limiting those students to particular courses or classes is permitted. However, other forms of sex discrimination by the institution against its opposite-sex students would still be unlawful.

Examples

- A women's college which admits only female students is not discriminating unlawfully against men.
- If the college admits a small number of men to make up the numbers on a particular course of study, it is still regarded as a single-sex college. It is not discriminating unlawfully by refusing to admit men to other courses.
- A women's college which admits men to certain courses but refuses to let them use the student cafeteria would be discriminating unlawfully against them.

Single-sex institutions turning co-educational: paragraphs 2 and 3.

Effect

878. These paragraphs enable a college which is going through the process of changing from a single-sex to a co-educational institution to apply for a transitional exemption order, to enable it to continue restricting admittance to a single sex until the transition from single-sex is complete.

879. Paragraph 3 sets out the procedures for applying for a transitional exemption order.

Background

880. These provisions are designed to replicate the effect of provisions in the Sex Discrimination Act 1975.

Examples

- If a transitional exemption order is made in accordance with the arrangements in paragraph 3:

  A women's college which decides to become co-educational by starting to admit a certain number of male undergraduates to the first year of its degree courses will not be discriminating unlawfully by limiting the number of men it admits, or by refusing men access to postgraduate degree courses.

  A college in the process of becoming co-educational must treat its male and female students equally once they have been admitted, since the transitional exemption order relates only to discrimination in relation to admissions.

Part 2: Other exceptions

Occupational requirements: paragraph 4

Effect

881. This paragraph enables a higher or further education institution to treat a person differently based on a protected characteristic in relation to providing training which would only fit them for work which, under exceptions in Schedule 9, can lawfully be restricted to people of a particular race, sex, religion, sexual orientation or age, or who are not transgendered or who are not married or in a civil partnership and for which they would therefore be ineligible.

Background

882. This is designed to replicate the effect of provisions in the previous legislation.

Example

- A Catholic theological college can refuse to admit a woman to a training course which was designed only to prepare candidates for the Catholic priesthood. However, a Church of England college could not confine training for the priesthood to men since women may also become Anglican priests.

Institutions with a religious ethos: paragraph 5

Effect

883. This paragraph confers on a Minister of the Crown a power to designate an institution if the Minister is satisfied that the institution has a religious ethos. If an institution is designated it may admit students who share the relevant religion or belief in preference to those who do not, but only in relation to admissions to courses which do not constitute vocational training.

Background

884. This is designed to enable the previous position under an exception in the Employment Equality (Religion or Belief) Regulations 2003 to be maintained. Schedule 1B to those Regulations modified the prohibition on discrimination for a small number of sixth form colleges with a religious ethos. The intention is that this power will be used to designate those colleges.

Benefits dependent on marital status, etc.: paragraph 6

Effect

885. A higher or further education institution which confines any benefit, facility or service – such as access to residential accommodation – to married people and civil partners will not be discriminating because of sexual orientation against people who are unmarried or not in a civil partnership.

Background

886. This is designed to replicate the effect of a provision in the Employment Equality (Sexual Orientation) Regulations 2003 so far as it related to higher or further education institutions.

Child care: paragraph 7

Effect

887. This paragraph provides that a higher or further education institution is permitted to provide, or make arrangements for, or facilitate, care for the children of students which is confined to children of a particular age group. This includes all kinds of assistance with child care including paying for or subsidising it, or enabling parents to spend more time caring for the child.

Background

888. The Act makes it unlawful for higher or further education institutions to discriminate because of the age of a person with whom a student is associated, and not the student's own age. The exception makes it clear that where child care for students' children who are aged 16 or under is concerned, it is not unlawful for this to be based on the age of the child.

Example

- If a college provides a crèche for the pre-school children of students, this will not be unlawful age association discrimination against a student who is the parent of an older child. The college will not have to demonstrate that the provision and the age limits are objectively justified.

Schedule 13: Education: reasonable adjustments

889. This Schedule provides for reasonable adjustments to be made by educational bodies in relation to disabled people.

Effect

890. Paragraph 2, which relates to admissions, the provision of education and access to benefits, facilities and services, requires schools to comply with requirements to:

- ensure that any provisions, criteria or practices do not place disabled pupils at a substantial disadvantage in comparison with non-disabled pupils:
- provide any reasonable auxiliary aids which might help remove any such disadvantage.

891. Paragraph 3 requires higher or further education institutions in relation to admissions, education, access to benefits, facilities and services, and the conferring of qualifications to comply with requirements to take reasonable steps to:

- ensure that any provisions, criteria or practices do not place disabled students at a substantial disadvantage in comparison with non-disabled students;
- take reasonable steps to change physical features which place disabled students at a disadvantage;
- provide any reasonable auxiliary aids which might help remove any substantial disadvantage.

892. Paragraph 4 defines who is an "interested disabled person", in relation to conferment of qualifications. It also sets out that a provision, criterion or practice does not include an application of a competence standard, which is also defined.

893. Paragraph 5 requires local authorities and maintained schools which are providing higher education or further education to take reasonable steps to ensure that any provisions, criteria or practices do not place disabled people at a substantial disadvantage, and provide any reasonable auxiliary aids to help remove any disadvantage in relation to enrolling people on courses of further or higher education, and to services provided once enrolled. Local authorities providing such services also need to take reasonable steps to change physical features which place disabled students at a disadvantage.

894. Paragraph 6 requires local authorities providing recreational or training facilities to take reasonable steps to ensure that any provisions, criteria or practices do not place disabled people at a substantial disadvantage. They must also take reasonable steps to change physical features which place disabled students at a disadvantage and provide reasonable auxiliary aids to help remove any disadvantage in relation to their arrangements for providing recreational or training facilities.

895. Paragraph 7 requires educational institutions to consider the relevant code of practice produced by the Equality and Human Rights Commission when determining reasonable steps.

896. Paragraph 8 requires that, when making any reasonable adjustment for a particular person, the educational institution needs to consider any request made by that person to keep the nature and existence of that person's disability confidential.

897. Paragraph 9 sets out that qualifications bodies must take reasonable steps to:

- ensure that any provision, criterion or practice does not place disabled people at a substantial disadvantage;

- change physical features which put disabled candidates at a substantial disadvantage;
- provide auxiliary aids to disabled candidates who are at a substantial disadvantage in the conferring of qualifications.

Background

898. These provisions are designed to mainly replicate the effect of provisions in the Disability Discrimination Act 1995.

Examples

- A school with a number of disabled pupils could negotiate special arrangements for pupils who are taking exams.
- A school could provide Braille texts to a blind pupil at the start of lessons so they have access to the same information as other pupils.
- A university has a revolving door which causes some problems for disabled pupils and under these duties it may be reasonable for them to replace the door with a sliding one.
- To ensure that a pupil who needs a wheelchair is not disadvantaged by being left out of PE lessons, a school consults a physiotherapist and devises special activities for the pupil to carry out in PE.

Schedule 14: Educational charities and endowments

Educational charities: paragraph 1

Effect

899. This paragraph provides for trust deeds or other instruments concerning educational charities which restrict available benefits to a single sex to be modified by a Minister of the Crown. This cannot be done within 25 years of the trust being created without the consent of the donor, or the donor's or testator's personal representatives. Applicants need to publish particulars of the proposal and invite representations for the Minister to consider before making the order.

Background

900. This paragraph replicates provisions in section 78 of the Sex Discrimination Act 1975. It is likely to happen when a single-sex school becomes co-educational, and so wants to enable both sexes to benefit from a particular charity connected with the school.

Example

- A single-sex (boys') grammar school now allows girls into its sixth form and wishes to modify a trust deed which offers scholarships and help with tuition for boys of the school wanting to go to university – so that it can also offer help to girls.

Educational endowments: paragraph 2Effect

901. A similar power to that in paragraph 1 is given to the Scottish Ministers to modify educational endowments administered in Scotland.

Schedule 15: Associations: reasonable adjustments

Effect

902. This Schedule explains how the duty to make reasonable adjustments in section 20 applies to associations. Paragraph 2 explains that the duty applies in respect of disabled members and guests including prospective members and guests and that the association must comply with all three reasonable adjustment requirements. It describes the types of adjustments an association must make, stipulates what the duty does not require and

provides further information on the meaning of "physical features". It is an anticipatory duty which means associations must anticipate the needs of disabled members and guests including prospective members and guests and make appropriate reasonable adjustments.

Background

903. This Schedule is designed to replicate the effect of similar provisions in the Disability Discrimination Act 1995.

Examples

- A private club with 30 members usually holds its annual dinner upstairs in a local restaurant. However, as there is no lift, the room is not accessible to two new disabled members who have severe difficulty in climbing stairs. Under the duty the club would need to think about changing the venue to a downstairs room to accommodate the new members. This is likely to be a reasonable adjustment for the club to make.
- A club has members who cannot read standard print. Under the duty it would need to think about providing information in large print and on audio tape for them. These are likely to be reasonable adjustments for the club to make.

Schedule 16: Associations: exceptions

904. Schedule 16 contains exceptions from the association provisions in Part 7 of the Act.

Single characteristic associations: paragraph 1

Effect

905. This paragraph allows an association whose main purpose is to bring together people who share a particular characteristic (such as a particular nationality, sexual orientation or a particular disability) to continue to restrict membership to such people, and impose similar restrictions on those who can exercise the rights of an associate, or who can be invited as guests.

906. It is however unlawful for an association to restrict its membership to people of a particular colour.

Background

907. An exception for associations which bring together people who share a particular protected characteristic was provided in previous legislation in relation to race and sexual orientation. This exception has been extended to cover all of the protected characteristics in line with the prohibition on discrimination.

Example

- A club for deaf people can restrict membership to people who are deaf and would not need to admit people with other disabilities, such as a blind person.

Health and safety: paragraph 2

Effect

908. This paragraph is designed to ensure that it is not unlawful for an association to treat a pregnant woman differently in the terms on which she is admitted as a member or is given access to benefits as a member if the association reasonably believes that to do otherwise would create a risk to her health or safety and the association would take similar measures in respect of persons with other physical conditions. Equivalent provision is made in respect of associates and guests.

Background

909. Provisions making it unlawful for an association to discriminate against a pregnant woman have been introduced for the first time in this Act. The provisions in this

paragraph, which are similar to those which apply in the provision of services to the public, are therefore also new.

Example

- A private members' gym may wish to restrict access to squash courts after a certain point in the pregnancy (for example, after 36 weeks).

Schedule 17: Disabled pupils: enforcement

Part 1: Introductory

910. This Schedule sets out the arrangements for making disability discrimination claims in respect of school pupils.

Part 2: Tribunals in England and Wales

Jurisdiction: paragraph 3

911. Disability discrimination claims in respect of school pupils are made to the First-tier Tribunal in England and to the Special Educational Needs Tribunal in Wales, unless they relate to admissions or exclusions. Claims are brought by the child's parent.

Time for bringing proceedings: paragraph 4

912. Claims need to be made within six months of conduct commencing. This period can be extended to nine months if the Equality and Human Rights Commission makes arrangements for conciliation in respect of disputes. In addition, tribunals could consider cases beyond this time limit.

Powers: paragraph 5

913. If a tribunal finds that a school has discriminated against a pupil, it can make any orders it sees fit, particularly in order to remove or reduce the problem. However, it may not award the payment of compensation.

Procedure: paragraph 6

914. The Welsh Ministers are given powers to make regulations to govern the procedure of claims heard by the Welsh Tribunal.

Part 3: Tribunals in Scotland

915. In Scotland the power to make procedural rules for the hearing of disability discrimination claims by the Additional Support Needs Tribunals for Scotland will be exercised by the Scottish Ministers.

Part 4: Admissions and exclusions

916. If the disability discrimination claim made is in respect of admissions to, or permanent exclusion from, a maintained school or an Academy, then the claim will be brought under independent education appeals panel arrangements as set out in education legislation, rather than going to the tribunals.

Background

917. This Schedule is designed to replicate the effect of provisions in the Disability Discrimination Act 1995.

Examples

- A school pupil is not allowed to join other children in the playground at break-times because of his wheelchair and his parents believe he is being discriminated against because of his disability. They are able to bring a claim against the school which is heard by the First-tier Tribunal (in England). The Tribunal rules in favour of the pupil and makes an order for the school to alter the practice which caused the discrimination and make arrangements for the pupil to join his peers at break time.
- A pupil is refused admission to a school and her parents believe that it is because of her disability and make a claim. The claim cannot be heard by the First-tier Tribunal and is heard by an independent education appeals panel under education legislation.

Schedule 18: Public sector equality duty: exceptions

Effect

918. This Schedule lists exceptions to the coverage of the public sector equality duty.

919. Paragraph 1 disapplies the equality duty with respect to age in relation to the education of pupils in schools and the provision of services to pupils in schools and in relation to children's homes.

920. Paragraph 2 disapplies the equality of opportunity limb of the equality duty in relation to immigration functions in respect of race (except as it includes "colour"), religion or belief and age.

921. Paragraph 3 disapplies the equality duty in respect of judicial functions or functions exercised on behalf of, or on the instructions of, a person exercising judicial functions. A judicial function includes judicial functions which are carried out by persons other than a court or tribunal, for example courts martial.

922. Paragraph 4 disapplies the equality duty in respect of any public functions (as that term is defined for the purposes of the Human Rights Act 1998) performed by the persons listed in sub-paragraph (2), or in relation to the functions listed in sub-paragraph (3).

923. Paragraph 5 contains a power for a Minister of the Crown by order to add, change or remove an exception to the scope of the equality duty. However, this power cannot be used to remove or limit the exceptions relating to judicial functions or those relating to Parliament, the Scottish Parliament, the National Assembly for Wales and the General Synod.

Background

924. This Schedule replaces the exception for immigration functions from the race duty in section 71A of the Race Relations Act. It also replaces sections 76A(3) and (4) of the Sex Discrimination Act 1976 and sections 49C and 49D of the Disability Discrimination Act 1995 relating to excepted bodies and functions and applies similar provision to the protected characteristics that did not previously have equality duties associated with them.

Examples

- A school will not be required to consider advancing equality of opportunity between pupils of different ages. Nor will it be required to consider how to foster good relations between pupils on different ages. But it will still need to have due regard to the need to eliminate unlawful discrimination, advance equality of opportunity and foster good relations between pupils in respect of the other protected characteristics.
- The UK Border Agency, when taking immigration-related decisions, will not be required to have due regard to the need to advance equality of opportunity for people of different

races, religious beliefs or age when taking those decisions. However, it will still be required to have due regard to the need to advance equality of opportunity for disabled people, for men and women, for people of all sexual orientations and transsexual people when making those decisions.

Schedule 19: Public authorities

Effect

925. This Schedule lists those public bodies which are subject to the public sector equality duty contained in section 149(1). It is divided into three Parts: public bodies generally; relevant Welsh bodies; and relevant Scottish bodies. There is provision for a fourth part to be added for cross-border Welsh and Scottish bodies. Subsection (2) of section 149 applies the public sector equality duty to other persons who are not listed in the Schedule, but who are carrying out public functions, but only with regard to the exercise of those functions. The powers in sections 153 and 154 to impose specific duties only apply to bodies listed in Schedule 19; they do not extend to persons who are subject to the public sector equality duty by virtue of subsection (2) of section 149.

Background

926. This Schedule uses as its starting point Schedule 1A to the Race Relations Act 1976.

Schedule 20: Rail vehicle accessibility: compliance

927. The provisions of this Schedule are tied to those of section 186 which provides for the Schedule to be repealed if not brought into force (either fully or to any extent) by 31 December 2010.

928. This Schedule was included in the Act because, during its passage through Parliament, the Department for Transport was consulting on draft regulations under section 46 of the Disability Discrimination Act 1995. These were prepared following a policy reappraisal which favoured a move away from compliance certification and civil enforcement powers for rail vehicle accessibility. The Government's preferred option, adoption of Health and Safety at Work etc Act 1974 enforcement powers with the Office of Rail Regulation being designated as enforcement authority, would make accessibility enforcement on light rail consistent with recent changes to accessibility enforcement on the main line rail system resulting from the introduction of new European standards which came into force in July 2008. The consultation period ended on 3 July 2009 but, in order not to pre-empt the outcome, the option to use compliance certification and civil enforcement powers was retained in the Act.

929. Consultation responses indicated that the Government's preferred option of non-commencement of this Schedule was widely supported by stakeholders. The Government therefore proceeded with the implementation of a package of secondary legislation under the Disability Discrimination Act 1995 which did not include compliance certification and replaced the originally envisaged civil enforcement regime with enforcement by the Office of Rail Regulation under their existing Health and Safety at Work etc Act 1974 powers. The enforcement provisions were contained in the Rail Vehicle Accessibility (Non-Interoperable Rail System) Regulations 2010 (S.I. 2010/432) which came into force on 6 April 2010.

930. Government policy is therefore not to bring this Schedule into force. However, the provisions are still explained in detail below to assist the reader's understanding.

Paragraphs 1 to 4

931. These paragraphs introduce the concept of "compliance certification" into the rail vehicle accessibility regime. The effect would be to require prescribed rail vehicles to

have a rail vehicle accessibility compliance certificate (which certifies compliance with accessibility standards).

Rail vehicle accessibility compliance certificates: paragraph 1

Effect

932. This paragraph provides for the introduction of compliance certification into the rail vehicle accessibility regime by prohibiting a regulated rail vehicle from being used in passenger service unless a valid compliance certificate has been issued for that rail vehicle. Regulations would be required to set out which rail vehicles would require a compliance certificate.

933. It also contains provisions to enable a penalty to be paid to the Secretary of State should a regulated rail vehicle, which is required to have a compliance certificate, be operated in passenger service without one.

934. In circumstances where the Secretary of State has refused to issue a compliance certificate, provisions are made for the applicant to ask for a review of that decision, within a maximum time period to be set in regulations, taking into account any written representations that may be presented by the applicant. A fee could be charged to recover the costs of undertaking such a review.

Background

935. This paragraph replicates the provisions of sections 47A and 47D of the Disability Discrimination Act 1995 inserted by the Disability Discrimination Act 2005 but not yet in force.

Regulations as to compliance certificates: paragraph 2

Effect

936. This paragraph enables regulations to be made setting out how the compliance certification regime introduced by paragraph 1, would operate in practice. For example, the regulations could specify who may apply for a compliance certificate, the conditions to which they would be subject and the period for which the conditions would remain in force.

Background

937. This paragraph replicates some of the provisions of section 47B(1) to (3) of the Disability Discrimination Act 1995 inserted by the Disability Discrimination Act 2005 but not yet in force.

Regulations as to compliance assessments: paragraph 3

Effect

938. This paragraph provides for regulations to be made for the undertaking of compliance assessments, including provision as to who may carry out assessments, and which may provide that assessments be carried out by persons appointed by the Secretary of State (to be known as an "appointed assessor").

939. Sub-paragraph (3) enables regulations to make provision about the appointment of appointed assessors, for them to charge fees in connection with their work, to prescribe procedures and for the referral of disputes between an appointed assessor and a person who requested a compliance assessment.

Background

940. This paragraph replicates the remaining provisions of section 47B of the Disability Discrimination Act 1995 inserted by the Disability Discrimination Act 2005 but not yet in force.

Fees in respect of compliance certificates: paragraph 4

Effect

941. This paragraph enables regulations to be made setting out the fees which the Secretary of State may charge to recover the costs of carrying out certain administrative tasks relating to the issuing of compliance certificates. Any fees which are received must be paid into the Consolidated Fund. Before making any regulations under this paragraph, the Secretary of State must consult representative organisations.

Background

942. This paragraph replicates the provisions of section 47C of the Disability Discrimination Act 1995 inserted by the Disability Discrimination Act 2005 but not yet in force.

Paragraphs 5 to 12

943. Paragraphs 5 to 12 make provision for a civil enforcement regime which would enable penalties to be levied for non-compliance with rail vehicle accessibility regulations.

Penalty for using rail vehicle that does not conform with accessibility regulations: paragraph 5

Effect

944. This paragraph sets out the procedure to be followed by the Secretary of State in respect of an operator of a regulated rail vehicle which appears not to comply with the construction requirements of rail vehicle accessibility regulations. The procedure would involve the issue of "improvement" and "final" notices and, if the vehicle is used despite still being non-compliant with those elements of rail vehicle accessibility regulations with which it is required to conform, the Secretary of State could impose a penalty. The various timescales leading up to the imposition of the penalty would have to be set out in regulations.

Background

945. This paragraph replicates the provisions of section 47E of the Disability Discrimination Act 1995 inserted by the Disability Discrimination Act 2005 but not yet in force.

Penalty for using rail vehicle otherwise than in conformity with accessibility regulations: paragraph 6

Effect

946. This paragraph makes similar provisions to paragraph 5 but in respect of vehicles used in a way which does not comply with the operational, rather than technical, requirements of accessibility regulations. For example, a regulated rail vehicle may have appropriate equipment to assist a disabled person in getting on or off the vehicle, such as a lift or ramp, but no member of staff is available to operate it.

Background

947. This paragraph replicates the provisions of section 47F of the Disability Discrimination Act 1995 inserted by the Disability Discrimination Act 2005 but not yet in force.

Inspection of rail vehicles: paragraph 7

Effect

948. This paragraph sets out powers of inspection, to be available where the Secretary of State has reasonable grounds for suspecting that a regulated rail vehicle does not conform with those provisions of accessibility regulations with which it is required to conform. The paragraph also grants similar powers of inspection following the issuing of notices under paragraph 6. "Inspectors" would be empowered to examine and test such rail vehicles and to enter premises at which it is believed they are kept. If an inspector was intentionally obstructed in the exercise of these powers by an operator, or someone acting on the operator's behalf, the Secretary of State could in certain circumstances impose a penalty on the operator.

Background

949. This paragraph replicates the provisions of section 47G of the Disability Discrimination Act 1995 inserted by the Disability Discrimination Act 2005 but not yet in force.

Supplementary powers: paragraph 8

Effect

950. This paragraph would allow the Secretary of State to issue a notice to a rail vehicle operator requiring it to provide information by a specified deadline to enable a rail vehicle which is described in that notice to be identified. A penalty could be imposed on the recipient of such a notice if it fails to provide the information required by the deadline, which must be a minimum of 14 days from the date on which the notice was given.

951. Provision is also included to incentivise compliance with notices served under paragraphs 5 or 6 (notices requiring rail operators to make vehicles, or their use, compliant with accessibility regulations). Operators could be required to state what steps they are taking to comply with such notices.

952. In default of providing this information, the Secretary of State is empowered to proceed to the "further notice" stage under paragraphs 5 or 6, a precursor to charging a penalty for non-compliance.

Background

953. This paragraph replicates the provisions of section 47H of the Disability Discrimination Act 1995 as inserted by the Disability Discrimination Act 2005 but not yet in force.

Penalties: amount, due date and recovery: paragraph 9

Effect

954. This paragraph makes provision in relation to the amount, due date and recovery of penalties imposed under paragraphs 1 and 5 to 8. It stipulates that the maximum penalty cannot exceed the amount prescribed in regulations, or 10 per cent of the turnover of the rail vehicle operator subject to the penalty, whichever is the lesser amount. "Turnover" must be determined in accordance with provisions set out in regulations and the Secretary of State is able to take court proceedings to recover any penalty payable to him. All penalties must be paid into the Consolidated Fund.

Background

955. This paragraph replicates section 47J (1) to (7) of the Disability Discrimination Act 1995 inserted by the Disability Discrimination Act 2005 but not yet in force. The other aspects of section 47J are replicated at paragraph 10.

Penalties: code of practice: paragraph 10

Effect

956. This paragraph would require the Secretary of State to issue a code of practice to set out matters that must be considered in determining the level of a penalty. The Secretary of State would be required to take account of the code when imposing a penalty under this Schedule or in considering any objections received to the imposition of a penalty. A court must also take account of the code in considering an appeal against a penalty (see paragraph 12).

957. Before issuing either the first or a revised code of practice, the Secretary of State would have to lay a draft before Parliament, and could bring it into operation by order.

Background

958. This paragraph replicates the remaining provisions of section 47J of the Disability Discrimination Act 1995 inserted by the Disability Discrimination Act 2005 but not yet in force.

Penalties: procedure: paragraph 11

Effect

959. This paragraph sets out the procedure for the imposition of penalties under this Schedule. In particular it specifies the information which the Secretary of State would have to provide when notifying a rail vehicle operator that it is liable to a penalty, and outlines the operator's right to object to the imposition, or amount of, a penalty. Should an objection be received, the Secretary of State would be under an obligation to consider the objection and take appropriate action.

Background

960. This paragraph replicates the provisions of section 47K of the Disability Discrimination Act 1995 inserted by the Disability Discrimination Act 2005 but not yet in force.

Penalties: appeals: paragraph 12

Effect

961. This paragraph sets out the right of an operator, on whom a penalty has been imposed, to appeal to a court on the grounds that either it is not liable to a penalty, or that the amount is too high. An appeal under this section is a re-hearing of the Secretary of State's original decision to impose a penalty, and may be brought whether or not the operator has given a notice of objection (under paragraph 11), or the Secretary of State has already reduced a penalty.

Background

962. This paragraph replicates the provisions of section 47L of the Disability Discrimination Act 1995 inserted by the Disability Discrimination Act 2005 but not yet in force.

Forgery, etc.: paragraph 13

Effect

963. This paragraph would make it a criminal offence for a person, with intent to deceive, to forge, alter, use, or lend a compliance certificate, to allow one to be used by another person, to make or have possession of a document which closely resembles one, or to knowingly make a false statement for the purpose of obtaining one.

964. It would also make it a criminal offence for a person, with intent to deceive, to impersonate an inspector authorised by the Secretary of State under paragraph 7.

Background

965. This paragraph replicates elements of the provisions of section 49 of the Disability Discrimination Act 1995 inserted by the Disability Discrimination Act 2005 but not yet in force.

Regulations: paragraph 14

966. This paragraph provides that any power to make regulations provided for in the Schedule is exercisable by the Secretary of State.

Interpretation: paragraph 15

Effect

967. This paragraph defines what is meant by the terms "compliance assessment", "compliance certificate" and "operator" in relation to this Schedule.

968. Under sub-paragraph (2), if a rail vehicle to which this Schedule applies is the subject of an exemption order issued under section 183, then a reference in this Schedule to a rail vehicle accessibility requirement would not include a requirement from which that vehicle is exempt.

Background

969. This paragraph replicates elements of the provisions of section 47M of the Disability Discrimination Act 1995 inserted by the Disability Discrimination Act 2005 but not yet in force.

Schedule 21: Reasonable adjustments: supplementary

Effect

970. The provisions in this Schedule apply to earlier Schedules in the Act dealing with reasonable adjustments where a person providing services or carrying out public functions, an employer, an education provider or an association is required to consider reasonable adjustments to premises which it rents and would require landlord consent to do so. It sets out what steps it is reasonable for a person to take in discharging a duty to make reasonable adjustments in a case where a binding agreement requires that consent must be obtained from a third party before that person may proceed to make the adjustment to let premises or the common parts of let premises.

971. Where a person wishes to make an adjustment in order to fulfil a duty to make reasonable adjustments but is unable to do so, the Schedule enables the adjustment to be made by deeming the tenancy to include certain provisions. For example the tenancy may have effect as if a tenant is able to make alterations with the consent of the landlord.

972. Where a landlord has refused consent to an alteration or gives consent subject to a condition, the person requesting the consent (or a disabled person who has an interest in the alteration being made) can refer the refusal (or the conditional consent) to a county or sheriff court.

973. The Schedule also provides for a landlord to be joined as a party to proceedings before an employment tribunal, county or sheriff court where a disabled person is bringing an action under the reasonable adjustment duty.

974. The Schedule provides a power to make regulations about matters such as when a landlord is taken to have refused consent, when such refusal is unreasonable and when it is reasonable. Words and phrases used in the Schedule are interpreted consistently with the parts of the Act to which it cross-refers.

Background

975. This Schedule replaces similar provisions in the Disability Discrimination Act 1995. It also applies in relation to the new duty to make alterations to the physical features of common parts of let and commonhold residential premises in England and Wales.

Examples

- An insurance company works from a rented two storey building and has plans to install a stair lift to make the building more accessible to employees with mobility impairments. The terms of the lease preclude alterations to the staircase. The company writes to the landlord for permission to make the alteration. The landlord consults the superior landlord who agrees to waive this condition of the lease thereby allowing the installation of the chair lift to proceed. However, as a condition of consent, the landlord requires that the chair lift is removed on surrender of the lease.

- A disabled tenant asks to have automated doors put in at the entrance of her block of flats. Her landlord would like to agree but is unable to do so as he is a tenant of a superior landlord who does not agree to the alteration. The tenant's remedy is to bring an action against her landlord in the county court where she can ask that the superior landlord is brought in as an additional party to the case. The court can order the alteration to be made and order the superior landlord to pay compensation if it finds he has acted unreasonably in refusing his consent.

Schedule 22: Statutory provisions

Statutory authority: paragraph 1

Effect

976. Paragraph 1 of this Schedule provides exceptions from several Parts of the Act, in relation to the protected characteristics of age, disability, religion or belief, sex and sexual orientation, for things done in accordance with what is, or may in future be, required because of some other law.

Background

977. Paragraph 1 replaces the separate exceptions for statutory authority in previous legislation. However, the exception in section 41(1) of the Race Relations Act 1976, which excused certain race discrimination done under statutory authority in areas with which European law is not concerned, has been removed but not replaced.

Examples

- An employer can lawfully dismiss a disabled employee if health and safety regulations leave him with no other choice.
- An employer can lawfully refuse to employ someone to drive a large goods vehicle who is not old enough to hold a LGV licence.

Protection of women: paragraph 2

Effect

978. This paragraph allows differential treatment based on sex or pregnancy and maternity at work which is required to comply with laws protecting women who are pregnant, who have recently given birth or against risks specific to women.

Background

979. The paragraph replaces separate exceptions for the protection of women in the Sex Discrimination Act 1975 and in the Employment Act 1989.

Examples

- A care home cannot lawfully dismiss, but can lawfully suspend, a night-shift worker because she is pregnant and her GP has certified that she must not work nights.
- It may be lawful for a road haulier to refuse to allow a woman lorry driver to transport chemicals that could harm women of child-bearing age.

Educational appointments, etc: religious belief: paragraphs 3 and 4

Effect

980. Paragraph 3 provides an exception from the provisions on sex or religious discrimination for certain posts in schools or institutions of further or higher education where their governing instrument requires the head teacher or principal to be of a particular religious order, or that a particular academic position must be held by a woman, or where the legislation or instrument which establishes a professorship requires the holder to be an ordained priest. In the case of academic positions reserved to women, the exception only applies where the governing instrument was made before 16 January 1990.

981. There is an order-making power conferred on a Minister of the Crown to withdraw the exception either in relation to a particular institution or a class of institutions.

982. Paragraph 4 provides that it is not unlawful discrimination for schools which have a religious character or ethos (often referred to as faith schools) to do certain things which are permitted by the School Standards and Framework Act 1998. This includes:

- allowing teachers who have been appointed to give religious education to be dismissed if they fail to give it competently;

- allowing a faith school to take account of religious considerations when appointing a head teacher; and
- allowing a voluntary aided school or an independent school to take account of religious considerations in employment matters.

Background

983. Paragraph 3 is designed to replicate the effect of provisions in section 5 of the Employment Act 1989.

984. Universities restrict Canon Professorships to certain religions since such posts can only be held by ordained Ministers.

985. Paragraph 4 is designed to replicate the effect of regulation 39 of the Employment Equality (Religion or Belief) Regulations 2003.

Examples

- Voluntary controlled and foundation schools with a religious ethos may appoint a head teacher on the basis of his ability and fitness to preserve and develop the religious character of the school.
- Voluntary aided schools with a religious ethos can restrict employment of teachers to applicants who share the same faith. For example most Catholic schools may require that applicants to teaching positions be of the Catholic faith.

Crown employment, etc.: paragraph 5

Effect

986. Paragraph 5 allows restrictions on the employment of foreign nationals in the civil, diplomatic, armed or security and intelligence services and by certain public bodies. It also allows restrictions on foreign nationals holding public offices.

Background

987. The paragraph replaces similar provisions in the Race Relations Act 1976.

Examples

- Posts in the security and intelligence services are automatically reserved for UK nationals.
- People who are neither British, Commonwealth or Irish citizens nor British protected persons are generally prohibited from serving in the armed forces, with the notable exception of Gurkhas.

Schedule 23: General exceptions

Acts authorised by statute or the executive: paragraph 1

Effect

988. This paragraph allows direct nationality discrimination and indirect race discrimination on the basis of residency requirements where the discrimination is required by law, Ministerial arrangements or Ministerial conditions.

Background

989. The paragraph replaces a similar exception in the Race Relations Act 1976.

Examples

- The points-based system which replaced the former work permit arrangements can discriminate on the basis of nationality in determining whether migrants from outside the European Economic Area and Switzerland should be given permission to work in the United Kingdom.
- The NHS can charge some people who are not ordinarily resident in the United Kingdom for hospital treatment they receive here.

- Overseas students at universities in England and Wales can be required to pay higher tuition fees than local students (there are no tuition fees in Scotland).

Organisations relating to religion or belief: paragraph 2

Effect

990. Paragraph 2 provides an exception for religious or belief organisations with regard to the provisions in the Act relating to services and public functions, premises and associations.

991. The types of organisation that can use this exception are those that exist to: practice, advance or teach a religion or belief; allow people of a religion or belief to participate in any activity or receive any benefit related to that religion or belief; promote good relations between people of different religions or beliefs. Organisations whose main purpose is commercial cannot use this exception.

992. The exception allows an organisation (or a person acting on its behalf) to impose restrictions on membership of the organisation; participation in its activities; the use of any goods, facilities or services that it provides; and the use of its premises. However, any restriction can only be imposed by reference to a person's religion or belief or sexual orientation.

993. In relation to religion or belief, the exception can only apply where a restriction is necessary to comply with the purpose of the organisation or to avoid causing offence to members of the religion or belief whom the organisation represents.

994. In relation to sexual orientation, the exception can only apply where it is necessary to comply with the doctrine of the organisation or in order to avoid conflict with the strongly held convictions of members of the religion or belief that the organisation represents. However, if an organisation contracts with a public body to carry out an activity on that body's behalf then it cannot discriminate because of sexual orientation in relation to that activity.

995. The exception also enables ministers of religion to restrict participation in the activities that they carry out in the performance of their functions as a minister and access to any goods, facilities or services they provide in the course of performing those functions.

Background

996. This paragraph replicates the effect of similar provisions in Part 2 of the Equality Act 2006 and the Equality Act (Sexual Orientation) Regulations 2007.

Examples

- A Catholic seminary can restrict places for students to those of the Catholic faith. This would not be unlawful religion or belief discrimination.
- A Church refuses to let out its hall for a Gay Pride celebration as it considers that it would conflict with the strongly held religious convictions of a significant number of its followers. This would not be unlawful sexual orientation discrimination.
- A religious organisation which has a contract with a local authority to provide meals to elderly and other vulnerable people within the community on behalf of the local authority cannot discriminate because of sexual orientation.

Communal accommodation: paragraph 3

Effect

997. This paragraph provides an exception to the general prohibition of sex and gender reassignment discrimination. It allows communal accommodation to be restricted to one sex only, as long as the accommodation is managed as fairly as possible for both men and women. It sets out factors which must be considered when restricting

communal accommodation to one sex only, and provides that discriminatory treatment of transsexual people must be objectively justified.

998. Communal accommodation is defined as residential accommodation which includes shared sleeping accommodation which should only be used by members of one sex for privacy reasons.

999. Where such accommodation is refused in the field of work, or a benefit linked to such accommodation is refused, alternative arrangements must be made where reasonable so as to compensate the person concerned.

Background

1000. This paragraph replaces similar provisions in the Sex Discrimination Act 1975. The scope of the exception has been extended from employment, education and services to all fields.

Examples

- A hostel only accepts male guests. It is not unlawful for it to refuse to accept female guests because the majority of the bedrooms are shared and there is only one communal bathroom.
- At a worksite the only available sleeping accommodation is communal accommodation occupied by men. A woman employee who wishes to attend a training course at the worksite is refused permission because of the men-only accommodation. Her employer must make alternative arrangements to compensate her where reasonable, for example by arranging alternative accommodation or an alternative course.

Training provided to non-EEA residents, etc: paragraph 4

Effect

1001. Paragraph 4 allows less favourable treatment because of a person's nationality in relation to training and associated benefits that are intended for people who do not live in an EEA state, as long as the training provider believes that the person will not subsequently use the skills obtained in Great Britain. This means that an EEA resident cannot claim to have been discriminated against in relation to this type of activity.

1002. Employment or contract work can be covered by this exception where its sole or main purpose is the provision of training in skills. Special provision is made in relation to defence training to reflect current arrangements to help provide other nations with the skills to assist the United Kingdom in addressing global conflict and supporting the United Kingdom on multi-national operations.

Background

1003. The main purpose of this provision is to enable people from developing countries to acquire vital skills which may not be available in their country of residence. It replaces similar provisions in the Race Relations Act 1976. The general rule on non-residence has been extended from Great Britain to include all EEA states, except in relation to defence training which is provided to forces from other EEA states as well as those outside the EEA.

Example

- It is not unlawful for a company specialising in sustainable irrigation that offers a training scheme in Great Britain for people who live in Mozambique, who then return home to put the skills learned into practice, to refuse to offer the same training to someone who lives in Great Britain.

Schedule 24: Harmonisation: exceptions

Effect

1004. This Schedule sets out the provisions of the Act to which the power in section 203 does not apply. These are largely provisions where all the equality provisions are clearly governed by European law or where power exists under other legislation to deal with any anomalies that may otherwise arise. Accordingly it will not be possible to amend these provisions using the power in section 203 to bring them into line, where needed, with changes in European law.

Schedule 25: Information society services

Effect

1005. This Schedule ensures that the provisions of the Act do not conflict with the requirements of European Directive 2000/31/EC of 8 June 2000, known as the E-Commerce Directive. The Directive concerns information society services, which are services provided from a distance by means of electronic equipment to businesses and consumers such as on-line shopping, direct marketing and advertising. It provides that where an information society service provider is established in Great Britain, the provisions of the Act apply to anything done by it in providing the information society service in another EEA state other than the United Kingdom. By contrast, where the provider is established in an EEA state other than the United Kingdom, then the Act does not apply to anything done by the provider in providing the information society service. Various exceptions to the provisions of the Act are provided in respect of intermediary internet service providers who carry out activities essential for the operation of the internet

Background

1006. These provisions are new. They are necessary to ensure the United Kingdom correctly transposes the Directive.

Examples

- An on-line holiday company established in Great Britain refuses to take bookings for shared accommodation from same-sex couples. In this instance a case of direct sexual orientation discrimination could be brought in the British courts regardless of whether the complainant was in the United Kingdom or another EEA member state.
- An on-line retailer, which provides tickets to major sporting events, provides discounts to large groups of men but not women when booking hospitality packages for the forthcoming football world cup. The on-line retailer is established in Germany, so in this instance a case of direct sex discrimination would have to be brought in the German courts regardless of whether the complainant was in the United Kingdom or another EEA member state.

Schedule 26: Amendments

Effect

1007. This Schedule sets out a number of amendments to the following acts: the Local Government Act 1988, the Employment Act 1989 and the Equality Act 2006. These amendments are necessary to ensure that these Acts refer accurately to the new provisions contained in the Act and work properly with those new provisions. For example, where a new term or a new definition is used in the Act and another Act refers to the same or similar term which is contained in legislation which is being repealed, that other Act needs to be amended to refer to the new term or definition. In addition to the amendments set out in this Schedule, sections 216 and 207 used together provide a power to make similar consequential amendments to other primary legislation.

Local Government Act 1988: paragraphs 1 to 4

Effect

1008. This paragraph amends Part 2 of the Local Government Act 1988 ("the 1988 Act") so as to provide that the public bodies to which that Part applies may exercise a function by reference to a non-commercial matter to the extent that the authorities consider it necessary or expedient to do so in order to comply with the equality duty.

Background

1009. Section 17 of the 1988 Act prevents public bodies to which that Part applies from introducing certain non-commercial matters into the procurement process; these are set out at subsection 5 of that Act. Section 18 of the 1988 Act ensured that section 17 of that Act did not restrict those authorities from complying with their duties under the Race Relations Act 1976. It achieved this by permitting those authorities to ask six approved questions of their contractors.

1010. The Local Government Best Value (Exclusion of Non-commercial Considerations) Order 2001 (S.I. 2001/9090) modified sections 17(5)(a) and (d) of the 1988 Act so that matters relating to the terms and conditions of employment etc. of a contractor's workforce, and the conduct of contractors or their workers in industrial disputes cease to be non-commercial matters only so far as necessary or expedient to permit or facilitate compliance with the best value requirements of the Local Government Act 1999 or the Transfer of Undertakings (Protection of Employment Regulations) 1981. Similar amendments were made for Scotland and Wales.

Examples

- A local authority which is not a Best Value Authority, which was previously permitted to ask only the six approved questions of its contractors on the race duty, will now be able to consider broader issues on equality when contracting for public supply or works as the authority sees fit in order to comply with the requirements of the public sector equality duty.
- A local authority wants to contract with a private company. It will be able to take into account the ethnic make-up of the workforce of that company, the behaviour of that company during an industrial dispute, and any other issue which is defined as non-commercial, when deciding to award the contract, but only if it considers it is necessary to do so in order to meet the requirements of the public sector equality duty.

Equality Act 2006: paragraph 13

Effect

1011. This amendment to the Equality Act 2006 allows the Equality and Human Rights Commission to use its enforcement powers, such as the power to conduct investigations and the power to apply for an injunction, in relation to unlawful direct and indirect discrimination under the Act, including the making of arrangements which would result in direct discrimination, if applied to an individual. It can also use its powers in relation to discrimination arising from disability and discrimination in cases where the relationship between the parties has ended; when an employer asks job applicants prohibited enquiries about disability and health; and to enforce any diversity reporting requirements imposed on political parties using the power in section 106.

1012. It allows the Equality and Human Rights Commission to use its powers whether or not it knows or suspects that an individual has been affected by the discrimination. It makes clear that nothing in the Equality Act 2006 affects an individual's right to bring a claim under the Act.

Background

1013. This amendment partially replaces provisions in previous discrimination law relating to discriminatory practices and discriminatory advertisements. The substantive prohibition against discriminatory practices and advertisements is no longer required as it is covered elsewhere in the Act. This amendment does however extend enforcement by the Equality and Human Rights Commission to cover both direct and indirect discrimination because of any of the protected characteristics, as well as discrimination arising from disability. It also extends the use of the Commission's existing powers to situations where employers ask job applicants prohibited enquiries about disability and health, and to any diversity reporting requirements that may be imposed on political parties.

Examples

- A golf club operates an informal but well-known policy of not offering membership to people from ethnic minority communities, which discourages people from these communities from applying. The Equality and Human Rights Commission may investigate this unofficial discriminatory policy even though it is not aware of particular individuals directly affected by it.
- A Bed and Breakfast (B&B) advertises for customers but includes a statement that it does not welcome people from the Gypsy and Traveller communities. Even though the Equality and Human Rights Commission can take action, an individual who is discouraged from staying at the B&B can still bring a claim in his or her own right.

Schedule 27: Repeals and revocations

Effect

1014. This Schedule lists the legislative provisions which will cease to have effect once the relevant provisions in the Act come into force.

Schedule 28: Index of defined expressions

Effect

1015. This Schedule lists the terms and expressions which are defined in the Act and refers the reader to the provision in the Act where the definition can be found.

HANSARD REFERENCES

The following table sets out the dates and Hansard references for each stage of this Act's passage through Parliament.

Stage	*Date*	*Hansard Reference*
House of Commons		
Introduction	24 April 2009	Vol. 491 Col. 476
Second Reading	11 May 2009	Vol. 492 Cols. 553-655
Committee	02 June 2009	Hansard Public Bill Committee Equality Bill
	02 June 2009	
	09 June 2009	
	09 June 2009	
	11 June 2009	
	11 June 2009	
	16 June 2009	
	16 June 2009	
	18 June 2009	
	18 June 2009	
	23 June 2009	
	23 June 2009	

Stage	*Date*	*Hansard Reference*
	25 June 2009	
	25 June 2009	
	30 June 2009	
	30 June 2009	
	02 July 2009	
	02 July 2009	
	07 July 2009	
	07 July 2009	
	(20 Sittings)	
Report and Third Reading	02 Dec 2009	Vol. 501. Cols. 1111-1233
House of Lords		
Introduction	3 December 2009	Vol. 715 Col. 842
Second Reading	15 December 2009	Vol. 715 Cols. 1404-1418
Committee	11 January 2010	Vol. 716 Cols. 298-351 and 367-392
	13 January 2010	Vol. 716 Cols. 518-566 and 574-600
	19 January 2010	Vol. 716 Cols. 878-949 and 964-986
	25 January 2010	Vol. 716 Cols. 1197-1266 and 1278-1290
	27 January 2010	Vol. 716 Cols. 1415-1472 and 1487-1512
	09 February 2010	Vol. 717 Cols. 634-660 and 689-724
Report	02 March 2010	Vol. 717 Cols. 1326 – 1442 and 1408 - 1414
Third Reading	23 March 2010	Vol. 718 Cols. 851 - 873
Commons Consideration of Lords Amendments	06 April 2010	Vol. 508 Cols. 926-942
Royal Assent	08 April 2010	House of Lords Vol. 718 Cols. 1738-1740
		House of Commons Vol. 508 Cols. 1256-1258

Adapted and published by GRANGIS under the OGL Licence 3.0.

www.nationalarchives.gov.uk/doc/open-government-licence/version/3/

GRANGIS - UK PUBLISHING 2022.
Thank you for taking the time to leave us a review regarding this version

★★★★★

For further inquiries, contact us at:
www.grangis.com / contact@grangis.com

www.ingramcontent.com/pod-product-compliance
Lightning Source LLC
LaVergne TN
LVHW060211210926
848481LV00008B/2700
* 9 7 9 8 8 8 5 5 9 0 3 8 9 *